Teresa Moorey is a practising counsellor, hypnotherapist and astrologer, and the best-selling author of over thirty books. For her entire adult life she has explored the magical and the mystical, drawing upon ancient knowledge to enhance modern life.

She lives in the Cotswolds, England with her husband and four children.

Selected titles by the same author

Silver Moon
The Little Book of Moon Magic
Spellbound!
Witchcraft – A Complete Guide
Herbs for Magic and Ritual – A Beginner's Guide
The Goddess – A Beginner's Guide

A Charmed Life

How to Make Your Life More Magical

TERESA MOOREY

RIDER

LONDON · SYDNEY · AUCKLAND · JOHANNESBURG

1 3 5 7 9 10 8 6 4 2

Copyright © Teresa Moorey 2004

All rights reserved. No part of this publication may be reproduced, stored in a retrieval system, or transmitted in any form or by any means, electronic, mechanical, photocopying, recording or otherwise, without the prior permission of the copyright owner.

Teresa Moorey has asserted her right to be identified as the author of this Work.

First published in 2004 by Rider, an imprint of Ebury Press, Random House, 20 Vauxhall Bridge Road, London SW1V 2SA

Random House Australia (Pty) Limited
20 Alfred Street, Milsons Point, Sydney,
New South Wales 2061, Australia

Random House New Zealand Limited
18 Poland Road, Glenfield,
Auckland 10, New Zealand

Random House South Africa (Pty) Limited
Endulini, 5A Jubilee Road,
Parktown 2193, South Africa

The Random House Group Limited Reg. No. 954009

Papers used by Rider are natural, recyclable products made from wood grown in sustainable forests.

Printed and bound by Bookmarque Ltd, Croydon, Surrey
Typeset by seagulls
Illustrations by Rob Loxton

A CIP catalogue record for this book is available from the British Library

ISBN 1-8441-3213-7

contents

1. Welcome to a Charmed Life — 1
2. What Sort of 'Me' Would You Like to Be? — 13
3. The Lore of Love — 46
4. A Feeling of Wellbeing — 96
5. Making Friends, Staying Friends — 128
6. Family Fortunes — 144
7. Making Your Work Work for You — 165
8. Money Matters — 192
9. Problem Areas — 212
10. Living a Charmed Life — 227

Appendix 1: Charm Correspondences — 233
Appendix 2: A Few More Helpful Scripts — 234
Further Reading — 242
Useful Addresses — 245
Resources — 246
Index — 247

Please note:
The information given in this book is not intended to be taken as a replacement for professional medical advice. Any person with a condition requiring attention should consult a qualified practitioner or therapist. If pregnant or suffering from allergies, always consult a doctor before using essential oils or other traditional remedies.

Candles: always place candles in safe places, in secure holders, well away from flammable materials. Fire is an unpredictable element, so *never* leave a lit candle unattended.

Fireworks: always read and follow the manufacturer's safety instructions carefully. Keep fireworks away from flammable materials, children, animals and sources of heat.

one

Welcome to a Charmed Life

'Life, like a dome of many-coloured glass
Stains the white radiance of Eternity.'
Shelley, 'Adonais'

'I compare human life to a large Mansion of
Many Apartments, two of which I can only describe,
the doors of the rest being as yet shut upon me.'
Keats, in a letter to J.H. Reynolds, 3 May 1818

a charmed life

Welcome! You have taken your first step towards making life better for yourself – maybe just a little bit, maybe lots.

We are told that we 'create our own reality', but it may be very difficult to see how this can be so in a world where we often feel powerless and overwhelmed. Being told to 'think positive' can simply make us feel that everything is our fault, because we can't manage to keep a smile on our faces! It's true that life is what you make it, but that subtle yet radical change of perspective may be very elusive.

In this book we shall be looking at some very old, yet very simple, ways of changing that perspective by a mixture of understanding, pragmatism, visualisation, gentle self-hypnosis and very simple rituals called 'charms'. It is important that we sort out what is going on in our lives and inside us before we take steps in another direction, so first of all we look at possible situations in an analytical and practical way. Sometimes it is possible to overlook some very simple things when we are distressed and pressurised. Often we need to 'feel understood' – and to understand ourselves – before we feel able to move on. With the best will in the world we cannot always alter our attitudes at an emotional level by logic alone. Performing a charm will make a strong statement of the change we want to make. Finally, we can make changes in our moods and outlook by self-hypnosis, again by the use of a very basic technique.

As we will see, a charm is, in effect, a small ritual. Ritual has a way of by-passing the conscious mind and getting through to the level we call 'sub-conscious' or 'unconscious'. What you do in a charm is actually a metaphor for what you want to achieve in a larger and more abstract sense. Often the connections are not obvious, yet deep in your mind, something happens. And maybe there is even more at work – after all, you are sending out a strong message to the Cosmos that you want something to happen. Could it be that someone is listening? Your attitude to this will depend on your belief system, but you do not have to put faith in anything specific for your charms to work. Just visualise and enjoy, for charms are usually beautiful things and working them will put you in touch with yourself and the pleasant things in the world around you, such as flowers, herbs, colours and essential oils.

welcome to a charmed life * 3

'Reality' is a strange thing. Let us look, for example, at something unpleasant (because these things by their very nature get more scrutiny than nice things!) – let us look at what happens when there is an accident. The police take 'statements' from observers, but it is a known fact that the people who have been on the scene will have perceived the event in many different ways, even though they were all detached bystanders. 'Well,' you may say, with some justification, 'that's just because some folk are more observant than others.' True, but could that possibly be only part of the picture? In the first place, whether what a person has seen is totally objectively 'true' or not, the impression received may radically affect their life. In the second place, could it be that 'reality' isn't quite as solid as we believe? After all, quantum physics is now showing us that the observer can actually affect the process of the experiment – for instance in the behaviour of a stream of photons (or particles of light). By narrowing a beam of light down to a single stream, scientists have shown that photons behave differently when being watched. That sounds incredible, because we are used to science being very 'physical' and we are surrounded by evidence that science manipulates our surroundings in a radical and enduring fashion – and who would have it otherwise? Few people would want to go back to a time without street lamps and central heating. But science may also have taken from us some of our faith in ourselves and our powers to use our imagination, widen our scope and say, 'Anything could happen!'

Very small shifts can give rise to immense changes. If your attitude shifts just a tiny bit, over a period of time, people will begin to react differently to you – not just to your altered facial expressions and body language, but also to something more subliminal, to a presence you radiate. As their actions change, so yours will respond likewise, and a process is set in motion, for good or ill. Sometimes what starts that process maybe something fairly small; and so from the acorn, the oak tree grows.

> **Top Tip**
> *Even a small change in you will mean that others see you differently – and this can be the start of something great!*

4 ✶ a charmed life

This book is about shifts – some of them small, it's true, but some of them may be larger. Of course, not everything in life can be easily sorted out. However, the focus of this book is principally 'ordinary life', and in ordinary life it is possible to make many things much better by first realising what is happening and then taking steps to change it. There is enough bounty in the Universe for everyone to feel fulfilled. And if life is about learning lessons, the Cosmic Curriculum states that school can be rewarding and fun.

So charm your way to success!

✶ the questionnaires

The first step in this process is to get to know yourself better. Throughout this book you will find questionnaires and simple exercises to encourage you to do just that. These are designed to help you to focus on yourself, to be more conscious of who you are and where you stand. But they are not designed to pigeon-hole you. Treat them light-heartedly, and if you really disagree with the results then at least you will have given the matter some thought. No questionnaire can unerringly discover the truth about a person, although in some cases they can be quite revealing. As long as they get you thinking, they will have achieved their purpose.

✶ visualisation & meditation

This chapter contains detailed advice about visualisation and how to start off on your own inner journeys. As you will discover, visualisation is a type of meditation. Meditating is not necessarily some demanding and mysterious Eastern discipline – it is a natural state, similar in some ways to the hypnotic state, and it can be cultivated.

When we meditate we empty our minds of the humdrum and the day-to-day. When you look at a patch of sunlight on your carpet and go off into a daydream, you are in a sense meditating. But unfortunately this state of mind is one that we often do not value, tending rather to see it

welcome to a charmed life * 5

as time-wasting. However, the ability to go off 'into another world' can and should be cultivated, because it can be very helpful.

You may have heard of various approaches to meditating. The term is used freely and we don't need to be pedantic about it. It can be a process of objectifying, in which we watch ourselves and our thoughts, realising that we have them, while understanding that *we are not them*, and that our essence is separate. The term 'meditating' may also be used for inner exploration of various sorts. These may be visualisations in which we focus on how we want things to be – a powerful tool in creating our reality. Or we may go into our inner landscapes in a fashion that is structured or fairly free – such inner voyages can tell us much about ourselves and can also be effective in expanding our perspectives and changing our state of mind. In this book, the type of meditating that we shall be looking at is structured visualisation, in which we follow fairly precise instructions about what we see in our mind's eye.

> **Top Tip**
>
> *As you think, so you become – visualise positive events to entice them into your life.*

Meditation and visualisation can be interesting, beautiful and sometimes breathtakingly revealing. Enjoy your own experiences of them as you create your charmed life.

* using charms

Throughout this book you will find many suggestions for charms to help improve specific situations. These are built on time-honoured principles and are fun to perform. However, there are a few considerations that you need to bear in mind before doing a charm if it is to work well for you.

Make sure you are in the right state of mind before you begin. This does not mean that you should be ferociously concentrating, taking it all very seriously and being pedantic about the instructions – in fact, rather the opposite. To do your charms you need to be fairly relaxed. Indeed a playful attitude can be good. It will help if you are in a slightly 'drifty' mood. If you need to chill, try a meditation exercise prior to the charm.

It is best to do your charms alone. If you involve someone else, make sure they are totally in harmony with your attitude and objective.

Try to have a small shelf or work area where you regularly do your charms. This will help you to build up associations, so that when entering that space you will become conditioned to be in the right frame of mind for charm-working.

As time goes by, you will learn to trust your intuition and make adaptations where they feel right to you. For instance, if you feel sure a blue candle would be better for your purpose than a pink one, go by your own feelings.

Don't talk to other people about what you're doing, although you might make an exception for someone very close and trusted.

Make sure you have everything you need for a charm before you start – if you have to break off to get something you will need to start again, and your state of mind may have been affected.

Never attempt charms that aim to directly influence another person, as this would be to meddle in their life path and will do you no good in the long run. For instance, a love charm should be for the sort of love you desire and about the *kind* of person you feel would be ideal for you, but should not target someone you already know.

Place definite boundaries around your charm-working. For example, as you start tell yourself, 'Now I am beginning.' It is good practice to get in the habit of visualising a protective circle around yourself for most charms by closing your eyes and imagining yourself enclosed in an egg of light. When you have finished a charm, close yourself down properly by imagining your circle fading. Place your palms on the floor and/or have something to eat or drink, to confirm that you are back with the here and now. Tidy away everything you have used afterwards; this serves symbolically as an act of finishing.

Assembling Your Charm Kit

For each of the charms suggested in this book, there is a short list of requirements, some of which will be specific to the charm in question. However, it is a good idea – and fun! – to collect a basic set of equipment

welcome to a charmed life * 7

for your charming ways. House these in a special box or cupboard if possible. Here is a list of basic items for charm-working.

* Candles and candle-holders. You will need candles in a variety of colours (although white can be used for any purpose if necessary).
* Matches.
* Oil-burner.
* Joss sticks and holder.
* Censer – if you want to use incense instead of oils.
* Pen/s in various colours.
* Paper in various colours.
* A calendar of lunar phases (see Further Reading and Resources for lunar calendars). The phases of the moon are believed by many to be linked to the ebb and flow of all kinds of energies on the earth, and so are important to bear in mind when doing a charm. The moon is waxing when it is going from new to full, and waning when it has passed full. As the moon wanes it is seen later and later in the night. Full moon is at the zenith round midnight and the waxing crescent is seen early in the evening (you can 'cup' its outline with your right hand if you live in the Northern hemisphere, or with your left hand if you live in the Southern). Charms that are to do with increase and growth are best done during a waxing moon, whereas the full moon may be best for love charms, and the waning moon is good for charms to get rid of something.
* Coloured cords/wool.
* Needle and thread.
* Scissors.
* Attractive bowls or jars in natural substances such as earthenware or glass (never plastic).
* Semi-precious stones – you can usually buy these in New Age shops at low cost. Rose quartz, crystals, amethyst, carnelian, agate, amber and apache tear are a good selection. Keep them in a soft bag.
* Herbs – a selection of dried herbs to use in the charms or as ingredients in incense will come in useful. Rosemary, mint, thyme, lemon balm, ginger, sage, lavender and basil are a good basic collection.

8 ✳ a charmed life

- ✻ Essential oils – these have many uses and can be obtained in alternative shops or natural therapy centres. Make sure that what you are getting is the genuine article, extracted from the plants, and not a synthetic imitation. Lavender, jasmine, ylang ylang, eucalyptus, patchouli and frankincense make a good starting collection. (See Appendix 1 for some of the associations of these oils.)
- ✻ Carrier oil – this is an oil to 'carry' the essential oils for massage (however, don't dilute them before using them in an oil burner or incense blend). Grapeseed oil or sweet almond are good. (Please note, baby oil is a mineral oil and should not be used.)
- ✻ Miscellaneous natural objects such as feathers, dried leaves, interesting stones and pebbles, wind-born seeds and any other item that catches your eye when you are out walking.
- ✻ You may also like to have statues as devotional objects. For instance, you might like to have a statue of Venus for love charms or just as a focal point in your working area, to remind you of the happy forces that are at work in life.

If you are pregnant or suffer from any allergies, always check with your physician before using essential oils or any other traditional remedies.

✳ hypnotherapy

One of the main tools this book uses for developing a more fulfilling life is hypnotherapy, and you will find suggested scripts in each chapter. Hypnosis is a very simple tool but is very effective. In fact it is deceptively simple – many subtle things go on between a good therapist and the patient that are hard to define. You could almost say a kind of magic is involved. If the therapist is also a counsellor, help and guidance will also be given on other levels, so that self-understanding can be reached and the hypnotherapy more accurately targeted.

There are many misconceptions about hypnotherapy, so let's clarify what actually happens. Firstly, although hypnotherapy makes use of a mental state similar to that used in stage hypnosis, that is where the similarity ends! Stage hypnosis is entertainment, and much happens out of sight of the audience. Furthermore, about five to ten per cent of people are what is called 'deep trance subjects'. This means they go into the hypnotic state very readily and deeply, so they are quicker to respond. A skilled hypnotist will quickly spot such subjects, often by a look in their eyes. In addition, those people who get up on stage and do weird things at some level actually want to do them! It is said that you can't be made to do anything you do not want to do under hypnosis, and while I'm not sure the mind is that simple, it is certainly not everyone who will walk like a chicken and eat raw onion believing it to be apple! As a deep trance subject myself, I know what it is like to be hypnotised standing up, I know the sorts of things I would do – and those I would not!

The state of mind used for hypnotherapy is one we all go through at least twice in every twenty-four hours, as we wake up and as we go to sleep. This is that pleasant state between sleeping and waking, in which the subconscious mind is very open and receptive. It will soak up positive suggestions like a sponge. It is often the suggestible, 'deep trance' souls who are most affected by negative conditioning in childhood, but it is these people who tend to respond well to positive statements in hypnosis. The hypnotic state can be induced simply by talking, and then all the necessary instructions can be given for the improvement that is desired.

For the purposes of this book, you will need to record your own self-hypnosis tapes from the scripts provided. This is nowhere near as good as having a skilled and experienced hypnotherapist treat you, but considerably better than any general tape you can buy – because it is targeted specifically at you! If you do not like the sound of your own voice then get a soft-spoken friend to record the tape for you. You need to play your tape every day, and if possible at the same time of day, so that your subconscious expects it.

To prepare yourself for your self-hypnosis session, lie down and make sure you are warm and comfortable – don't be afraid to wriggle as much as you need to. Make sure you won't be disturbed by other family members, pets or the phone. If there is a knock on the door, ignore it. It isn't particularly good for you to hop up in the middle of a session – let the process take its course. Close your eyes from the outset if you like, or stare at a spot on the ceiling until you feel your eyes need to close.

Self-Hypnosis Induction

Here is the script for the first part of every tape. It is called an induction. Use this to induce the drowsy feeling, then use the rest of the script as therapy. Finally use the Wake-up section to bring you back to the here-and-now.

You are lying comfortably. Let that wonderful feeling of relaxation flow all over you. Gently going down, down, down, sinking, feeling drowsy, feeling so sleepy. So very, very sleepy. All the tension just draining away, leaving you free, leaving you blissfully relaxed. Beautifully relaxed....

[If you like you can extend this, using imagery and repetition.]

Feel the relaxation flow over you, taking away every last scrap of tension. Nothing matters, only the sound of my voice. Feel the relaxation starting at the top of your head, flowing down over your face and neck... wonderfully relaxed as all the cares and worries melt away... flowing down over your shoulders, down your arms and out through your fingertips... wonderfully relaxed... and down your chest and back, over your abdomen, thighs, knees and down your legs flowing out through your toes. Completely, utterly relaxed.

Soon I am going to count slowly from one to seven and after each number I shall use the word 'sleep'. But this won't be an ordinary sleep for you – instead you will become very deeply relaxed. Very, very relaxed. You will still be aware of things happening near you, still hear noises inside and outside, but all of this will gradually mean less and less to you. Gradually less and less, until all you are aware of is the sound of my voice. So listen to the sound of my voice and let it take you deep into the wonderful place where everything is so tranquil and peaceful. Beautifully relaxed. And you know you could wake up if you wanted to. If something important needed your attention you would wake up. But for now all you want to do is let go and relax... relax.

One... sleep... two... sleep... feeling relaxation flowing all over you...

three... sleep, delicious sensation of being totally, perfectly relaxed... four... sleep... wonderfully relaxed, relaxed in mind and in body... five... sleep... feeling yourself going deeper and deeper... six... relaxation so pleasurable, so tranquil... seven... and beautifully relaxed, truly, deeply relaxed, all your limbs feeling so comfortable. Floating... floating.

Such a wonderful feeling. Peace and serenity, peace and serenity. Nothing matters, nothing's important. Just listen to my voice, listen to my voice.

And while you're lying there so very relaxed, relaxed in mind and in body, I'm going to give you some instructions, some suggestions that you have chosen, instructions that you desire to hear, because you know they are right for you, and you allow them to sink deep inside you and to become part of you.

[Insert specific script.]

Wake-Up Procedure

Now I am going to count down from seven to one, and on the number one you will wake up, feeling wonderfully refreshed, invigorated, positive and energetic. Your body will be feeling rested and vigorous and your mind will be happy and at ease. You will keep with you all these good feelings and put into practice all the good things you have heard. Seven... six... five... four... three... two... one – awaken.

Working with the Scripts

You may find that the hypnotherapy scripts sometimes seem a bit repetitive. This is because they are helping you to re-programme your thoughts at a subconscious level. Although you may be tempted to skip over them if you are reading straight through the book, do come back to them later and have a go at recording them so that you can listen to them when you are ready. You may be pleasantly surprised by the results.

using this book

You can read this book from cover to cover or dip into it to address some specific issue – or just flick through it out of curiosity! You will find a variety of approaches, including some case histories that may serve to reassure you that you are not alone in your experiences! All of these are based on true stories, but obviously details have been altered to protect confidentiality. Feel free to use what works for you and to leave the rest – it is not intended that you should feel you have to do everything, all the time, and use every charm, every visualisation, every self-hypnosis that might apply. Make your choice! However, if you want to do everything, then please do. Monitor your progress and focus on what you find most effective.

You can charm your life, but hopefully you, in turn, will be charmed by life as you find new dimensions to existence. Enjoy!

two

What Sort of 'Me' Would You Like to Be?

'Where my heart lies, let my brain lie also!'
Robert Browning, 'One Word More'

'We hold these truths to be self-evident: that all…
are created equal; that they are endowed…
with certain unalienable rights; that among these
are life, liberty and the pursuit of happiness.'
American Declaration of Independence, July 4, 1776

can i be happy?

Happiness is the goal of everyone, and yet for many people it is very elusive. Many wise things have been written about 'happiness'. Sages tell us we cannot find it by looking for it, but we may be fortunate enough to uncover it as we look for – or struggle against – something else. Happiness means different things to different people, of course. We all have individual levels of tolerance, and there is a difference between a situation not being perfect and there being something profoundly wrong.

Happiness is, to a great extent, a matter of attitude. For many people true happiness is found only through an awareness of spiritual meaning. There is little doubt that pursuing a list of 'I wants' tends not to make people happy in the long term. Pursuing fulfilment is rather a different matter, however. Being fulfilled is often a challenge, is rarely purely pleasurable, and yet it makes for happiness. Becoming the 'me' you were meant to be is rather like a pinched rose-bud opening out into a glorious flower. It's a blessing to everyone.

> **Top Tip**
> *Happiness is more a matter of attitude. The trick is to find your personal way into that attitude.*

I was brought up to believe that 'we were not put here to enjoy ourselves' and spent so many years in confused rebellion against this that I had little idea of what I wanted and precious little ability to have a nice time! This has made me aware of all the obstacles we put in our own way and all the ways we mislead ourselves. Therapy will not help unless we are prepared to take some steps, make some changes, however small, to improve our life.

So how prepared are you to take the bull by the horns and start making some real changes? You probably already have a fair idea of how dynamic an attitude you have towards improving things. The following simple questionnaire is designed to help you gauge your attitude to working on your life.

what sort of 'me' would you like to be?

1 You walk downstairs in the morning to see a single letter lying face down on the mat. The first thing that goes through your mind is:
   a) Interesting news,
   b) More junk mail,
   c) Another bill.

2 On the way to work you are caught in the traffic. You use the time to:
   a) Listen to your Teach-Yourself tape,
   b) Listen to music or phone a mate,
   c) Get all steamed up and frantic.

3 When you arrive at work your boss has a new assignment for you. How do you react:
   a) Great, a new challenge gets me interested,
   b) Oh, well, it'll soon be five-thirty,
   c) Oh no, not something else to get my head round!

4 Someone new moves in over the way, so you:
   a) Go over and say 'Hi' – they could turn out to be a good friend,
   b) Won't bother them, and they won't bother you,
   c) Hope they aren't going to park their car over your drive.

5 At your favourite restaurant your usual meal is unavailable:
   a) You don't have a 'usual' meal,
   b) You dither a bit and let someone choose for you,
   c) Your evening is spoilt.

6 You need something extra-special to wear for an important occasion:
   a) You keep looking until you find something spot-on,
   b) You buy the first reasonable thing you try on,
   c) Something in your wardrobe will probably do.

7 You are quite sure that a course now being offered will lead to the career of your dreams, but going on it means taking a considerable drop in salary for a while:
   a) You don't hesitate – this is a means to better things,
   b) You aren't sure what to do and ask everyone's advice,
   c) You feel resentful that you have to manage on less and decide not to do the course.

16 ∗ a charmed life

8 A friend sets you up with a blind date, but you hear from a third party that the date is a boring no-hoper:
   a) You go along, looking your best, determined to get the most from the evening,
   b) You go along, without bothering much, expecting it to be a dead loss,
   c) You cancel the date.

9 Your principal thought when sold a raffle ticket is:
   a) I might win!
   b) Oh well, it's in a good cause,
   c) I suppose I must.

10 Your attitude to your health is:
   a) It's up to me to keep as healthy as I can,
   b) One day I'm going to sort out my lifestyle…,
   c) Health is mostly genetic.

11 Here comes that bank statement, so you think:
   a) It's up to me to make sure I get the money I need,
   b) I can't seem to get to grips with money,
   c) I'm just unlucky – I never can seem to earn enough.

12 Day-to-day life is very stressful, so you:
   a) Do things that help you relax, from meditating to working out,
   b) Slob out whenever you can,
   c) Feel unable to relax with all the demands made on you.

Your Score

Mostly A: You don't need to be told that you're a pretty dynamic person. You tend to look on the bright side and you make the most of your opportunities. Perhaps your greatest asset is your sense of responsibility. You feel you have the power to make changes; or if you don't, you're prepared to find out how. Make sure you keep realistic goals in mind.

Mostly B. You can be a tad apathetic at times. It isn't necessarily that you can't be bothered, but often that you feel confused. It seems easier to take the line of least resistance. But is this easiest in the long run? Perhaps if you take the time to find out what you want and how to get it you will find things a lot easier.

what sort of 'me' would you like to be? ✲ 17

Mostly C. What has made you so negative? You can have much more effect on your life if you will only believe that you can do so. Your expectations of the worst are a self-fulfilling prophecy – and yet you probably feel, deep down, that this does not have to be. Start by making small changes – what have you got to lose?

✲ ringing the changes

If you are reading this, the chances are you would like to change something – or many things – in your life. You may know what these are, or you may have only a general feeling that something isn't right. Maybe you reason yourself out of these feelings with arguments like 'Why should I be any different? We all know life isn't perfect. Look at the starving millions…' etc. Most of us say these things. More often than not such arguments arise from our own feelings of unworthiness and guilt and fear of failure – and, let's face it, our laziness! Before the first step on the road to the rest of your life, identify and clear away some of your own self-imposed obstacles.

Clearing the Path

What stands in your way? To see where you're at on the 'Should I?/Shouldn't I?' spectrum, ask yourself which, if any, of the following statements you agree with.

1. It's greedy to want too much.
2. I should be thinking more about other people instead of wanting more for myself.
3. The fact is 'Life's a bitch' – you can't change that!
4. Life isn't about enjoying yourself; it's about learning lessons.
5. It isn't very spiritual to focus on what one wants.
6. I'm not clever or talented enough to get what I want.
7. I'm not beautiful/handsome enough to get what I want.
8. I'm not rich enough to get what I want.

18 * a charmed life

9 I don't have the time to work towards what I want.
10 I'm too lazy to get what I want.
11 If I got what I wanted I might lose my friends and/or my familiar surroundings.
12 I just don't know how to get what I want.
13 I've always been thwarted in the past.
14 I just don't know what I want.

Let's now look at these statements, one by one, to see where they arise and why none of them are valid!

Greedy? If you agreed with Statement 1, you are probably reacting to something imposed on you by your upbringing or culture. This begs the question of what is 'too much'. Nothing that you want that it is not at someone else's expense is 'too much'. Being greedy is having more than you can deal with and enjoy – that is unlikely to be your situation! Please rest assured that having what you want can also do other people the power of good as you will have more to give, from smiles to hard cash. While some resources in the world are finite, that does not mean, in essence, that bounty is limited. Besides, there are many different sorts of bounty and not everyone wants the same. As your bounty increases, your satisfaction will spiral outwards – believe it!

Selfish? If you agreed with Statement 2, then some of the comments from the previous paragraph also apply to you. Why are you less worthy of your own attentions than other people? How are others really going to experience you if you think only about them? How can you be sure what everyone wants? Will the world be saved by your martyrdom? And who might, in fact, prosper from your happiness and good fortune? Safety experts advise us always to fasten our own lifebelt first, because without that in place not only is our ability to help others limited, but we may also be a danger to them.

Life is a Bitch? If you agreed with Statement 3, that life is a bitch, well, yes, it can be. Often it depends on how you look at things and what you make of them. For instance, I have had more than one relationship that was pretty bad by most people's standards. So has life been a bitch to me? No, I think not, because as a result of those relationships I have wonderful children, I've learnt a great deal about myself – and those experiences are part of the pattern that has enabled me to write this book. As another example, some months ago I had the chance to have a prominent part in a TV series. I very much wanted this. The journey to get there was quite horrendous, the audition nerve-racking and when I did not get the job I must admit I had a bit of the 'life is against me' feeling. However, I made a contact with a lovely person there whose company has been interesting and who has brought me other work. Besides, I have since learnt things about the job that make me realise I was actually very fortunate not to get it. Call life a bitch and you'll feel like a dog. Believe there is a positive side and life will come to heel when you whistle.

Life is about Learning Lessons? If you agreed with Statement 4, why should the two be mutually exclusive? Must it always be the stick, and not the carrot? The idea that some divine power insists that we learn through pain is quite pervasive, and yet educationalists and people involved in management increasingly acknowledge that rewards work better than threats. Surely God, Goddess or whatever you want to call the Higher Power of the Universe isn't less wise than we are? Bad things often do teach us, but they do not have to be the sole point of life.

Unspiritual? For Statement 5, the comments for Statement 4 may also apply. It is worth reflecting that having what we want in a material sense can only be defined as unspiritual if the world of matter is seen as devoid of divine spark. If we see the world as a manifestation of something divine, then enjoyment can be an act of worship. Maybe spirit and matter are not split, but are parts of a spectrum.

Not Gifted – and/or Coping with too Many Demands? Agreeing with any of Statements 6, 7, 8 and 9 implies that you have to have something in the first place before you can get what you want. If that is the case, you need to get the intermediate requirement – or realise that it is not relevant. Feeling that we are not clever or good-looking enough is usually a manifestation of lack of self-esteem. It can also be an excuse for giving up. Extreme good looks are only a requirement if you will settle for nothing less than being a top model. If you really do not have the appearance for that, is there something else you could do (apart from extensive plastic surgery!) that would bring you the same fulfilment? What is it about modelling that seems so wonderful? For the vast majority of other roles, attention to presentation and manner will work wonders. As for talent, it is rare for a person to dream about something for which they have absolutely no aptitude, for it is often the aptitude that gives rise to the yearning. The tone deaf person is unlikely to dream of being a concert pianist. So concentrate on developing your existing talents and brushing up on your education. Do you need more money? Are you quite sure? Is there not some other way? If not, earning the money will have to come first. In the case of time, you need to prioritise. Even if it seems you have no time, there are probably many things you do during the day that are far less important than achieving your heart's desire, so stand back and exercise choice in your life.

This seems a good point to pause and look at something that applies to so many people – lack of self-value. This isn't the same as lack of self-esteem – you may be pretty confident and positive in general, but still not value the things you do well, because you do them too easily! You may envy your friend's ability to draw, but think nothing of your skill in accounting – it's easy, boring and 'anyone can do that'! But they can't! Meanwhile your artistic friend probably laments the chaos of her finances and truly envies your skill (and income!). For years I dismissed my ability with words: 'Oh, that, yes, well, I've always been good at English – it's easy,' I'd say to many people who said, 'You should write

> **Top Tip**
>
> *For the next month, make a note of all the things you do easily and well, even if it's 'only' the shopping. Congratulate yourself. Ask yourself how you could make this work better for you.*

what sort of 'me' would you like to be? * 21

a book.' Meanwhile, I struggled to be Housewife of the Year and wondered why I never quite made it. The message is to value what you can do, *and use it*! You may not even know what your talent is, so easily do you dash it off.

Lazy? If you agreed with Statement 10, then give yourself a pat on the back for your honesty! Now ask yourself if you are happier being lazy – maybe you are one of those easy-going people who are easily satisfied in life. Or maybe you were told so often as a child that you were lazy that you now believe it. Ask yourself what being lazy really means. If you are truly dissatisfied by your lack of motivation and action then you need to tackle this first, in small ways, before doing anything bigger. For instance, if you are a true couch potato then get in the habit of taking a ten-minute walk each day before attempting any more demanding physical projects. If you always slob out in front of the telly instead of studying, start by turning it off for half an hour each evening, to read or do crosswords. Activity begets energy – it does not drain it!

Afraid of Change and the Reactions of Others? A 'yes' to Statement 11 denotes a real fear of change and the destructive aspects of envy. Consider that if your friends are not the sort to delight in your success then maybe you need better friends (see Chapter 5). Consider also that a little envy can spur people on to better things and some of your mates might thank you for widening their horizons. Read through these phrases:

* Feel the fear and do it anyway.
* Don't let your fears stand in the way of your dreams.
* Better to regret what you have done than what you have not done.
* Change is the only constant.

Make one of these (or another that sounds better to you) your motto, and start by making small changes until you feel comfortable with the idea.

Fear of the unknown keeps many people in situations they do not like. 'Better the devil you know,' they say. If we find ourselves in such a place long-term, then we are in danger of selling our souls to 'the devil we know'. If life seems scary to you and any uncertainty bodes ill, instead of offering possibilities for improvement, something or someone has made you fear the process of life. This conditioning is probably at a deep level and may be tackled by self-hypnosis or by a charm (see page 39). Pure logic is unlikely to have much effect against such angst. However, you can fight – and win – a few skirmishes by being open to new things on a day-to-day level, such as going to new places, trying new food and so on.

Can't Take the First Step? Did your response to Statement 12 reveal that you just don't know how to get what you want? Have you ever heard the saying 'If you wander around in enough bewilderment you will soon find enlightenment'? The trick is to wander around and not stay rooted to the spot! Holding in your mind as clear an image of what you want as possible, start networking, asking questions, making phone calls, reading anything you can and watching anything you can that will give you some clues. Ask people who have got what you want, or at least part of it – successful people, providing they feel secure, are often only too pleased to tell other people how to find their own fulfilment. (See the comment on Statement 1, where we saw that bounty tends to beget generosity.) If you have a talent, put it on display, and let as many people see it and know about it as you can, because you never know which contact is going to pay off. Finally, once you have some idea, make a resolution to take a step each day, however small, whether it's making a list, ordering a book or talking to someone on the phone, that will take you just a little bit closer to your goal – or at the very least reveal any blind alleys.

Braced for Frustration? If you have always been thwarted in the past, then you have become programmed for failure. You may not be aware of just how you are setting yourself up for it. You may feel that you are doing your best. But all the while your inner voice is saying you can't win, and without realising it you are surely doing little things, making little gestures, using a tone of voice that sends out loser signals. This is the first day of the rest of your life! Self-hypnosis and the right charm will help you turn your life around.

Haven't a Clue? Finally, if you don't know what you want, your situation is complex. While a happy happenstance may well come along and drop you right into your niche, it is also true that it is hard to hit the target if you don't know what – or where – it is. Possibly you are a pretty contented person with a relaxed and playful attitude to life. In that case you will, in all probability, wind up where you want to be – and then recognise it! However, if you are conscious of considerable discontent then it is quite probable that in some way you feel disempowered. Your subconscious mind may be telling you that you can't win, so what is the point of identifying a goal? Maybe you are avoiding the pain of possible failure by telling yourself you don't want anything. Maybe you are arguing yourself out of ambitions before they are fully formed. Often when people ask themselves what they want they go over half a dozen or so goals that they'd 'quite like' or think they ought to want, before admitting what really lights their fire – something they have almost given up because it seems so unreasonable. Or if you simply aren't sure, then maybe you need more information about life and what is on offer – this may be the case if you are quite young. Cast your net as wide as you like to see what you catch. Maybe you do not need a definite direction as yet.

At this point you hopefully have a better idea of your basic dynamism and the things you feel stand in your way. Before we progress to some charming ways, let's look at the negative side of 'positive' thinking.

when playing pollyanna doesn't pay

Cliché though it is, positive thinking does work wonders. However, there is a difference between the positive thinking that recognises suffering and neediness and the other sort that disregards them. If you feel really dreadful because you have lost your job or your partner, you will want to shoot the person who says, 'Look on the bright side; don't be so negative!' Being told that is liable to make you feel even worse because not only have you 'failed' in your career or your love life but you are also 'failing' to be 'positive'. Even worse, you may feel to blame because not being positive in the first place might have brought this about!

If things go wrong for you, you are entitled to a period of mourning. No-one feels good all the time, no-one succeeds all the time and no-one is lucky all the time. Moreover, feelings of misery, regret and anger are healthy and normal. In fact, to be relentlessly cheerful all the time may even be a sign of pathology, because such a person is in denial of their deepest feelings. Little that is authentic, meaningful and deeply fulfilling can materialise in our lives if we do not recognise how we feel. It is true that shit happens. It's insulting to the victim – who may very well be ourselves – if we do not give recognition and sympathy to suffering. When things go wrong and we feel awful, we need empathy. A 'cheer up!' said by someone who understands and sympathises is very different from the same phrase said by someone who does not! It is well known by counsellors that 'feeling heard' is a necessary step on the way to improvement and that not 'being heard' may mean the person stays in the negative place because their first need is for their pain to be recognised.

> **Top Tip**
> *Being positive doesn't mean lying to yourself about your negative feelings and emotions; it means having the faith to work through them.*

However, a period of mourning does not mean wallowing. Depending on the nature of the trouble, after days, weeks or months we can expect

> **Top Tip**
> *For the next month, vow to yourself that you will face up to your own fears and negative feelings. What really scares you? What are you really worried about? How are you really feeling when you tell yourself you don't care? Be brave, only you will know! And when you know your 'enemy' you will know what you are dealing with.*

to begin to come out of the extremely negative phase, to begin to learn from our experience and even to say, 'Yes, there were positive elements in that.' Occasionally something really awful can happen that in fact turns out to be good. For instance, a child who loses their mother is considered, rightly, to be in a tragic position. However, if the adults around are sympathetic, helpful and loving, the message of a friendly, accepting and supportive world may be internalised and this child may actually grow up to expect good treatment from all and sundry, thereby eliciting it. Even people who have lost children of their own have been known to describe themselves as enriched by the experience, although it would be unforgivably crass and callous ever to suggest to someone in such a situation that this might be the case.

So the bad things that happen *are* dreadful. We are entitled to cry, rage and scream. But sooner or later we owe it to ourselves not only to pick up the pieces but also to see meaning in what has happened, because in so doing we turn things – sometimes amazingly – to our advantage.

Sandra's Story

Sandra was a single mum with a difficult teenage son. Needless to say, life was a struggle. Sandra worked to pay the mortgage and often felt tired and worried. However, she was a positive woman who always took good care of her appearance and retained as many interests as she had time for. Not surprisingly, she hoped she would soon meet a man that would be a suitable partner for her. When she met Bob at her yoga class she really thought she had found the guy for her. Bob was interested in many alternative subjects. He seemed to share many of her values and was in the process of starting several small businesses about which he was very positive. 'Life is what you make it,' he would tell her, smiling, and she felt cheerful just looking at him. After they had been going out together for six months, however, Sandra was becoming increasingly depressed, although she had no idea why. At weekends they often attended self-development seminars together and her son liked him. But Sandra's job was going badly and she would come home exhausted and anxious, only to be told by Bob to 'think positive'. 'You're making things worse for yourself by your negative outlook,' he would say. Although none of his businesses had taken off, Bob was still most optimistic. If Sandra was very upset he would often leave her alone 'to get over it' and he was always telling her to 'snap out of it'.

One day on the way home from work Sandra had a car accident and was taken to hospital. She had suspected concussion, multiple bruising and a broken arm. She was kept in hospital for observation and was in some pain. Bob came to visit, but didn't stay long. 'Cheer up, you'll be fine,' he said. One of the nurses overheard him and said to Sandra, 'Oh yeah, it's okay for him, isn't it love?'

Like many of us, Sandra needed a little word from someone else to wake her up. During her stay in hospital (with no further visit from Bob) she realised that it wasn't so much that Bob was a wonderful, positive and cheerful person, but that he was so afraid of emotional pain that he could not even let himself experience it. Far from strengthening him, his unrealistic and relentless 'optimism' was preventing him from seeing the reality of his business mistakes and stopping him from giving her the support and empathy she needed. She ended the relationship and made room in her life for someone who valued her true feelings, not a painted smile. Being given the opportunity to explore, validate and fully experience her 'negative' feelings put Sandra in a far better position to see herself and her situation clearly and to make the job changes she needed.

rescue me!

Sometimes a need to be heard may grow until it becomes a need to be rescued, which is a more difficult and disturbed position. It is natural to want to be noticed, but it may be childish and destructive to want to be rescued – although often understandable! Many of us hit points like this in life, when outside circumstances drag us into a time warp and we feel three years old again. If we did not experience the kind of rescue that every child needs at times, or if other circumstances have been difficult for us, we may, as adults, require rescuing all the time. This need for rescue (which may be a desperate, paralysing longing) will in all probability prevent us from progress for the simple reason that if we do make progress and get out of the mess we are in, then we can never know the comfort and bliss of rescue! This may be totally subconscious, of course.

If you think this may apply to you, be brutally honest with yourself. Have sympathy for yourself and the life experience that has led to your feeling like this. Then face up to the choice – spend your life in the dumps, looking for what only a child can ever really have, or find a way to rescue yourself, possibly through therapy initially. Remember that although there is no Big Momma or Daddy to make it all okay, you can get the support you need from a variety of willing resources, from friends to welfare organisations – but you need to be adult enough to co-ordinate all of this.

life scripts

Earlier in the chapter we looked at fourteen obstacles that we may create for ourselves. Most of these could be termed 'life scripts'. These are messages about life that we have internalised, things we repeat to ourselves, ways we look at ourselves and the events that surround us. Although they may seem to represent our life, in truth they do no such thing. They bear as much relationship to reality as the view from a tiny basement window reflects the lively, teeming city that lies around it. The view may be not only partial but also extremely distorted. For instance, if all you had ever seen from your basement were the feet and ankles of the people going by, what might your picture be of what a human being looked like? Many of us go through life with such crippled perceptions.

If you have a message you continually repeat to yourself (it always happens to me... nobody likes me... I'm always in a mess, etc), this is probably a life script. To take the last example, at some point in the dim-and-distant past you internalised the message that you were untidy and disorganised. After that you failed to see the times when you were tidy and in control of things – to you they did not exist. As time went by you probably grew increasingly messy as you lost touch with the part of you

> **Top Tip**
>
> *For the next month keep a notepad with you and jot down any little phrases that keep coming into your mind – things like 'I never win', 'It's always me who gets the rough end', etc. You will probably find, after a very few days, that the same phrases are repeated. Leave plenty of room in your notebook in between the statements. When you have a quiet moment and feel in a good mood, sit down and fill in the spaces with instances when the statements were not true! Now think again!*
>
> *If you conclude that the statements are true, ask a trusted friend to help by reading them through and offering a more reasonable perspective. If your friend agrees that they really are true – which is unlikely – then explore the ways in which you create this reality. Providence has not singled you out for a beating – promise!*

that could be organised. Starved of light, it ceased to exist. Depending on your circumstances, this might matter only a little bit or it might matter a great deal, to the point where it is quite crippling.

Tina's Story

Tina's basic life script was that she was 'stupid' and 'a mess'. She felt that most things in her life had gone wrong because she had no strength or common sense. Her self-esteem was rock bottom – so much so that she had effectively cut herself off from any positive input by deciding that she wasn't good enough to have any friends, and so avoiding them! She had three children, one from each of her disastrous marriages. The first man she married to prove her stepmother wrong when she told Tina that no-one would ever want her. He was unfaithful and ultimately left. The second became violent and she left him to protect her children, and the third became involved in some dubious business deals, leaving her with only the house when he departed to foreign climes along with his 'swag'. She was smoking heavily, her youngest child had been caught shoplifting, she detested her job and she described herself as 'empty'.

In many cases it is not helpful to compare a client with others for it may get in the way of them feeling heard and seen as a true individual. However, I felt that Tina needed a dose of reality. I told her that I knew many women who had had similar experiences to her, and several who had done much worse! She was very surprised at this, feeling she was the only woman in the world who was so 'pathetic'. I pointed out all the successes she had achieved. She had proved her stepmother wrong – a bad reason for marrying, but significant nevertheless. She had had the guts to leave her violent husband to protect her children – something all too many women do not do. And she had salvaged the house from the wreckage of her last marriage.

Hearing these basic things spelled out formed the beginnings of a new viewpoint. Actually Tina had not done as badly as she thought – in fact, taking into consideration her upbringing and her available resources, she had done well. This simple change of perspective turned her around. Her new glimmerings of self-esteem were encouraged by hypnotherapy and she brought the same practicality and dogged approach to her current problems that had worked in the past. Tina found the best counselling for her child (along with the patience to understand her), started an evening class and decided to give up smoking. Currently she is looking for another job – which I am sure she will find, as she now realises what a determined and effectual person she has always been and can build on this. Her new life script is 'I work at it until I get there.'

that little thing called luck

'I'm always unlucky' is a frequently encountered life script. Some people believe luck is mere chance, while others are convinced that fate is at work and we cannot change it. Others say, 'You make your own luck' and use that belief either to empower themselves or make themselves feel bad for not 'making' it. 'You make your own luck' is another one of those clichés that in fact is probably quite accurate.

Studies by Dr Richard Wiseman (see Further Reading) indicate that there are indeed some people who are lucky and others who are unlucky but instead of this depending solely on something mysterious, lucky people have certain definable characteristics that make them attract good fortune, while those who are unlucky are the opposite.

To maximise your luck, put the following tips into practice:

* Try always to look on the bright side and expect even bad things to work out for the best.
* Don't waste energy dwelling on what has gone wrong – instead learn from your mistakes and build on these lessons.
* Try to expect that things will go well – or at least behave as if you do.
* Be open to new experiences of all kinds. (Naturally this increases your chances of happy happenstance!)
* Be as relaxed as you can.
* Regularly listen to your intuition. Most lucky people actually take steps to increase their intuition, by meditating or giving themselves space to reflect. Lucky people are not necessarily more intuitive; they just tend to listen to their intuition when it speaks to them.

Luck School

If the pointers listed above were easy for you to follow, you might like to try some more advanced techniques before progressing to the more esoteric realms of charms and meditation. There are several things you can do to maximise your general good luck. If you are feeling very down you may find some of them difficult at first. Just try a few at first and build upon your efforts.

* Keep a 'good things' diary. However awful the day has been, there will always be good things – a flower, a ray of sunshine, a warm bath.
* Keep a diary of what you have achieved each day – make no mention of what you have not achieved. You can use the same diary as for

'good things'. List everything you have achieved – telephoning a friend, doing the shopping, completing a day at work – not just achievements you consider especially noteworthy.

* Smile as much as you can – smile at yourself in the mirror, smile at strangers, smile at children. Just smile!
* Chat to strangers (with obvious caution!). Don't worry about rejection – it isn't personal, so try to get used to it. Many people want to talk and you may make friends or pick up some interesting information. (For instance, today I have heard about a new vegetable hair-dye that is wonderful for your hair, and found out about a good band performing locally – both from folk I had never met before.)
* Set yourself sensible goals and go for what you want. When you get there, set further goals.
* Don't give up on something you want – keep on trying new approaches.
* Make a list of things you are going to achieve, large and small.
* When something bad happens give yourself time to feel awful. Then, when you have recovered, make yourself think of one good thing that has come out of it. The time you will need to recover depends on how bad the event – missing a train might take ten to 20 minutes to get over, while not getting a job you wanted might take you 24 hours, for example.
* Take responsibility for what goes wrong and take steps to change it – don't blame Fate.
* Imagine important things (and even relatively unimportant ones) working out in your favour.

Of course, it would be great if you could follow all the above points in an instant. For now, just do what you can. With the best will in the world, it is not always easy to change one's state of mind. The mind may be willing, but the imagination – which is a much more powerful and unruly animal – may pull in the other direction. Visualisation, charms and self-hypnosis can work the magic with the imagination that reason cannot accomplish.

visualisation and meditation

You may feel clear about what you want and ready for a fresh start. But creating a new 'me' on the outside will be much easier if the inside also has a wash and brush-up. It will greatly help you if you learn to relax, because tension is a great barrier to creative thought and obtaining results of all descriptions, including plugging in to the vast reservoirs of power in your unconscious mind. This process will have started with self-hypnosis. Learning also to meditate will open inner landscapes and enable you to have an inner dialogue with the deeper, wiser side of you.

Meditation, as we have seen, is a fairly general term, usually used for 'inner journeys'. It is also used for techniques that clear the mind, such as a mantra, or phrase that is repeated over and over again. What you are doing is quietening the conscious mind so that the unconscious may come out to play. When you do your self-hypnosis you are following a similar procedure, but it is more passive in the sense that you are using the meditative state to programme yourself. When you meditate you are, to some extent, exploring.

General Introduction Technique

Before you start, have available a notebook in which to write what you experience while meditating. Make sure you will not be disturbed for a while, then use this method to put yourself in a meditative state.

Light a candle if you wish, play some soft music (no lyrics) and/or heat some lavender oil in a burner. Settle yourself comfortably, lying or sitting well-supported, and close your eyes when you feel ready. You may wish to have taped the following instructions.

Feel all the tension draining away from you. Pay special attention to your body. Imagine the tension as muddy water that is draining slowly out of you, starting at the top of your head, going down from your face and neck, down your arms and out through your hands, down your chest and back, down your legs and feet and out through your toes. Keep going through this procedure until you feel that your tension has all gone.

what sort of 'me' would you like to be? * 33

Now imagine that you are sitting in an auditorium, looking at a curtained stage. The curtains are going to part on a new world – the world of your imagination. Let the curtains slowly swing wide, revealing the stage. What is it like? What can you see there? Watch for a while, noticing the colours, the shapes. Make changes if you want to. Now let the curtains close again. That was your first effort. Come back to the everyday and eat or drink something or pat your body to affirm you are back.

You may try this several times if you like, then proceed to the next stage when you are ready. This involves going up onto the stage and entering your inner world. There are several ways of looking at this inner world. Occultists tell us it is the astral plane or astral light – another plane of existence, more rarefied than the everyday, where things first come into being before they translate to ordinary life. Some believe that beings exist on the astral plane that do not have corporeal form. To other people it is simply imagination. However you view this, you are going inside yourself in order to get outside yourself! – your imagination is what makes the connection, and whether you believe the astral plane is real or not, you can still get results.

Visualisation for Self-Discovery/Problem-Solving

Go out into the world that you see on your stage and find yourself at the foot of a grassy hill. At the top of the hill is a temple, shining in the sunlight. Walk slowly up the hill, noticing the grass, the blue of the sky, the warm stone of the temple basking in the sunshine with birds wheeling around it. Hear the cries of birds, the sound of the grass scrunching under your feet and the sound of soft chanting from the temple. Smell the open air and the faint spicy scent of incense. Feel the sun on you, the breeze and the firm earth beneath your feet.

When you reach the top of the hill, enter the temple. In here it is shadowy, fragrant and tranquil. The chanting sounds louder now. Within a shrine ahead of you, you see a figure sitting peacefully, with a large book on his or her lap, holding a staff. Beside the figure, on a small altar, there is a chalice, a candle, a censer and a large, beautiful crystal. You approach this figure and kneel before it.

Now you may speak with this figure. You may ask it any question you like. Or you may just talk without asking for a response. Speak about anything that is on your mind. (If you need clarification on a single specific issue, then it is best to keep to that issue alone.) The figure may answer or it may remain silent. Either way, you will probably find that as you speak you feel somewhat clearer about things.

When you have spoken as much as you wish, tell the figure that you must now take your leave. There may be a response or you may be offered a gift, such as a ring or a book, which will have a symbolic meaning. Alternatively, there may be no response on this occasion, which is fine. Take your leave respectfully, make your way out of the temple, down the hill and find yourself on your stage. Come down into the auditorium and into the body of the theatre. Mentally close the curtains onto the stage and come back to the everyday as described above. Make sure you write down your experiences – it is best to have a special book that you keep for your meditation record.

You can use this little exercise whenever you feel confused or stressed, or when you need an answer to something specific that is troubling you. In all probability you will find it amazingly helpful.

Meditation for a New Start

You can use this exercise if you want to give yourself a bit of a boost in creating a new future for yourself. It gives you more scope than the Self-Hypnosis for a New Start (page 43), stressing more the aspect of self-discovery. It will help if you do this to music. Choose a piece in which the tempo changes after about five minutes, signalling that you are about to find the archway. Try it when you need some inspiration, are not sure which direction to take or don't really know what is available to you.

Imagine yourself in your auditorium. The curtains slowly swing apart to reveal your magical world. In this case it is a wonderful garden. Do you want to enter it? If so, climb the steps onto the stage and find yourself in this radiant and colourful place. Wander around, just looking and touching, as you might have done as a child. Simply enjoy the place, smell the flowers, feel the sunshine, watch butterflies, and admire the profusion of multi-coloured flowers and the mysterious tangle of the paths.

Now you are coming to a more overgrown part of the garden. Although the flowers are equally luxuriant, here there is less evidence of cultivation. Stems straddle the path, hedges overhang, blooms wrestle with each other for space to grow and the buzz of bees and insects is even thicker.

Ahead of you, you see an archway formed by the intertwining branches of two cherry trees. The path to the archway is lined by lavender bushes. Beyond the arch there is a delicate silvery mist. Try as you may, you cannot see beyond this mist.

You walk towards the archway and your clothes brush the lavender as you go, making a sweet fragrance. You find yourself beneath the cherry trees, but still you cannot see through the mist. Do you wish to continue?

If the answer is 'yes', step beneath the cherry branches. As you do so, you realise that the mist is composed, in part, of sandalwood smoke, smelling spicy and exotic. You come through the mist and find yourself in another landscape entirely.

Wander round this place, noticing its details. As you wander, look for three things left for you on the ground. They may be very ordinary or very unusual. Gather them up and keep them with you.

When you are ready, look for the archway and the mist. Wherever you are in this new place, the archway will be there when you call for it. Walk through the mist and back into the garden, carrying your three articles. Walk through the garden and find yourself back on the stage.

Step down into the auditorium and place your three articles somewhere safe, for example in a special box hidden away at the back of the room. Give thanks. Come back to everyday awareness, eat or drink something and pat your body. Write down what you saw and felt. It may well be that you have no idea what the three things meant. On the other hand, you may recognise many meanings in both the landscape you were exploring and the things you picked up, and may feel you have found an answer or are on the way to one. Whatever the case, you have 'opened a door'. In the days and weeks that follow, you may well find you understand better.

charms for the new you

Cheer-Me-Up Charm

If your answers to the questionnaire at the start of the chapter were mostly Cs, then you may be very sceptical about things improving. There may even be a kind of grim satisfaction in saying to yourself, 'See, I knew it wouldn't work!' – whatever 'it' may be. Before you attempt to make any changes, try this charm.

You will need a gold or orange scarf – colours should be deep and vibrant, not muddy. Also have available some honey, a sachet of St John's wort tea, a mug, a candle that matches the colour of your scarf, and your favourite video or book.

Choose a time when you have no pressure and when you feel as relaxed as possible. Light the candle and make the tea – if you really hate the taste then do not steep the bag for more than a second. Add honey to taste and stir it saying, 'Sunshine and smiles for miles and miles,' at least three times. Smile as you are saying it (even if this is a smile at the absurdity of what you are doing!).

Now settle yourself with the scarf over your lap and sip your honey tea as the candle burns down. Then relax with your video or book, if you feel like it. Repeat this three nights in a row if you can and thereafter as necessary.

Charm for Self-Understanding

The inscription over the initiation temple in Eleusis, in Ancient Greece, read 'Know Thyself'. Knowing ourselves is essential in beginning to explore the mysteries of the Universe; unless we do, all we encounter are the shadows of our own fears and desires. Self-knowledge may be the most difficult thing to achieve in life, as we peel away the layers of the onion to reveal yet more layers. It can be very hard to be completely honest with ourselves, and even if we are – or almost are – there are still different levels of us and different parts of us that do not seem to agree with each other.

There is a wonderful line from Ralph Waldo Emerson that reads 'A foolish consistency is the hobgoblin of little minds.' You do not have to be the same today as you were yesterday, nor do you have to have one viewpoint – in fact the ability to hold opposing viewpoints may be a sign of a varied and open mind. However, the point is to be able to explore, to see different sides of ourselves and to discover things we may have repressed. It is a great help to adopt the outlook 'A part of me is/feels/wants…', for then we are able to work with unpleasant bits of ourselves without feeling we are utter villains. For instance, if you are a step-parent you will probably have ambivalent feelings towards your partner's children. On the one hand, you probably want to care for them, you want to be a family and you may want to make friends with them. But a part of you may be very jealous and resentful – even violently so. You can admit to that and contain it, letting it walk alongside the rest of you without feeling that it is the final statement on you.

If you really are not sure what you want or how you feel, try this charm. You will need to obtain the most beautiful piece of crystal you can afford. This may be literally a crystal ball such as used by fortune-tellers (although these are now very expensive if they are of any size). A glass ball will also do, or you may prefer other crystals in other shapes – an amethyst geode would be a perfect tool. You will also need access to a stream, a piece of black velvet, two purple candles, jasmine oil and an oil-burner.

Take your crystal or glass to the stream and hold it in the running water, imagining anything negative leaving it – this is especially to be recommended if you know someone else has been using the crystal.

Take your crystal back home and place it on a piece of black velvet in a softly lit room and light two purple candles. Burn some jasmine oil in your oil burner and relax, letting yourself enter a drifty state. Formulate a question as clearly as you can – this does not have to be an ultimate question because you can ask others at a later time for more clarification. Look into your crystal, letting your eyes focus not on the surface but deep inside it, as if you were looking into a magical land.

Now just note what you see or what comes to mind. Try not to disturb your relaxed state or get excited – just carry on looking, travelling into the crystal to see what you see. It is possible you may see an inner message or even hear something in your head. Whatever you experience will be important. If you experience nothing, this is still a helpful charm because the peace you are bringing to your mind will make space for an answer to come at some later time and you may be surprised at what pops into your head in the days that follow.

When you are ready, come back to everyday awareness, have a sip of water, write down anything you have experienced, put out your candles and wrap your crystal up in the velvet cloth.

If you use your crystal regularly, cleanse it anew from time to time in running water.

Charm for Life Scripts

Identifying your life scripts may take a while. Get yourself a small notebook and keep it with you over the course of a month. Jot down any life scripts as they go through your mind. You may even have quite a giggle when you see the list of your 'unfortunate circumstances'.

For your charm, choose a waning moon. You will need some black cord, your notebook, a black candle, patchouli oil, some tongs, sheets of notepaper and a pen. You will also need something nice to eat or drink.

Light your black candle and sit before it, quietly meditating. Be aware that a phase is coming to an end. When you feel ready, open your notebook and copy out one of your life scripts onto a piece of paper. Screw this into a taper and ceremoniously burn it in the candle flame. Do this one by one with each of the scripts. If you get tired, can't concentrate or find this a bit strenuous, leave off to complete the charm the next day, or spread it over several days of the waning moon.

When all the scripts are burnt, dab some patchouli oil on the notebook, bind it round with the black cord and bury it in the garden or in wasteland, along with any ashes you can gather up from the burnt scripts. Celebrate with your food and drink – what a good job you have done!

Rome not always being built in a day, you might like to get another notebook and repeat this charm a few times until all those boring scripts are gone.

Charm to be Rid of Negativity

Do you have a tendency to look on the black side? Are there behaviour patterns that you want to be rid of? Do you want to get primed for a new start? This simple and rather un-charming charm will help. This is a quicker charm than the one given above, and can also be used to cleanse your life.

Just write the thing you want to be rid of on a scrap of soluble paper, screw it up and throw it down the toilet. Flush the toilet and say goodbye to the negativity. You can repeat this as often as you like, but do make sure that the paper you use is really flushable. Toilet paper, if you have a pen that will write on it, is the best choice.

Charm for Confidence and Faith in Life

For this charm you will need some natural gold or orange food colour, a piece of natural amber or an amber necklace, a little orange oil, nine gold or orange candles and a large, soft orange or gold towel.

Simply run yourself a warm bath with a few drops of the food colour in it. (Natural food colour isn't usually very strong, but be careful not to use too much of it if you are worried about staining.) Add a few drops of orange oil (having tested for allergy first, as this oil can cause adverse reactions). Then light the candles all around the bathroom and place the amber in the bath. Lie in the bath enjoying the sensation of luxury and watching the candle flames dancing in the water, and affirm to yourself that you are surrounded by warmth, held suspended in a caring and benevolent Universe. Feel the warm water supporting your body and feel the unseen support of the Powers of Life. Affirm to yourself that you are safe and warm, whatever you do, that you are radiant with confidence and faith, and as glowing as the water around you.

When you are ready, get out and wrap yourself in the towel. Dry off the amber and keep it with you whenever you need a special feeling of faith and confidence. Repeat this every so often, for a boost.

Lucky Charm

For this charm you will need three white or silver candles, a small mock-silver horseshoe such as is used to decorate wedding cakes, some table-confetti stars, a small green cotton pouch (you can make this yourself; it does not have to look smart), some hazel twigs (or some hazelnuts and a green scarf), green thread and some cinnamon oil.

This charm should be undertaken at the time of the full moon. Begin by having a leisurely bath, so you feel relaxed and warm. Make the hazel twigs into a rough crown – you can bind them together with green thread, or stick them together if you wish. If you cannot find any hazel wood, tie a few hazelnuts in a green scarf and place this on your head or neck. Settle yourself comfortably, with the hazel crown on your head, and rub a few drops of cinnamon oil into each of the candles, while you repeat the word 'Lucky, lucky, lucky'. Sprinkle the stars round the candles and light them, smiling as you do so. Hold the little horseshoe so that the 'horns' point upwards and imagine good fortune shining down and being caught in the bowl of the horseshoe. Hold the horseshoe between your palms and imagine a lucky outcome to something that you are going to do. Continue to imagine for as long as is comfortable. If negative thoughts come to you, put down your horseshoe and breathe them out, visualising a grey mist on your out-breath – do this until you feel clear, and then do it a few extra times. Take up the horseshoe and continue visualising a great outcome.

When you feel you have done all the visualising you can, place the little horseshoe in the pouch, with some or all of the stars, and place three drops of cinnamon oil on the pouch. If possible leave this out in the light of the full moon. Carry the pouch with you, for all the luck you need.

It is a good idea to keep a stock of these horseshoes, to charge up for different occasions. You can use the hazel crown as often as you like.

self-hypnosis for the new you

Self-Hypnosis for Relaxation

If you do no other exercise in this book, you owe it to yourself to do this simple one. Tension is a great barrier between us and the things we want to achieve. Tension is a prison. It is part of the package of fear and negativity that immobilises us. While our fears cause us tension, a vicious circle is created because the presence of tension intensifies anxiety. But you can break the feedback loop! Tension also forms a barrier between us and our intuition and natural instincts; it distorts our perspectives, twists our priorities, stunts our creativity, cramps our enjoyment – and it is bad for our physical health. Convinced? Read on!

Make the most of your self-hypnosis relaxation session by making extra sure you won't be disturbed. Dim the lights or draw the curtains, light a candle and heat some lavender oil in an oil-burner. Alternatively you can choose a good lavender-scented candle, or perhaps place a few drops of the essential oil on a tissue and place it near you. Take your phone off the hook and put the cat out. This is your time.

Play some soft music while you prepare the room and get ready to relax before you play your self-hypnosis tape. You could even leave the soft music playing in the background while you listen to the self-hypnosis tape – or alternatively you could record the self-hypnosis with music in the background.

[Usual induction]

You are so relaxed, so beautifully relaxed, and your relaxation is growing. There is a sensation of gentle warmth all over you and you are floating, light, free, light as a feather, feeling so free, so comfortable. Beautifully relaxed.

Relaxation is growing inside you. Feel it spreading down from the top of your head, flowing down and around your face and neck, so wonderfully relaxed, free from tension, blissful, comfortable, flowing over your shoulders – aah, how relaxed they are – and down your arms, hands and fingers. Now the relaxation is flowing down over your chest and tummy, down your back right down to the base of your spine and through your buttocks. All the tension is being washed away by this beautiful feeling of relaxation. Going down your thighs, over your knees, down your legs, ankles and feet and even to the tips of your toes. There is no tension left – not a scrap. All there is room for is wonderful relaxation.

You are walking through a meadow. The sun is shining, the sky is blue and everywhere there are blue flowers. You walk lightly, springing from foot to foot almost as if you were flying. Your feet stir the blue blossom, releasing a fragrance – a sweet, calming scent. All around you there is gentle blue and wonderful fragrance.

You come to a silver stream and sit beside it. The water shines like jewels and where it falls over small rocks it makes a sound as clear as a bell. You watch the water flowing, flowing, finding its way round stones, into cracks and crevices, moving onwards and onwards, always flowing, always moving, always there. The water is always moving on, the water is never gone.

As you sit beside this peaceful stream you know that everything and everyone will be easier from now on. You realise that so many of the things you get stressed about do not matter. In a few years time they will be gone, lost in the mists of time, while this silver water keeps on flowing, keeps on flowing. Everything is easier; everyone is easier to deal with. You feel relaxed and free.

As the days go by, this feeling of relaxation is growing, deepening, becoming more habitual. You are serene, you keep things in proportion, you keep a sense of wide perspective. You have the wisdom to know that very, very few things are worth any concern at all. Your attitude is positive, your mind is free and your body is relaxed. You are open to the beauty and the wonder of life. Everything and everyone is easier to cope with; everything and everyone is manageable, nothing and no-one upsets you. Naturally, at times you experience annoyance, but these times become less and less frequent, for you are indeed becoming a much more relaxed person, a person with a free and harmonious mind, a person with a wide perspective, a person with a comfortable and relaxed body.

Now you take up a leaf from beside the stream and you drop it into the running water. The stream takes it, bobbing on the silver current, downstream, into the distance. That leaf is your tension, your concerns and worries, carried away, out of your sight, out of your mind, down to the vast ocean of being where it will dissolve. And all is well, all is well. You are so relaxed, so comfortable, so aware of all the bliss that is available in life.

All around you now you are aware of the blue flowers and their sweet fragrance. So relaxed, so serene, and all is harmonious, all is peaceful and tranquil and you are floating, so deeply relaxed, so pleasantly relaxed, so gently relaxed. And this feeling of relaxation you take with you, into daily life, in just the quantity that you need it to feel your best, to be at your best. And you do retain this feeling of relaxation, you do retain this feeling of harmony and you do retain this wide perspective on life.

[Waking-up procedures.]

Self-Hypnosis for a New Start

[Usual induction.]

You are standing in a country lane and there is a heavy pack on your back. Look around you – see the green hills, the blue of the sky and the graceful branches of the trees. Hear the birds singing, the distant hum of a tractor, the drowsy buzz-buzz of bees, the lowing of cattle in the distance. Smell the scent of the country, the freshness of the breeze, the fragrance of the hedgerows. Feel the sun gentle on your face, the cool breeze on your cheeks, the weight of the straps from your pack cutting into your shoulders. *[Elaborate, if you like, paying attention to all the senses.]*

Here you stand in this country lane. Now you are starting to walk backwards. Walk backwards along the lane – oh so carefully. You have to strain your head to look over your shoulder. How awkward it is, how unpleasant and frustrating! You can see all the pathways you have missed, all the gates you could have climbed, all the things you could have stopped to examine, and now all you can do is look at them go by as you struggle to make your way.

Now, this is like the pathway of life. This is just like the pathway of life, where you go along thinking about the past, going over and over the past and the things that went wrong, all the things you missed. And while you are going over and over the past you cannot get anywhere – all your energies are going into keeping your footing, reflecting on what you've missed, repeating your mistakes because you can't see any other way of doing things.

So now just turn your head and face forwards. Ah! – that feels better. And now drop that backpack. That pack is filled with all the negative experiences, all the unhelpful beliefs and habits, all the burdens of the past. You do not need these any more. They are not relevant, they are no use to you. All you need for the future is what you can carry in your pockets. You have everything you need. Drop that heavy pack, feel it land with a thud on the path. One more look round and you see it dissolve into dust, on the path. It has turned to dust, disappeared, gone. And you feel so free, you feel so liberated, you feel so light and carefree.

Square your shoulders, look forwards, take a deep breath and start walking. Walking towards a good future. Feel the solid earth beneath your feet – how good it feels to be moving, to be in control, to be getting somewhere. You can see all the paths you could take; you can see the gates, the stiles, the hills you can climb if you wish, the shady nooks you can explore, the sunny expanses that you can stride over. You have choices, you have control, you have options. Walk on, steadily, happily, in a balanced way and feel really good about your decision – that wise decision to leave the past and its burdens behind you. All those past experiences, they have gone, they are no longer relevant, they have nothing to do with the present and the future and all the options that you have.

Now stride on, looking around you. What a wide, wonderful world it is, and it is yours to explore. Walk on, until you find a comfortable seat where you can sit to look out over a beautiful view. Sit in that seat feeling the sun playing upon you. Look into the blue horizon and imagine one thing that you are moving towards, one thing that you want to explore and achieve. Imagine it in detail, feel the joy of achieving it. *[Elaborate if you wish.]*

And now you relax, and you feel good, so very good. And this feeling of relaxation, positivity and achievement stays with you with every day that passes. It is growing with every day that passes. And you know you can move towards a good future. You know that you can create a good future. You know that a great future is there waiting for you to move into it.

[Waking-up procedure.]

In Appendix 2, you will find additional hypnotherapy scripts for improving your luck and your sense of self-esteem.

* final thoughts

In this chapter we have looked at what we want and what might stand in our way. We have considered several ways of changing our approach, using the practical methods of charms, self-hypnosis and visualisation. There are many tools at our disposal for making creative change. How can we keep all of this in mind with the many demands and hectic pace of life?

It is a truism that no-one ever said on their death-bed that they wished they'd spent more time at the office! So if you were 85 right now, this minute, what would you wish you had done in your life?

Do it!

three

The Lore of Love

'…Yet all love is sweet,
Given or returned. Common as light is love,
And its familiar voice wearies not ever.'
Shelley, 'Prometheus Unbound'

✱ this little thing

The worst – and the best – moments of our lives often come through one-to-one sexual relationships. Full of complexity, paradox, agony and ecstasy, often we wish we could do without them, only to change our minds again as the strange alchemy begins and we are caught up in something that is as elemental as rain and wind.

Love has given rise to majestic poetry and interesting philosophical perspectives. It has inspired heroism and crime. It has been given metaphysical powers and biological definition. We all know it makes the world go round. One thing we cannot do is control it. The best we can hope to do is have some understanding of our role in the drama of our loves, to see that love can be a teacher and to learn to steer our personal boat on the currents of love so that we have some influence over where we are going. Yes, we may get what we want in relationships, but then we find that we, and others, are changed by them. Love is a journey and destiny is at work. Wanting a relationship can in no way be seen as similar to wanting a possession, but let's try. Compare love to a Ferrari – you may get the car but then it is up to you to drive it, and it will take you on a journey – to where?

Relationships are a spiritual, even karmic experience. Often we draw to ourselves those relationships that will teach us something about ourselves. The quicker we learn these lessons (sorry, it sounds like school, but it's usually more fun!), the quicker we can develop and move on to a more fulfilling place, for the quality of the love we give and appreciate depends on our own essence. If we are afraid, self-centred (as opposed to self-valuing), manipulative and caught in unconscious repetition of childhood patterns then all this will be reflected in our relationships. Even if we were to meet our soul-mate we would not be able to relate properly to him or her because we would be looking through clouded and distorting lenses. The love is only as good as the lover. Of course, we do not have to be perfectly evolved beings in order to love and be loved. But we do need to be prepared to look at ourselves bravely and truthfully and to be especially honest about what we really feel.

Loving relationships are as complicated as the human personality, and nothing is more complicated than that! The purpose of this chapter is to isolate some issues, to give you some basis for further exploration and also to help you make this savage yet tender, scary yet comforting thing called love work better for you.

the 'me' generation

Our situation in the developed world at the start of the twenty-first century is unique in a lot of ways for we have many freedoms not enjoyed by our forebears. We may think we have money worries, but we don't have to fend off starvation; despite nuclear threat, we do not have to be prepared to defend our community in hand-to-hand combat against marauders. Our society is comparatively free and tolerant regarding sexual morals and relationships. This is great – who would wish to go back in time, to be poor, threatened and constrained? While today we have the open misery of divorce, it is reasonable to assume that in former times there was untold misery behind closed doors, within relationships that 'no man could put asunder'. Our problem now is that we have freedoms and choices that we don't always know how to manage, and we may chase impossible ideals and impractical schemes, then wonder why we feel let down.

Astrology has an interesting perspective on this. Changes in the values and attitudes of the collective are mirrored by the passage of the outer planets through the signs, particularly Neptune and Pluto, which take approximately 165 years and 248 years respectively to make a tour of the Zodiac. The theory of astrology is outside the scope of this book, but it can help us to see our lives as part of a cosmic tide affecting the developing consciousness of humankind. Each generation has something new to experience and to explore and in many ways the baby-boomers are fated to explore and discover what it means to be an individual, and a passionate one, in ways pleasant and not so pleasant. This correlates with the passage of Pluto through the sign of Leo, from 1938 to 1957. Leo is a sign associated with self-expression, self-esteem, love and creativity – also with egotism, self-importance and general bossiness. Leo also heralds the need to find what one really is, as opposed to drawing one's identity from the appreciation of others. People born with Pluto in Leo are reacting to the legacy of the Pluto in Cancer generation, who were more accepting of the status quo and prepared to put their 'family' (i.e. their mother country) before their own welfare during the Second World War. These were the parents who were all too keen to say, 'After all I've done for you!' to a son or daughter, who might then arrogantly respond, 'I never asked you to. Look at the mess you made – I can do better!' Pluto in Leo has been followed by Pluto in Virgo, giving a much more analytical group of people, determined to get to the root of things and often sceptical and critical of the Pluto in Leo determination to make things, especially themselves, wonderful! This is the generation that was especially concerned with the implementation of technology, giving way in the early 70s to Pluto in Libra, and a generation of people who are reforming very radically our ideas on relationships and political correctness. Hence gay marriages and emphasis on the rights of minority groups.

The process is ever-evolving, but it is doubtful whether change has ever been so swift in recorded history or has ever presented us with so many challenges to our identities and standards. This has nothing to do with the movements of the planets as such, for Pluto has been through Leo, for instance, approximately eight times since the beginning of the Christian epoch. What does correlate with the apparent acceleration of change has been the discovery of the planets Neptune in 1846 and Pluto in 1930, which seems to have brought their themes more into our consciousness.

Whether you are an astrological animal or not, there is no doubt that different times have their own characteristics, challenges and subtle essence. In our times we are often left with the task of forming our own standards about what is right for us, exploring what our relationships can do – and cannot do – for us, what rights we have, what our duties are, and how best, if at all, to formalise relationships for ourselves and within our culture. May the Goddess be with us!

begin at the beginning

You can only begin with yourself. We have all been told over and over again in childhood not to be selfish. Sadly, this tends to have the effect of making many of us feel guilty about wanting things, ashamed of putting our own interests to the fore. This can have the odd effect of making us more truly selfish, because subconsciously we may be taking things through the back door and being greedy because we feel deprived.

True self-love and self-esteem are not distorted and certainly not wrong. What else do you have but yourself as a starting point? How can you give to others if your own well is empty? Can you really make other people feel good if you put them before yourself, continually sacrificing your own needs in order that they might meet theirs? At any rate, who wants to live with a martyr? The fact is, truth will out. However much we suppress, deny and hide our own feelings, they still ooze out to contaminate the air around us, and all we give carries a sub-text. True sacrifice, of course, brings joy, but that is a matter of spiritual awakening, seeing the division between self and other dissolve. That cannot be induced, and is often prevented by 'shoulds' and 'oughts'. On the other hand, a person who is able to enjoy life, be honest about what they want and take pleasure in getting it, where possible and suitable, is able to bring joy to others and to create an aura of contentment. It is natural, when we are happy, to want to give to other people.

Loving Number One Questionnaire

First of all you need to find out how much you like yourself and are prepared to treat yourself. Work through the following questions.

1. Stand before a full-length mirror and list six things you like about your appearance – you have half a minute to do this. Was this possible?
2. Write down six things you are proud of achieving in your life. You have one minute to do this. Was this possible?
3. When you get a compliment, does it make you feel great?
4. Do you give yourself at least three small treats every day?
5. Do you give yourself at least one big treat every week?

6 If there is something that you really want, do you do everything reasonable to get it?

7 If you really hate the thought of doing something, do you almost always refuse?

8 Do you never socialise with people who make you feel bad? In work/family situations do you never socialise more than you need to with such people?

9 Are you happy to ask for a favour if you need it?

10 Are you prepared to ignore the phone or the doorbell on the odd occasion when you are absorbed in something enjoyable?

11 Do you feel you have a right to do work that you enjoy, most of the time?

12 If someone says they like you, do you believe them?

13 If someone says they love you, do you believe them?

14 Do you always try to make sure you have something to look forward to?

What is your score? If you answered 'Yes' to twelve or more questions, your self-esteem is in good nick; for eight to eleven 'Yes' answers, you need to think about why you gave those 'No' answers – could you work towards feeling better about yourself? For seven or less 'Yes' answers, you need to put up the scaffolding straight away to build that self-esteem!

Quickie Self-Love Tips and Exercises

* Keep a Compliments Diary in which you write all compliments you receive, small or large. Flick through this when you're feeling down.
* Keep a list of things you have done that you reckon make you really lovable.
* Look in the mirror, find your best feature and spend a minute or two admiring it.
* Look in the mirror and give yourself a big smile.
* Get a group of your friends together. Each of you should have a piece of A4 paper with your name written at the top. Pass this around for each person to write one of the things they most admire about the person whose paper they have (the paper should be folded so that the other comments are not visible). This is sure to surprise you pleasantly!

- Buy yourself a present.
- If being with a person gets you down, avoid them. You may, it is true, be imagining things, but you may also be sensing some real feelings from them that are not in your best interests, whatever the reason. They may well not be aware of this, but no matter. Give yourself permission to keep away.
- By the same token, mix with up-beat types who encourage you to make the best of yourself.

> **Top Tip**
> *You must first love yourself before you have the spiritual resources to bring to loving someone else.*

so you really want a relationship?

Looking for a relationship, coping with problems within relationship, getting out of a bad relationship – these are the issues that beset most people at some point in their life. Sometimes these problems are not so much our own as other people's – friends and relatives seem to think we should be in a relationship, especially if most of them are. Our culture assumes that most people will, sooner or later, pair up, and even today single people, especially women, are occasionally looked down upon.

It is worthwhile asking yourself why you want a relationship. What will it give you that you don't have on your own? What will it take away? What is the attitude of your family to you, single or hitched? What is the attitude of your friends? What things are most important to you in life and will a relationship help or hinder you in achieving them? What things do you most enjoy, and will a relationship help you to enjoy them more?

Relationships are wonderful things, but they are also an enormous source of heartache, problems, disappointments, demands and dilemmas. They take hard work and time. If you can be contented without a steady, permanent relationship, do not feel that you *should* be looking for one. Give yourself permission to be splendidly single.

Getting Involved

If you have not yet had much in the way of long-term partners, or if you are now between partners, this is a good point to take stock and ask yourself what you want out of a relationship.

First, it is useful to look at your family of origin, for these experiences will undoubtedly colour what you hope for, expect or even dread in a relationship. That is your template for a couple, and to some extent you will be working with this, either positively or negatively. The permutations are endless, but here are some pointers.

* An apparently happy relationship between parents can cause you not to look too deeply at underlying issues. For instance there may have been manipulation, hypocrisy and pretence. If we feel sure our parents were happy and that our childhood was happy, it can be very hard indeed to look more closely. We may fear being disloyal or having our impressions shattered. Many counsellors feel their hearts sink when a client comes to them for help and asserts they had 'a very happy childhood'! Of course, many childhoods are happy, although fewer people who have had these seek therapy. Try to be very honest here, because if things weren't quite right you are very likely to repeat the same pattern unless you are conscious of it.
* If your parents were really happy, ask yourself why. Could this work for you? If not, what changes would you like to make?
* Don't let a bad parental relationship blind you to the possibilities of great partnerships. If your childhood was not happy, you may not be programmed for happiness, but at least you have no rose-coloured specs.
* Beware of trying so hard to have the opposite kind of relationship that you end up making a mirror-image of the same mistake. For instance, a child of parents who rowed all the time may vow to have 'never a cross word'. However, the atmosphere of pent-up feelings may be as

bad as overt violence. The best way is the middle one, where issues can be honestly aired.

* Look at your relationship with your parent of the opposite sex. If it was great, then it may be hard for anyone to 'follow Daddy'. An awful lot may be expected of partners. Ask yourself, do you really want a partner who is like your parent? Ask yourself also if you have separated from your parents and really grown up, because if you haven't (and this can be true well into middle age) then you cannot fully relate to someone else as an adult. Of course, we all like to be babied at times, but this needs to be in proportion.
* If you had a bad relationship with the opposite sex parent this can, unsurprisingly, put you off relationships big-style. However, it can have the opposite effect, too. You may look for a substitute. Also, if you had no proper relationship with this parent, and you know this to be the case, then you have no proper template. So your imagination gets to work and you may in fact idealise members of the opposite sex, simply because in your formative years you had so little meaningful contact with it.

Look also at past relationships – do they have a pattern, or is there a characteristic that you can discern in retrospect? Here are some possible issues.

* Were you acting as a parent figure, or was your partner?
* Was there ever any form of violence or cruelty? Who by? Why?
* If you were on the receiving end of bad treatment, why did you put up with it? (Think about this carefully, as there may be several answers.)
* Did either of you lay guilt trips on the other? Why? How did you react?
* Was money an issue? Why was that? What could you have done differently? (Remember that money is power, money is energy. Money issues need to be thrashed out openly in relationships. That isn't being mercenary; it's being sensible.)
* Did either of you manipulate the other – i.e. covertly, getting them to do things by arousing certain feelings rather than asking outright.
* Did your partner make you feel good or bad about yourself? Why?

* Was jealousy an issue? Was it yours or your partner's? How did you handle it? Would you like to have done it differently?
* Did you want the same things in life or were they very different? If the latter, what made someone so different attractive to you? Was this a problem?
* Was there any deception involved?
* What were your fears, if any, when around your partner?
* Did you leave or did your partner, and why?

These are just some triggers for self-exploration. The point is to try to see what wasn't right about past relationships. It is not about pinpointing what you did and did not have in common with your partner and deciding that from now on you will avoid people who snore or love footie! It is about seeing in what ways you went into relationships with hang-ups and unhelpful patterns of behaviour. It is even better if you can connect this with something you absorbed as a child. If you can understand your hidden scripts and agendas, you will be more able to re-write these, or at least be aware enough to come clean when you next form a close relationship.

Of course, some relationships simply fizzle out. People out-grow each other and move on, or find they are 'just friends' and split amicably. Sometimes there is a conflict of interest such as demanding careers heading in different directions, and sometimes a desire for children on the part of just one partner can cause a split. By no means are all splits due to pathology! It merely helps to be as clear as possible. After all, the real point of the study of history is so that we may better understand where we are right now!

Laura's Story

Laura was in her early forties, facing yet another relationship break-up. Once more she had chosen a man who let her down badly and her self-esteem was at rock-bottom. Through talking it over with her therapist, she realised that she was continually selling herself short in relationships. She did not feel good enough because her father had consistently ignored her. Consequently she subconsciously chose partners who were inferior to her in almost every way so that she could feel sure of keeping them. Her greatest fear was that she would have to face the final proof of her un-lovableness – being alone. But the behaviour of her current man was making it preferable to go solo. She realised that although she felt terrified, her terror was not really about her present circumstances but about what she had experienced in the past, when she had been a forlorn child. She then found the courage to strike out alone. Less than a year later, a much better relationship had come her way, but this time she was determined to give herself time before committing.

what you really, really want

You're looking for a relationship and probably you have some idea of the kind of person you want. Hopefully you have thought about what we said in the earlier section Getting Involved. If there are negative patterns, you will be doing your best to be aware of them and not to repeat them and you will be trying to think clearly about what would make you happy. Of course, love is something you can never control and there is always that 'certain something' that makes relationships gel – and that cannot be defined or predicted. However, don't be afraid to bring common sense in – if entertaining but unreliable characters have tended to attract you and then let you down, why go like a lamb to the slaughter again, saying 'I can't help it – I'm in love!' You owe it to yourself to find a way to help it if you are going to have a chance of happiness.

A strange magic occurs when we fall in love. It seems that this wonderful person is the answer to our dreams and everything is the stuff of legend. What is actually happening is that we have an inner image of the ideal man or the ideal woman, which we project onto a likely partner. It is this – and a bit of good old chemistry – that makes them appear larger than life. As time goes by we tend to take back our projections, and the person 'shrinks' – they aren't so magical and perfect after all, and the cracks begin to show. It is at this point that loving takes over from being 'in love'. Or, if things go badly wrong, we just fall out of love completely. If we are very needy and/or if we have a stack of bad experiences behind us, then the gap between the image we project and the person who receives the projection may be very great and we wake up one day to find the face on the pillow next to us is that of a stranger. If we can be positive, cut our partner some slack and realise that no-one can be a god – or goddess – all the time, then we may keep some of that magic and find it still lingers through the years.

Try one of the following questionnaires to see what your ideal image might be.

For Women

1 The most important quality in a man is:
  a) Capability and strength,
  b) Courage and enterprise,
  c) Cleverness and mental resourcefulness,
  d) Supportiveness and understanding.

2 You like to be wooed by:
  a) Being moderately wined and dined and having your shelves put up,
  b) Being whisked off to the Seychelles at a moment's notice,
  c) Being taken to social events involving successful and entertaining people,
  d) Having your hand held and a cuppa poured for you.

3 A man should dress:
  a) In a way fitting to what he does – no fuss,
  b) Sharp dress or flamboyant – you like a bit of character,
  c) Smooth and smart,
  d) Casual, with cuddly jumpers and jeans.

4 It turns you on to:
  a) See a guy doing whatever he does, well,
  b) See a man doing something outrageous or dangerous, especially if he wins,
  c) Witness intellectual prowess, for instance a lawyer in a courtroom drama,
  d) See a man holding a baby, being tender.

58 ✻ a charmed life

5 **Which of these phrases have the greatest ring with you in regard to men (don't think, answer quickly):**
   a) Handsome is as handsome does,
   b) Faint heart never won fair lady,
   c) Manners maketh man,
   d) Two's company.

6 **All women want to be listened to when they are upset, but when you've dried your tears you'd like him to:**
   a) Look for ways to fix it,
   b) Take your mind off it,
   c) Keep talking about the ins and outs,
   d) Make dinner.

7 **His priorities should be:**
   a) Coping with the nitty-gritty of life,
   b) Exploring, looking for meanings,
   c) Getting a good education,
   d) Caring for others.

8 **You most want him to make you feel:**
   a) Secure,
   b) Excited,
   c) Communicated with,
   d) Understood.

Your Score

Mostly A: Your image is that of the 'Hero' – a guy who can cope with anything from tigers to tax returns. You like a man who is capable, protective and solid. You don't mind too much if he watches the footie and resorts to monosyllables sometimes, as long as he carries out the rubbish and carries you upstairs.

Mostly B: Your image is that of the 'Magician'. You like the idea of a larger-than-life man who'll try anything once and bring some excitement into your life. You're prepared to put up with the fact he's a big kid deep inside as long as he brings you armfuls of roses and takes you out in his Aston Martin – when he remembers where you live!

Mostly C: Your image is that of the 'Courtier'. You really like a man who can handle himself in civilised society, make an impression with his charm and wit and be clever enough to out-argue anyone. You don't mind if it's a bit above your head at times as long as you can queen it on his arm – and feel he also respects your views, of course!

Mostly D: Your image is that of the 'Father'. You like a man who is in touch with his feelings and can empathise with you, get close and cuddly and give you emotional support. You like him being sheltering and you don't mind if he prefers his pinny to his pin-stripe. You feel safe and comfortable with him, and that's what counts.

For Men

1. **The most important quality in a woman is:**
    a) Coping with life and being sensible,
    b) Being exciting, like a page 3 girl or a film star,
    c) Being able to talk sense,
    d) Looking after you.
2. **At the beginning of the relationship she should be:**
    a) Well-dressed and moderately sexy,
    b) Just a bit unpredictable and hard-to-get,
    c) Great company,
    d) Inviting you round to dinner.
3. **A woman should dress:**
    a) In keeping with what she's doing,
    b) To turn heads,
    c) Fashionably, and with great dress sense,
    d) Casually – you like to feel at ease with her.
4. **You find her sexiest when she's:**
    a) Cool, calm – and wearing stockings,
    b) When she's acting wild, and teasing you,
    c) When she's keeping all your mates' attention with her sparkling personality,
    d) When she floating around at home in a negligee.

60 * a charmed life

5 Which of these phrases rings true the most (don't think too hard)?
   a) When the girl I love's not here, I love the girl that's near,
   b) Absence makes the heart grow fonder,
   c) Keep it light and cheerful,
   d) Home is where the heart is.

6 When something's bothering you, you'd like her to understand and then:
   a) Talk through some solutions with you,
   b) Take your mind off it by lap-dancing,
   c) Make you laugh,
   d) Pour you a beer.

7 Her priorities should be:
   a) Keeping life sorted out so you don't have to worry about her as well as yourself,
   b) Blazing a trail – you want to catch a shooting star,
   c) Making a good career,
   d) Having children and home-making.

8 You want her to make you feel:
   a) It's safe to rely on her,
   b) Intrigued – what will she do next?
   c) Listened to, without too much of the slushy stuff,
   d) Understood.

Your Score

Mostly A: Your image is of the 'Amazon' – a gal who can cope with anything, before breakfast. You like a woman who is practical, strong and very in tune with her body. You don't mind if she concentrates on things like money and security – it leaves you free to be a bit of a playboy yourself, perhaps.

Mostly B: Your image is that of the 'Witch' – someone a bit magical, out-of-the-ordinary, who keeps you guessing just a little, and who has a crazy side. Tempestuous and passionate too – you can take it! You'll put up with her being a tad unreliable as long as you know she'll come back to you.

Mostly C: Your image is that of the 'Lady' – a girl who's at ease in any company, who has wonderful manners and always knows the right thing to say. You don't mind if you have to do the shopping while she's out at her evening class – she's always so interesting to be around and your mates really rate her.

Mostly D: Your image is that of the 'Mother'. You don't mind admitting it – you want someone who'll cook the Sunday roast and wash your socks. Home comforts are what count and you quite like the old-fashioned idea of the woman being at home – it means you know where you are in life.

If your answers are equally split between two letters, you like an amalgam of the two types. The important thing is to have some idea of your inner image – try not to be so starry-eyed that you can't check this out against the real, live person when he or she arrives. Are you fixing your image on someone who is miles off the mark? If they really come close, remember that everyone is human and they are bound to deviate very markedly from the image, very often. Also, are you blessed with the inner serenity that will enable you to be happy with someone who – broadly speaking – fits your type, or are you storing up heartache and trouble for yourself? If your ideal tends to bring you pain, then maybe you lack self-esteem or feel you deserve to be hurt, you have to compete, or that real love always means suffering. If so, give yourself permission to be happy by choosing what will make you content, rather than full of excitement and yearning. Remember what is obvious – but often over-looked – that there is always some compromise, some price to be paid. For instance, if you really resonate with type B, you need to be fairly secure inside and long-suffering; if type D, you may need to find mental stimulation elsewhere; type C might leave you looking for emotional support among your friends; and type A will be exciting only in a crisis (but don't create one!).

Regardless of what conclusion you came to, there are several important factors in any good relationship.

* You need to have shared values, or at very least deep respect for the values of your partner.

- Important life issues such as money, housing and having children should be fully discussed and agreed upon.
- Be straight about what you want – avoid game-playing and manipulation.
- Be as honest as you can.
- Make each other feel good. Of course, no-one can *make* you feel anything – we all make *ourselves* feel things. However, if someone is regularly pushing your buttons, it's a struggle. The Feel-Good Factor comes when you are valued, respected and when the other person is putting your comfort, at all levels, on a par with their own.
- True love, the wise men say, is not two people gazing at each other but two people looking towards the same goal.

Chris's Story

Chris had what appeared from the outside to be a stable and loving relationship with his partner, and he came seeking treatment for stress within his job. In the course of his treatment, it became apparent that although Chris worked hard, he wasn't playing hard – in fact he wasn't playing at all. At weekends and evenings he was making himself a servant to his partner's requirements, doing shopping and housework almost as an apology for his demanding (and very well-paid) job. It transpired that the true cause of Chris's tension was extreme frustration within his relationship, for which he blamed himself, describing his partner as 'an easy-going soul who didn't want much'! After talking things over, Chris realised that his current attitude was due in great part to his fear of causing the same conflicts within his partnership that he had witnessed between his parents. His philosophy was 'anything for a quiet life' although his mind and body were telling him that inside he was not quiet at all. He confronted his partner with his need to have interests and activities outside the partnership – to find she was not quite as easy-going as he had described her! His partnership did not survive his change of attitude, but he is now free to seek a much better relationship in which there is a true sharing and respect for individuality.

✸ keeping the feeling

There is a special way that we feel when we are in love – why doesn't it go on? As we have seen, part of falling out of love is that we take back that image we have projected onto the other person and they are left with their unadorned humanity – blackheads and all. But even more may be going on here – occultists tell us that when we are in love we are vibrating at a higher rate. Two people in love vibrate in tune like the taut strings of a Stradivarius. As they fall out of love their vibrational rate slows and they go out of sync. The music goes out of life and it becomes tedious, unexciting. If you think about it, that's just how it feels – everything goes flat and ordinary.

So is there anything we can do to keep that magic alive? Magic is something we create in our minds, so what we need to do is generate the right atmosphere for that to happen. To keep that enchantment it is best if we can start in the right way, before the fizz has gone. However, if you both still want to, you can get it back. Not every night, maybe, but enough to make it worthwhile.

✸ Keep a little mystery. There is no need for the bathroom door always to be left open. (But don't worry if you're ill – that's a separate issue. You aren't 'you' when you're ill, and you're entitled to be babied.)

✸ Although shared interests are great, it can be a good idea to have something you regularly do on your own.

✸ Let it be known that you have other admirers. Please note, this does not mean you play games and manipulate your partner through jealousy – that is not what it's about at all, and some people are very easily made agonisingly jealous, so act with consideration for the response you may arouse. But everyone likes to think they've got something that others want!

✸ Make time for each other – a cliché, I know, but true. A morning in bed together at weekends and a night out together once a fortnight gives you the chance to explore your relationship.

✸ Dress up, like you did on that first date.

✸ Laugh together – it makes everything seem rosy.

✸ Explore your fantasies together and act them out if you can.

When Trouble Comes Knocking

We all open our hearts and make ourselves vulnerable when we fall in love. However, if we have been significantly damaged we are even more in danger for it is all too often those wounds that grow suckers and attach to someone – anyone – who might make us feel better for a while. When we pick someone for all the wrong reasons, the relationship is, obviously, not well-starred. Besides, we often have the unhappy knack of attaching to someone who will actually reinforce all the bad messages we have internalised.

We all cling to what is familiar, even if it is ghastly, simply because it *is* familiar. Thus abused people regularly repeat the mistake of getting into abusive relationships. This certainly is not because they like being abused! Naturally they hate it – they may even consciously avoid it, and be puzzled and desperate that it has happened *again*. Here is one way it may happen.

A woman who was mistreated by her father (severely or otherwise) will probably have a conscious wish to make a relationship with a considerate, gentle man. (That is if she wants a relationship at all, which is another story.) Because of the way she has been treated, she may be needy; her self-esteem will probably be very low, and she will be looking for someone to lift it. When someone takes an interest in her, she is grateful, and very ready to respond. Naturally her prospective partner looks pretty good at the start. He has his own internal agenda, his own tragedy and insecurity that make him relate in his particular way (like her father, if the truth were known). Quite possibly he sees himself as a sensitive person, and his neediness and wish to get close may make him charming. Subliminally, there is something in him that our heroine recognises but she does not see it that way – she just feels great. As they both become committed and the relationship develops, another side of him gradually makes itself evident. Just like her father he begins to abuse her. This is familiar, she readily falls into role, blaming herself, being afraid, feeling cowed, her self-esteem taking a continual battering along with the rest of her.

If she is fortunate, has supportive friends, is not financially dependent and has the will to see that this is not the way things have to be, she will get out of this relationship. Alas, five years down the line she may again find the same old thing happening. This time it will be worse. The first time could have been an accident, whereas repeating the pattern points to something more. Realising this only does more damage to her self-image. At this point, hopefully, our heroine decides to do some serious work on herself. Why is she attracted to these men? What is it about the way she views life and herself that causes her to end up in this scenario? What is it about the situation that somehow feels okay even though it is anything but? Once she has achieved some self-understanding, she will be in a much better position to get out of the abusive relationship, however difficult that may be, and not to repeat the mistake. It can be done!

recognising an abusive relationship

We all have pockets of pathology and we all may be abusive, or abused, at times. Abuse isn't just physical. Nor does it have to be extreme, or dramatic. Sadly, there are many abusive relationships and a great proportion of these are never identified as such because neither party has any idea that abuse is going on.

When is a relationship abusive? This is hard to define. A partner may be lazy, neglectful, unreliable, selfish, untrustworthy and downright bad company without being precisely abusive. Such a one may be more readily dealt with as simply a bad partner, while abuse may be much more subtle. Of course, physical abuse is very obvious, although the undercurrents may be harder to define. The man who comes in drunk and bad-tempered and punches his wife is being physically abusive – evidently. However, if he is genuinely sorry, does not lay any sort of blame on his wife or manipulate her as a result then his abuse is merely physical.

I would like to make it clear that I am very old-fashioned about violence by men on women. As far as I am concerned it is *never* okay for a man to hit a woman unless she is actually attacking him physically and he has no option but to defend himself. A woman may slap a man in temper, and that is quite a different thing – maybe a tad unfair, but not reprehensible. Despite Buffy, Lara the Tomb Raider, et al, the fact is that the average man is considerably stronger than the average woman. And even if there is not that much difference in strength, by virtue of testosterone and thousands of years of conditioning, men have a different reaction to bodily attack – in general they simply cope better. In the biology of our species, the woman carries the offspring and the man protects her. In a more abstract fashion, women are the bearers of creativity and men are guardians of this. For a man to hit a woman where there is another available course of action is a violation. Of course, many men are so acutely aware of this that they are not even able to stand up for themselves in a relationship with a woman and it is often the larger men, animals on the rugby pitch or in the boxing ring, who are physically abused by their partners, because they are afraid of their own strength. However, that is another issue, and one cannot help feeling that such a man is a much nobler, if rather comic, figure than the six-stone weakling who viciously attacks his partner. (Of course, humanity is infinitely varied; there is no space here to examine issues such as homosexual relationships or people whose gender is not sharply defined, etc.)

To return to the issue of abuse, we might define this best as an attempt to gain unfair power in the relationship by any means, or the unfair use of the power we do possess to get our own way. The man who beats his partner is using his physical strength quite simply to get his own way – he is a bully. The woman who beats *her* partner is probably doing something more subtle – she is using his fear of his own destructive potential to keep him cowed (unless she is 6'4" and he is 5'2"!). A person who repeatedly arouses jealousy and insecurity expressly (although maybe subconsciously) in order to keep power over their partner is being abusive, however physically gentle they may be. However, someone who is unfaithful simply because they are unhappy is not being abusive, although they may be unfair. The person who regularly gets very upset over very little and who constantly demands time and attention from their partner for reassurance may be abusive, in effect. They are abusing the bonds and responsibilities within the relationship and depriving their partner of the ability to progress and develop in life. Often the abused person has no idea what is happening and may blame themselves for being over-sensitive. In fact they may be, and that just gives the abuser more of a handle.

Might your relationship be abusive? Answer the following questions:

- ✣ Does your partner ever physically abuse you?
- ✣ Do you often feel fearful of your partner?
- ✣ Do you feel you have little control over what happens to you in the relationship?
- ✣ Do you feel that your partner hinders you in growing as a person?
- ✣ Does your partner regularly put you down?
- ✣ Does your partner use the things you fear to control you?
- ✣ Does your partner shift responsibility for his/her feelings onto you?
- ✣ Do you feel that your partner wants to control you and the relationship?
- ✣ Do you feel that your real needs and welfare are of little true concern to your partner?
- ✣ Do you feel that you cannot get out of this relationship? (Practical issues like children and mortgage are out of the scope of this question.)

If you answered 'Yes' to any of these questions, then there is probably an element of abuse. If you are a woman and you answered 'Yes' to question 1 then you are definitely being abused (unless this is part of sex-play, and if so, be careful!). If you answered 'Yes' to three or more, then it is likely that the relationship is abusive. The more 'Yes' answers, the greater the extent of the abuse.

Ending Abuse

There is only one way to end abuse and that is by refusing to be a victim any more. Once you have reached that point, your problems can be solved, however hard this may be. It takes two to tango and abuse is a two-way street between victim and attacker. Some people are never abused simply because there is no part of their mind that says, 'I'm a victim, come and have a go at me'. If you are abused *it is not your fault*, but it is your responsibility to recognise your own part in this. In all probability you have attracted this abusive relationship in a subtle, subconscious fashion, because deep within you feel that you deserve it! You don't!

It is best not to confront your abuser in any direct way because the hooks are too strong and you will, in all probability, be drawn back into the dynamic. Instead, focus on the positive, on what you can do, on sources of self-esteem, on alternative avenues. While you can, and should, try to understand, this victimhood will not be reasoned away. It is best to deprive it of energy by directing your focus and attention elsewhere. If you are a physically abused woman you will, of course, need a place of physical safety. If the relationship is worth salvaging then this can only be done by the abuser recognising what is going on and taking genuine steps to develop self-awareness and change at a deep level. It is important that this is real and not just another power play to make the victim feel bad and/or to retain control.

You will be able to end the abuse when you truly see that your own welfare and your own right to recognition and to have your needs met is as great as that of your abuser. More than this, you have a responsibility to yourself that you have to no other person – that of discovering and following your own true path.

affairs

Every agony column and self-help book I have ever seen has been strongly, totally anti-affair! However, statistics show that many people – perhaps the majority – have had or are having an affair. This adds up to a huge number of isolated, unhappy people who are receiving little support and understanding and are simply being told, 'Don't!'. In these days of political correctness, we treat many criminals better!

We all know that the best way to run your relationship/s is not by deceit. It is too uncomfortable and heartbreaking for all concerned. But we don't need to be told this. Presumably if you are having an affair, you have your reasons, and for now – shock, horror, probe! – they may be good ones.

We live in a society where monogamy is the order of the day. We are encouraged to pair up for love and to stay that way, preferably indefinitely. If our partnership does break down we are encouraged to be honest and up-front, negotiating a fair break-up and letting the dust settle before embarking on another liaison.

But what if the whole idea of one-to-one relationships is based on a misapprehension? Maybe it is quite unrealistic to expect bonds to last. Some cultures, such as that of one Central African tribe, have a different structure in which there are two marriages – one socially sanctioned for child-rearing and another for the emotional, love stuff. The former is permanent; the latter may change many times, against a background of security and emotional support. In other tribal cultures a woman may go to a man that is not her husband for a night, and she does this with pomp and celebration for the fact that she is desirable, has been sought after and is going to enjoy herself. The tribe recognises this. Later she goes back to her husband. While both these alternative scenarios have their drawbacks, they do recognise something that we do not – at least not at all effectively – that 'Love is like a gypsy boy' and 'for ever' may not be literal.

If you are having an affair, it may be that the dilemmas of our culture have put you in a position that you cannot for the moment resolve. It is all very well to talk about honesty, but issues like children and mortgages are very real. Perhaps you owe it to yourself to find a fulfilment, within an affair, that you cannot find elsewhere. But at the same time you cannot bring yourself to cause unhappiness to others by terminating your live-in relationship. Does this make you weak and wicked – or does it mean you have the courage to live with ambiguity?

It isn't my intention to say 'way to go!' to any amount of deceit or selfishness that anyone may contemplate. If your affair is for fun and excitement, because you like living dangerously and having an extra string to your bow; if you truly love your partner but have got drawn into this situation for reasons that are comparatively trivial; if you have strings of affairs, are repeating some sort of pattern, are enjoying a sense of power or in any way being plain self-centred – you will know. Is it worth it? Do you like yourself? But if there is more to your situation, if there is a genuine dilemma, the chances are you are suffering considerably. Maybe you could be easier on yourself. Here are some points to consider.

* You got into this situation for a reason. Is the reason still valid? Ask yourself this every day if you like, and if the answer is 'yes', give yourself permission to continue.

- ✳ Are you putting your own needs too much to the back of the queue? Is this preventing you from finding a solution? Consider this aspect.
- ✳ If you are single but your lover is in a relationship, are you being taken advantage of? Do you genuinely feel you understand their issues or do you just feel you aren't good enough to deserve someone's total attention?
- ✳ Be as honest as you can be within the confines of what you are doing, *especially* with yourself.
- ✳ Find people you can talk to. These will need to be *very* carefully chosen, but you need company and an outlet for your emotions.

coping with heartbreak

So it's happened – that totally wonderful, irreplaceable someone has left you. You can't stop crying and you feel the world has ended. Everything seems different. You look around at all the fortunate, happy 'ordinary' people and it seems they're in another world, from which you are excluded. You feel hollow and panicky. It's as if you're falling, falling all the time, toppling over the edge of an invisible cliff. You can't eat anything – or perhaps you can't stop eating, just to try and fill yourself, which never succeeds. Possibly you're drinking far too much. When you sleep you have nightmares – but you don't want to wake up all the same, because reality is worse. It feels like it will never end – how can it? The only way things can improve is if s/he comes back, and that won't happen. So you despair.

Possibly the worst thing about this situation is the powerlessness of it. Oh yes, there's the loneliness, the longing, the feeling of rejection and worthlessness – all of these and more haunt you perpetually. But the point is that in few other situations in life can we do so very little to get what we want. If you lose some money, you can earn some more. If you are out of shape, there's usually plenty you can do about that. The only thing that can compare with losing that incredibly special someone is a bereavement, and bereavement (although it carries its own heavy issues) doesn't usually make you feel so bad about yourself.

the lore of love * 71

Let us assume, for now, that whatever the issues and the reasons for the split, trying to get your lover back isn't an option. But that doesn't leave you with nothing to do – far from it. Taking some action, however small, will be the first step towards seeing light at the end of the tunnel, for light there is, truly. Here are some pointers.

* Losing a lover is like being ill – very ill. So look after yourself as if you were ill. Wrap yourself up, pamper yourself, go to bed with a drink, cuddle a cushion, eat your favourite food (if you can swallow), watch telly, read an absorbing book, keep warm. Some of these things will be difficult, but choose anything you can cope with.
* Talk about it! This is a time for calling in the debt for all those times you've supported your friends through their crises. Feel free to lament, swear and bore them with your heartbreak. Listen also to what they say, for some of it may make sense.
* Make a list of all the things about her/him that weren't right. Obviously s/he wasn't right for you or the relationship wouldn't have ended, and when you think about it there will be many things about her/him that annoyed you, disappointed you or were simply not compatible with your personality.
* Make a list of other times in your life when you have felt like this. Go as far back as you can to your father/mother or close relatives when you were growing up. Try to realise that some of what you are feeling now is about earlier stuff – the child in you has been activated and this seems worse than it is because of this. Also the present situation is fed and amplified by past experiences – you are no longer merely a hurt and powerless child but an adult who can take steps to repair her life.
* Make a list of all the things you can do, now s/he's gone, that you could not do with him/her around.
* Try to realise, however dimly, that the creature you loved so and thought so very wonderful existed in your imagination. This is not to say that s/he deceived you, never loved you and was never any good. It is to say that when we fall in love it is *always* with some internal image. That is where the magic comes from. (See the earlier questionnaire where we discovered the inner image – this is what you

have pinned onto your lover.) That is why being 'in love' is different from 'loving'. That is why someone we are in love with has this larger-than-life, electric quality. Of course that is not to say that there aren't some very special magnetic people around or that the chemistry between two lovers is not real. But when we are in love we project something of our own inner, mythological landscapes on the beloved. Tell yourself you will start to take that back.

* Make some sensible changes in your life so you are not relentlessly exposed to too many reminders.
* Seek out situations and people that boost you and avoid ones that do the opposite – for now you are vulnerable, but it won't always be like this.

> **Top Tip**
> *All broken hearts have one thing in common – in time they mend.*

When You Are the One who Leaves

If you have taken the decision to end a relationship, you may feel almost as bad as if you were the one dumped. In some cases you may feel even worse, because of the burden of guilt you may carry for having caused hurt. You may be grieving for the things that were good about the relationship, such as company and having someone to share with, even if you have been brave enough to decide the relationship isn't going anywhere. Add to this the fact that friends are not usually as sympathetic to the dumper as they are to the dumpee – in fact some may even blame and condemn. In the case of a long-term relationship, leaving your partner may mean losing some friends who take sides.

Keep reminding yourself of all the reasons why you have decided to move on – they still hold good. If you are feeling very sorry for your ex it might help you if you can get angry. This is a conscious coping mechanism to help you through a difficult period that you need to negotiate because it is right for you – probably it is right for both of you. If you can recall times when your ex made you angry and all the bad or unsatisfactory things that existed in the relationship, you will be able to transfer some of your sympathy to yourself.

You can use the charm for a broken heart (page 88) if you are grieving, even though you have done the leaving. Try also the simple Charm to Break the Ties (page 89).

Moving on from a Relationship

There are as many different ways of moving on as there are people, and no-one can tell you precisely what is right for you. While it is very important not to enter another relationship on the rebound, there is no need to put yourself through a period of enforced loneliness in order to find yourself – unless you feel quite sure that is necessary. Many people make a very big deal about self-discovery, being okay with yourself before you are with someone else, going into relationships for the right reasons, not the wrong ones, etc. While many of these attitudes are very laudable, I feel that too much stress is laid on working on yourself, to the point where many people spend their lives disappearing up their own posteriors! Do you want to spend your life finding yourself? Or do you want to live?

Our perspectives on relationships have gone through immense changes over the last 50 years. Financial, practical and moral issues have all shifted so that there is much greater scope to be without a partner, whatever your circumstances. Obviously that is a good thing – but have we lost sight of something even Winnie the Pooh was clear about – 'It's much more fun for two'? Maybe life is too short to be agonising over what's the most self-aware thing to do.

Moving on is not, of course, solely about finding another relationship as quickly as possible. It is about:

* Really letting go of what is past so that you see it as past, not something that you are desperate to resurrect.
* Learning from the mistakes you made.
* Learning from the things you did right.
* Counting the good things about the past.

- Thinking about what you have learnt about life and incorporating that into your scheme of things.
- Thinking about what you have learnt about yourself and adjusting accordingly (remember that even if you do not feel okay with the bits of yourself you have seen, you are not alone in this, and will be stronger as a result).
- Seeing the future as something you can create.
- Exploring your options.

If you enter another relationship:

- Make sure you are relating to the new person as a person, not just as someone to fill a gap (i.e. on the rebound).
- Resist making comparisons with the past.
- Never try to recreate the past.
- Resist any impulse to do the opposite of what you did in the past just because it is the opposite; you have nothing to prove.
- Make sure this new relationship is one that makes you feel good, not something that you have been sucked into because your self-esteem was low.
- Explore anything that could help you to get more out of life.

dealing with jealousy

In life and love, jealousy can be one of the most painful things we have to deal with. We all want to be 'the best'. Specifically, we all want to be Number One in the affections of a loved one. This need can have many implications for us, both good and bad. We need to be aware of exactly what the jealousy is doing to us and how it is affecting the way we live our lives. For any charm to be effective we need to be very clear about our motives and what lies beneath them.

Often it is possible to trace jealousy back to childhood, for the most unbearable thing that ever happened to us may have been the arrival of a younger sibling who took away some of our parents' attention. In fact, this may have felt so bad that it was terrifying – for as children we were dependent upon our parents for survival. We may have felt things then that made us afraid of ourselves, for instance a wish to murder this horrid little baby that shattered our lives. When something happens in adult life that sparks this off, we may react out of all proportion to the circumstances because it is as if dark, invisible arms are pulling us back into some shadowy place full of monsters – i.e. our own childhood conditioning. Strangely, we may be conscious of violent feelings that are far too extreme for the current situation, as if all those scary emotions from early childhood are now being let out of the bag. However, if we had no siblings, this doesn't mean we feel no jealousy, for sometimes it can be harder to process rivalry if we have had no experience of it – the human mind being anything but a simple thing.

Here are some points about jealousy.

* Jealousy is a normal human reaction and it can spur us on to productive rivalry in the best possible scenario. We see what another person has and that makes us realise that we also want this person or thing. So rivalry can encourage us to make the best of ourselves, using our talents to the full.
* Rivalry can also be very destructive when motivated by pure jealousy. We are all familiar with jealousy as a motive for violence – even murder. What is not so obvious is that jealousy can destroy the person that feels it, robbing them of their peace of mind and what remains of their self-esteem.
* We might ask ourselves what is truly behind our feelings of jealousy. Are they simply a result of not feeling good enough? If not, why not? Do we really want to compete, or is it merely that we haven't yet found our own individuality? Do we want what someone else has or want what they are?
* It can also help a little bit to realise, intellectually if not emotionally, that if our feelings of jealousy have a childlike intensity; they are not merely about what is happening right now and we need to try to hang on to the adult in us. This is not about repressing how we feel, but about getting it in perspective.

Using a charm in such a case can activate our subconscious in a healthy manner and it can strengthen us, so we can find self-understanding and fulfilment independently from anyone else.

going it alone

Sometimes nothing seems to gel and there seems to be no alternative but to face the fact that, for the moment at least, you have to be content with your own company. Is that so bad? Try to be very honest with yourself and ask yourself the following questions:

* Do you really want a relationship or do you just think you ought to want a relationship because everyone else thinks you should?
* Is there really room in your life for a relationship? This room has to be emotional as well as physical. For a relationship you need time and attention. Are you subliminally giving out signals that you are too busy, your mind is elsewhere, you are too aloof?
* Are you in fact carrying a torch for an old love?
* Are your standards realistic?
* Do you have a life script that says you have to be/are destined to be alone?
* Are you punishing yourself?
* Are you simply not going out enough?
* Do you have a sneaking feeling that there is something in life that is more important for you to accomplish at the moment?
* Are you afraid of the exposure and commitment of a relationship and is it easier to tell yourself that no-one wants you rather than to face your fear?

If, on reflection, you feel you are placing obstacles in your own path, try the Charm for Making Room for Relationships on page 81.

If you decide that actually you do not want a relationship, at least not at the moment, then congratulate yourself on all the opportunities you will have to do as you want, and go on your way, rejoicing!

visualisation and meditation for love and relationships

Meditation to Form a Loving and Supportive Relationship

You can do this meditation whether you are already in a relationship or wish to find one.

Sit quietly in your familiar auditorium. Before you the curtains swing wide and you see a smooth, broad and shining pathway made of many-coloured mosaics. You walk up to the stage, step onto it and find your feet on a pathway.

Ahead of you there is a great, white temple. Although it has obvious devotional characteristics, it also has an air of beauty and opulence. The mosaic path is lined on either side by marvellous marble statues and at regular intervals fountains play in the centre of the path. *[Pause.]*

Now you are approaching the archway into the temple. It is shadowed and fragrant. Beyond you see a wonderful chamber, ringed by stained-glass windows. Here there are more statues, even more exquisite than those that lined the path, inlaid with jewels and delicately painted. *[Pause.]*

You walk into the chamber and approach an especially wonderful statue at the far end. It is a Goddess, robed in blue and smiling gently. Her arms are outstretched in welcome and she is wreathed in incense. *[Pause.]*

As you draw near the statue, you see that in front of her there is a pool, surrounded with lapis lazuli. In front of the pool there is a pile of small crystals. You walk up to the pool and kneel down to show respect for the Goddess. *[Pause.]*

As you face the Goddess, with the pool before you, you are aware that a figure has come to stand beside you. You know that this figure is your partner. You cannot see them directly, only their shimmering reflection in the water. You know what you must do. You must take up a crystal from the pile, name it for something you will bring to the relationship and cast it into the pool. Your partner will do likewise. Taking your time, pick up a crystal for each of the gifts you will bring. Ask for certain things from your partner. Take it in turns to cast your crystals into the water, until you have pledged all you can and received promises of the things you will be given. Look into the water – the crystals are now shining at the bottom of the pool.

You look up at the Goddess and find that her eyes are wide and smiling – in fact this is no statue but a living being. Gracefully she bends down and gives you a precious ring.

Place this ring within your clothing and give thanks. Never directly looking at your partner, turn and walk back the way you came, down the mosaic path and past the statues, until you find yourself on the familiar stage.

Go down into the auditorium and place your ring somewhere safe.

In the everyday world you might like to acquire a Goddess statue and bring fresh flowers regularly, and/or burn incense as an offering, to connect you to the bounty of Love.

Visualisation for Moving on from a Broken Relationship

Find yourself in your auditorium. The curtains on stage are swinging open and you see before you some steps. Go up onto the stage and start climbing the steps.

The steps are ancient and worn, going up the side of a mountain. Soon you come to a door cut in the stone. The door is surrounded by strange writing that you do not recognise. It is some ancient language that the world has forgotten. You tap on the door and suddenly the heavy stone swings wide, allowing you to pass through.

You go inside and the doors behind you close by themselves. You are in virtual darkness. As your eyes adjust to the lack of light, you become aware that there is a door to your left, encrusted with jewels that glint in the shadows. The handle of the door is made of smooth, solid ruby. What wonderful scenes lie behind this jewelled door? You step towards it and grasp the ruby handle. You turn it and the door begins to open. In comes a shaft of bright light; you hear music and laughter and smell flowers and delicious food cooking. You try to pull the door wide to enter that

the lore of love

happy scene, but somehow the door-handle slips from your grasp and the door slams shut, leaving you again in darkness.

Then to your right you spot another door. This one is much more humble, just an ordinary door. But when you touch the handle it feels warm. You open the door easily and the light pours in. You find yourself in a wonderful landscape, such as you have never before seen. There are fantastic towers with pennants waving, people pass by smiling and greeting you, the flowers are especially brilliant and the sky is blue in every direction.

Wander around this bright countryside for a while… Speak to the people you see… Explore and enjoy. If anyone speaks to you, be sure to note what they say. If you are given a gift, treasure it.

When you are ready, go back through the door and find yourself again in the dark chamber. Go out through the stone door and see the ponderous doors shut themselves in your wake. Go carefully down the mountain steps and find yourself again on the stage.

Go out into the auditorium as the curtains behind you swing shut. Treasure any gift you have been given and make a note of your experiences. Do you understand them? It does not matter if things do not make sense immediately – they will fall into place later.

You will find a further meditation for coping with abusive relationships in Appendix 2.

charms for love and relationships

Lovely Me Charm

Of course if you feel really low it is very hard to dredge up good feelings about yourself and almost anything you do can feel hollow. It is best not to try too hard to reason yourself out of this, because it may simply make you feel worse. The best thing is to target the subconscious mind, which is where the problem has usually arisen. The self-hypnosis script for self-esteem (page 237) will start you off in the right direction. Charms also work on this unseen part, convincing the Inner Child that all is, in fact, well.

This charm involves essential oils and you will need a carrier oil such as grape-seed or sweet almond in which to dilute the oil. If you wish to feel very calm, use lavender oil; if you have emotions that need soothing, ylang ylang is wonderful; if you want to feel majestic, use frankincense. Always test for allergy by placing a dab on the inside of your wrist 24 hours before using the oil. Dilute your chosen oil in the carrier in a ratio of two drops per teaspoonful – it is best to mix the amount you will need for each massage, for while the oils keep for some while, they can go off after a few weeks.

In this charm you can incorporate as many pleasant things as you like, but don't go over the top or you might rush things – save them for another occasion! Best to begin this evening of self-worship with a bath. The central part of the charm then follows, involving self-massage followed by your choice of treats. For instance you may want to plan a special meal, have a drink you particularly enjoy, read a book, watch a video, shop on the Net or by phone, phone a friend or snuggle up for an early night.

Make sure your bathroom and bedroom are warm and that anything that might remind you of work or anything unpleasant is well out of the way. Light your bathroom with plenty of candles, preferably in a deep rose colour. Stock up with the most gorgeous bath oil you can find and a pair of luxurious, velvety towels. Play your favourite CD. Stay in the bath as long as you like. When you are ready, dry yourself off and place a dry towel on your bed.

Using your chosen oils, begin to massage yourself. Starting with your feet, gently smooth the sweet oil around your toes, into your arches and round your ankles. Picture all the things your feet enable you to do, such as walk and dance – all these things you may take for granted, but really they are wonderful. Say, 'Feet, I love you!'

Do the same with your legs, working upwards and saying, 'Legs I love you... Knees, I love you... Thighs I love you,' etc. Carry on, at your own pace, working up your body. Think all the time about good things that have happened to you, pleasurable experiences that part of your body has brought you. If negative thoughts do come into your mind, just stop your massage, move your hands away, close your eyes and take a deep breath. Breathe out the unpleasant thought, smile and say, 'Goodbye,' as you imagine it drifting away on your out-breath. Only continue when the thought has dispersed. If there are parts of you that you don't like, try to give them a little extra love, and massage any bits that hurt with special care!

When you feel your massage is complete, now is the time for your treat. Raise a glass of wine, eat chocolates – whatever you fancy. This is your night! Look out at the night sky and contemplate the fact that life really does have some good things in it!

Repeat this charm at regular intervals – perhaps at every full moon – to give yourself a regular boost.

Charm for Making Room for Relationships

We may be very sure that we really do want a relationship but at the same time be putting obstacles in our own way. Is there time in our lives for a relationship or are we always working or embroiling ourselves in family matters? Are we going to places where we can meet other suitable singles or somehow hoping we'll just bump into someone in the supermarket? Are we setting our sights too high (as in the 50-year-old man who won't consider a woman over 30) or too low (giving attention to people who are truly less personable than ourselves)? Are we mentally clinging to old lost loves? How easy are we to get close to?

Here is a charm to cleanse your life of anything negative that is past its sell-by date and is keeping relationships away. You will need a white candle, a pink candle, essential oils of myrrh and lavender, paper and pen, a small heat-proof bowl or an ashtray, a glass of wine or fruit juice. Some tongs may also help.

Light the white candle and settle yourself in front of it. Look at the flame until you feel quite peaceful and your mind starts to roam. Let yourself reflect on your life and the important things in it. What do you think is keeping you from having a relationship, from drawing close to someone and forming bonds? (Please note, this will have nothing to do with your height, weight and similar issues! In fact you may be keeping closeness at bay through your negative self-image.) Some other factors may be that you are too busy, irritable or uptight; you may be in a world of your own, have few interests or be too absorbed in an isolating hobby; you may be too afraid of something that relationships hold, you may feel you are letting someone down, or you may even be just too lazy! Fear of failure is another possibility – perhaps it is easier to be alone than to try and to fail. Be as honest as you can, take your time and write everything you can think of on your piece of paper, even if it seems silly. Things may come to mind that don't make sense, but write them down anyway.

When you feel sure you have finished, roll the paper up into a tight taper and anoint it with three drops each of myrrh and lavender on each end. Imagine the things you have written all compacted and twisted up inside the taper. Light the paper in the candle-flame and use it to kindle the pink candle. Let the paper burn out and drop the ashes into the little pot or ashtray. Gaze at the two candle flames, imagining all the good things that will come to you once you have a relationship. Drink a toast of your favourite wine or beverage to all the new opportunities to which you have now opened the way. Later on take the little pot outside and let all the ashes be carried away on the breeze.

This charm can be repeated from time to time. If you like, you may do it each month a few days before the new moon. When the first sickle appears in the sky, light your candles again and let them burn down.

What Do I Want? Charm

The earlier questionnaires and advice notwithstanding, what you want in love will be highly individual and special to you alone. It is hard to get anything you want until you know what it is, and love is no exception. This doesn't mean that we should have very definite ideas about exactly how our lover will look and act. What we can be specific about is the way we want to feel about the relationship. This charm can be done again after a while because views and tastes may change. If you are still single, perhaps you could have an annual review at the start of each May – traditionally the month of love.

Buy yourself several sheets of attractive, pink paper, some deep pink ribbon to match and a special pen that you enjoy writing with. Burn some lavender oil in an oil-burner, for a clear head and peaceful heart. Have also some patchouli oil to hand, for its grounding qualities. Light a pink or white candle.

Write down all the ways you want to feel in a relationship and all the things you would like it to bring into your life. Don't sell yourself short or be afraid of being greedy. On another piece of paper write the characteristics you would like in a lover – best to list things like kindness and honesty rather than majoring on physical characteristics. On a third piece of paper write all the qualities and gifts you will bring to the relationship – you don't have to make sacrifices, just state what you have to offer.

When your lists are complete, roll them up together and tie them in a scroll with the ribbon. Dab each sheet of paper and the ribbon with patchouli, as a seal. Keep the scroll somewhere safe with your personal belongings. When you meet your lover, burn the scroll and give thanks to the Goddess of Love or Powers of the Universe by planting a fruit tree, a rose bush or some wild flowers in your garden.

Is S/he Right for Me? Charm

You may have met someone you think is God's gift, but if you've been wrong in the past you may be afraid of repeating mistakes. Deep within, you will not be fooled. Your subconscious knows all it needs to know about this new love. Try this charm to uncover your own inner wisdom. It is based on old folk custom, but works equally well in the modern world.

You will need two leaves of fresh basil, of as equal a size as you can manage to find, and an open fire. If you do not have this, you could use barbecue charcoal, two pieces of incense charcoal (obtainable from New Age shops and shaped like small disks) or even a thick, heated pan or hob.

All you do is take the two leaves and place them on the heat source. If they lie still and burn without delay, it's all systems go! If they crackle and sizzle there will be arguments. If they fly apart – well, that's self-explanatory.

Have the leaves confirmed your inner voice? Or are you still unsure? Sleep on it – there is no need to commit until you are happy.

A Love Talisman

If you take the time and the trouble to make a talisman to wear or carry, you will have completed a very powerful charm that convinces your subconscious that you are willing and able to get what you want. This talisman is made of rose quartz, which is a beautiful stone with gentle, loving vibrations. You can wear this as jewellery or keep it in your bag or pocket. Rose quartz is said to open the heart of the one wearing it, and so attracts love in return.

Rose quartz can be bought in New Age shops and in some jewellers. A piece that has been left rough is fine if you like it. Choose a piece that just feels right when you hold it. Now you need to plan a little ritual to charge it up. For this you will need two wine-red candles, some oil of rose, jasmine or ylang ylang, perhaps a statue of Venus or any figure that looks like a Love Goddess, and as many representations of love as you can find. Cover your working area with a pink or red cloth and on it place rose petals, erotic pictures, Valentine cards (but *not* ones sent to you by former lovers), romantic images of lakes, flowers, turtle doves, swans, rings, hearts, wine-glasses and anything that conjures up romance. If you have made the scroll from the What Do I Want? Charm, have that with you as well.

Light your candles and heat the oil so the fragrance rises. Start making your charm by breathing out, imagining all negativity being blown away from you. Do this until you feel sure you are cleansed. Then breathe out again, imagining your breath condensing to form a pink egg around you. Hold your quartz crystal between your palms and imagine the love you want coming to you. Affirm that the crystal is a magnet for just the right lover for you. Imagine him or her coming close – do not imagine detail, just a vague shape, but do imagine as clearly as you can just how you will feel. Feel joyful that this is coming your way. Place the quartz back on your working area and tilt the two candles carefully so their flames become one for a few seconds.

When you have finished, leave your rose quartz overnight on the rose petals. Next day place it in your bag, or on a chain round your neck, and strew the rose petals outside as an offering. Let the candles burn down a little each day until they are finished and bury the stumps. This charm is best done during a waxing moon and completed when the moon is full.

Mandala Magic for an Existing Love

A mandala is a circular shape that signifies completeness. The great thinker and psychotherapist Carl Gustav Jung identified the mandala as one of the archetypes – or highly important symbols – of the subconscious mind, and patients in therapy who start to dream about one are becoming whole. The meanings of the mandala go straight to the subconscious part of our minds, with a powerful message. Creating such a shape in a charm for your relationship is a message to your inner self that your love will grow, last and be as complete as can be. Your mandala will be even more effective if you and your lover make it together.

Buy a household notice-board and hang it in a carefully chosen part of your home, then pin on it an embroidery hoop and cover it or paint it deep pink – or a colour of your choice. Around the hoop pin anything you can find that is special to your relationship – photos, theatre programmes, holiday tickets, restaurant menus and old Valentine cards you have sent each other. Decorate it also with things that are merely pretty and romantic, such as red hearts, semi-precious stones, pieces of ribbon, etc. Divide the circle into eight segments by stretching ribbons across the hoop, using pieces of dowel or whatever seems easiest. These eight segments represent eight parts of the year and will correspond to the eight traditional festivals – Yule (21 December), Imbolc (2 February), Spring Equinox (20 March), Beltane (1 May), Midsummer (22 June), Lammas (31 July), Autumn Equinox (22 September) and Hallowe'en (31 October).

There are many associations, customs and mythology linked to these festivals that are outside our scope here, although you will find a little more detail in Chapter 6. (See also Further Reading.) However, it is not hard to see that the cycles of Nature are played out here and celebrated. At Yule the Sun is reborn, at Imbolc light is noticeably growing, at Spring Equinox the green shoots of new plants are appearing, at Beltane excitement is in the air with the first scent of summer, at Midsummer we have the glory of all the flowers, at Lammas the fields are gold with wheat, at Autumn Equinox we have harvest, and at Hallowe'en the eerie, ghostly time as darkness takes over.

During your first year together, pin a memento relating to something you did as a couple around each of these festivals/times in the correct segment. As time goes by, you can build and build, showing what you have experienced, how you have grown together. If times are bad, don't avoid or neglect your mandala – showing these times in as positive a way as you can within the mandala will be very helpful.

On special days light candles near your mandala and toast your life together with your favourite tipple!

Renewing Your Vows

'For ever' is the language of love and lovers want to swear eternal devotion – it goes with that feeling of being head over heels in love. These days we are more realistic than our forebears and do not try too hard to hold people to the formal vows they make in the church or registry office. However, that doesn't mean that vows count for nothing. Pagan relationships and folk customs use the term 'for a year and a day' in relation to vows. After that time they can be renewed or reaffirmed if that feels right.

It is probable that the expression 'a year and a day' links with the motion of the moon as compared with that of the sun, for the moon makes thirteen rounds of the Zodiac with a day to spare for every one circuit made by the sun – which takes a year. So 'a year and a day' probably means simply a year, with a little salute made to the moon. Whatever outward forms your relationship has to conform to, it is a good idea to renew your vows to each other in this way. This will keep the freshness and the magic alive and well between you.

Choose a time and a place that is special to you, possibly in woodland, where you first met, or even in company with your friends. Choose a time when the moon is waxing or almost full. First talk candidly about the things you are not happy with and discuss making changes. Remember that honesty is part of your togetherness. It is important that you are each prepared to change if things aren't quite right. When this part is completed, tell your lover all the things about him or her that you particularly value, appreciate and admire. It is a good idea to write some or all of this down on some special paper, perhaps pink paper, and tie it into a scroll with matching ribbon that you can then present to your partner. Swap rings, precious stones, small gifts and anything that you want to give as a love-token. Name one project that you will tackle together. Share a fruit, feeding each other the segments.

Spend the evening together celebrating in whatever way you like.

Charm to Help End Abuse

If you are being physically abused in any way, you need first to get practical protection in place for yourself. This charm will help things on their way.

You will need a besom (the type of broom traditionally associated with flying witches, made from a wooden handle and a bundle of twigs and often sold at garden centres!) and a pen that writes easily. You will also need some firm dried leaves (use scraps of paper if you cannot find anything suitable), a heat-proof dish, some wine or fruit juice, a saucepan and source of heat, a bay leaf, a black candle and a white candle.

First heat the wine or juice with the bay leaf for five minutes.

Light your black candle. Name a dried leaf for each element of the abuse that you intend to end – for instance guilt, control, powerlessness. Think about this for as long as you like. Now draw out a hair from your own head for each of the leaves and bind it round, as best you can. Place them all in the heat-proof dish and burn them. Watch the smoke rise and affirm that the abuse and its power to upset and hamper you is vaporising.

Take the dish and empty it outside. Come back in and, in an anti-clockwise direction (clockwise in the Southern Hemisphere), firmly sweep out the room where you have been performing your charm, saying, 'All traces of abuse are swept from my life.'

Light the white candle from the flame of the black candle and extinguish the black candle. Take this round the room very slowly in the opposite direction to your sweeping out, protecting the flame with a cupped hand. Drink the wine or juice while saying, 'I drink new strength, new heart, new goals' three times.

New things have now been set in motion.

Charm to Help Cope with an Affair

If you are involved in an affair, your greatest fear may be of causing hurt to others and to yourself. Use this charm to help protect all concerned.

You will need a gold five-pointed star – for this you can use a Christmas decoration. You will also need a square piece of very dark green or brown cloth, a candle of the same colour, some patchouli oil and an oil-burner, some dried lavender and a stone for each person concerned, including children if there are any involved. (You can pick up stones from the ground or invest in some semi-precious ones that seem appropriate.) Some dark green or brown ribbon or twine will also be helpful.

Light your candle. Spread out your cloth, arranging it so that each corner points roughly to one of the compass points. Anoint the cloth with a drop of patchouli on each of the corners. Start with North, saying as you do so, 'May the powers of the North give blessing and protection,' then East, South and West in turn, asking for the blessing of each. (If you live in the Southern Hemisphere, start with South, then East, etc.)

Place the five-pointed star in the centre of the cloth, so that one apex points upwards and two downwards, like legs. Baptise each of your stones with the name of the person they represent. Place them on the star and sprinkle lavender over everything. Say, 'May all involved be safe and content. May this matter work out for the best for all concerned.'

Carefully fold over the points of the cloth in the same order in which you anointed them, so that you make a neat package. Bind this with the ribbon or twine.

Place this somewhere safe until the matter is resolved.

Charm for a Broken Heart

That old saying 'It's better to have loved and lost than never to have loved at all' sounds a bit thin when you're feeling shredded and bereft. We've all been there, and you can come through this. Let your feelings flow – don't try to bottle them up. Allow yourself a sensible mourning period – this may be anything from a few hours to a few months, depending on the importance and duration of the relationship.

This charm is a bit complicated, but is worth the effort. You'll need your oil-burner, some oils of ylang ylang, lavender, eucalyptus and cypress, a chalice, some spring water, some wine or fruit juice, a soft green candle, some hot chocolate and a hot water bottle! You will also need access to a stream or other flowing water.

Burn the ylang ylang first, as it will help to release all your feelings, including those of jealousy and resentment. When you feel exhausted, burn cypress for consolation. Friends can help you with this – get them to pamper you, for example by filling the hot water bottle and making hot chocolate.

You now need to make a conscious decision that from this moment you will move on. Choose a new moon to make a ritual of burning any letters and mementoes. Fill your chalice with spring water and drop three drops of cypress oil into it. These represent tears – for joy that is past, for loneliness in the present and for loss of the future you dreamed about. Empty the chalice into a running stream. Now fill your chalice with your favourite wine or juice and drink a toast to all the possibilities open to you.

Burn lavender oil for peace and eucalyptus for healing. Fill your hot water bottle (again!) and place a few drops of eucalyptus oil in it. Make your hot chocolate and try to ensure the top is frothy. Light your green candle, saying, 'Peace, and a new start for me.' Sit cuddling your hot water bottle and write happy messages for yourself in the froth with a teaspoon or cocktail stick – this is the start of a new phase.

As the blessed scent of the lavender surrounds you, let yourself dream of all the wonderful things that could happen to you in the near future – some of them truly will! Sip your chocolate and feel content.

Charm to Break the Ties

For this you will need a picture of your ex or some other object that represents him or her, a length of black thread, a picture or other representation of yourself, some rose petals (dried or fresh), a pair of scissors, some pink cloth and a heat-proof container.

Tie one end of the thread to the representation of your ex and the other to your own symbol. Say:

> *'I break the ties 'tween thee and me;*
> *Never more we two shall be.*

> *Blessed be you, blessed be me,*
> *A better future we shall see*
> *Apart and happy – so may it be.'*

Cut the thread with the scissors. Wrap the end of the thread round the object that represents your ex and scatter rose petals on it. Burn all of this in the heat-proof dish. If there are ashes left, take these carefully outside and let the wind blow them away. Take your picture or representation and wrap it in a pink cloth with some rose petals for you. Put the package somewhere safe until you feel the separation has been properly established, then empty out the petals and do what you will with the rest.

Charm to Cleanse Yourself of Jealousy

Try this simple charm to get rid of jealousy and negative feelings. You will need a green glass filled with water, a green drinking straw and a white candle. Let yourself experience your jealousy for a moment – feel yourself full of it. Take a deep breath and place your lips to the straw and blow the jealousy out, visualising it as a green vapour that dissolves into the water. Keep blowing for as long as you feel it is necessary, plus a bit longer. Empty the water out onto wasteland and burn the straw.

Light the candle. As you look at the flame, think about a new and absorbing project that you feel will improve you, independent of your jealousy issue. You can repeat this as often as you need to.

Charm for Going It Alone

You have decided to be alone, but that does not mean you have to be lonely. Being solitary gives you more opportunity to make real contact with the world around you that you may not achieve within a relationship. Try this charm to feel serene and complete. Do this charm when you see the first sliver of the new moon in the sky.

You will need several teaspoons of a carrier oil such as grapeseed or sweet almond, some essential oil of lavender and a large white candle.

Dilute the lavender oil in the carrier oil, two drops to a teaspoon. Take off your clothes. If possible, stand facing the moon and say: 'Silver moon, you journey alone, yet your beauty lights up the night. May I also shine bright, and may my strength and serenity grow.'

Now dip your fingers in the oil and dab some on your feet while saying, 'Feet be blessed and take me on the right path.' Anoint your heart while saying, 'Heart be open to give and receive love and joy.' Anoint your forehead, just above and between your eyes, while saying, 'Mind be free to find the ways of wisdom.'

Now say, 'Though I am alone I shall not be lonely. I am surrounded by the wonders of life. I am held in the embrace of the Universe. I am always watched over, in love.' Light the candle and be aware that your guardian angel is with you.

Watch the flame dance for a while, imagining the many nice things you will do on your own. Light the candle on successive nights as the moon waxes, until it has burnt down.

self-hypnosis for love and relationships

Self-Hypnosis for Sex Appeal

Please note, parts of the following script may need to be intelligently adapted – for instance if you are a bald man you can still be very sexy, but talking about your hair is a nonsense! Also if you have a particular hang-up about a body part that is mentioned, then leave out the relevant section, for this script is not about addressing inadequacies, but boosting pulling-power!

[Usual induction.]

As you are lying there so beautifully relaxed, you are aware of your body – powerfully, enjoyably aware. You feel the life-force glowing strong within you. Feel it growing – you are positively glowing with vitality and energy and sexual magnetism. You are radiant, smiling, gorgeous – who could resist that charm? Feel the warmth rising within you and flowing round your body. How vital you are! How alive you are! How much you enjoy life! How vibrant you are!

Be aware of your hair. It is soft, it frames your face so attractively, it is wonderful to touch. At all times you take a pride in your hair because it is one of the most noticeable things about you. You make sure that your hair looks as good as can be – it is your crowning glory. You take the trouble to make sure that your hair is shining, clean, fragrant and well styled all the time, because you know this makes the most of your attractiveness.

Be aware of your face. Your personality shines here. It is a sensual, warm, irresistible personality. You are smiling. You have a ready smile. You enjoy smiling. You take special care of your teeth because you know how important they are to your lovely smile. You take special care of your facial appearance so that you can radiate the wonderful person that you are. Your facial expression is pleasant, open and relaxed. You are pleasant, open and relaxed. Who could resist that open expression, that relaxed smile, that lovely face?

Be aware of your shoulders. How relaxed they feel at this moment! At all times you hold your shoulders comfortably straight, so making the most of your appearance. You keep your shoulders straight and balanced; you keep your head erect. Your shoulders stay back as you stand and walk, making you look your very, very best.

Be aware of your belly and hips. These are the cradle of your sexuality. Here your sexual power is housed. Here you are at your most feminine/masculine. Feel the strength within your hips and belly. How your femininity/virility shows when you walk and move. It is subtle but powerful. It is a magnet for members of the opposite sex. Feel the heat within your belly. Feel your sexuality. Feel the warmth of your own sexuality. This is radiating around you. This will radiate around you with each day that passes. The strength and power of your sexuality is a magnet to members of the opposite sex.

[For women only.] Be aware of your breasts. How beautiful they are. How wonderfully they curve. They are a showing forth of your femininity. You feel proud of your breasts, proud of their curves. You are aware of the power they have to attract the opposite sex and you know how to use that power, in a wise and balanced way, to get what you want. You are aware of the

the lore of love * 93

wonderful sexual statement that your breasts make and you enjoy this.

Be aware of your hands. What a gift they are, to touch and feel! At all times you look after your hands, you care for them, keep them clean and manicured because you know that you can give and receive warmth with your hands. Your hands can give pleasure, your hands can express love. At all times you care for your hands so that they may express your feelings so pleasurably.

Be aware of your legs and feet. Feel their power to move, dance, walk. Feel their strength and shape – how good they look, how they convey your sexuality when you walk and move about. You are aware of the power and beauty of your legs and you know just how to use this, in a balanced way, to attract the opposite sex. You use the beauty of your legs to emphasise your sexuality. You appreciate and are aware of the strength and contours of your legs.

You feel confident of your ability to attract the opposite sex. You know that you are warm and sensual. At all times you look after your wonderful body in all ways, because it is important. Your body is precious. You are precious. Feel your sensuality – feel your body bathed in it. Imagine the touch of a lover, all over you, and imagine your response to it. What a lover you are! How much love and pleasure you have to give! How warm and sensual you are! You are strongly, vibrantly aware of your ability to give and receive pleasure. Your sensual warmth radiates around you. At all suitable times you are aware of your sensuality, you radiate it, you glow with it.

And you are interested in life and in other people. You listen and respond. You get involved with things that interest you. You become so interested in the good things in life and in other people that you forget about your own unimportant concerns. Life is enjoyable, it is rich, it is satisfying. You are interested in others, interested in life – you love life!

You are great to be with – you are warm, pleasant, responsive. You have a healthy balance between concern for others and concern for yourself. You are aware that your body is a temple and that the bodies of others are also temples. You respect and love yourself and you respect and love others. You are ready to celebrate all the sensual gifts that life has to offer.

You are sensual, vibrant and charming. Every day, in every suitable way and every suitable place, you radiate charm and appeal. You are gorgeous, vital and sensual and you are going to enjoy life more and more with every day that passes.

[Usual waking-up procedure.]

Self-Hypnosis for Moving on from a Relationship

[Usual induction.]

While you are lying there so beautifully relaxed you feel safe and secure in every way. You are surrounded by love and warmth. Feel that warmth now, surrounding you. Feel the comfort of your body. All is well, all is well. You feel at peace, tranquil, serene. All is quiet, within and without. There is nothing to fear. You feel peaceful, calm and very relaxed.

With each day that passes you feel more joyful, more free, more full of hope. You are leaving behind you all negative emotions. You are seeing things differently. You are seeing everything in a fresh light. How different the world looks! See, the sunshine is spreading over everything. This is such a big, wide beautiful world. Everything is sunny and fine and waiting for you to explore it. You are looking forward to exploring it. You feel free, at peace, confident and contented.

With each day you feel better and better, more positive, more confident, more determined to create a better life for yourself. Every day you become more aware of the many opportunities that you have. You are going to take some of those opportunities. You are going to make the best life you can for yourself. It will all turn out fine – better than you imagine. There are so many possibilities out there for you and you are going to explore the ones that seem most attractive to you. You are going to follow what feels right for you, in a calm and balanced way. You have nothing to prove, nothing to divert you from simply finding the life that is going to bring you most contentment. And your contentment is growing. Your interest in life is growing. You are feeling more positive. With every day that passes, you feel more positive, more full of hope, more determined to create the best possible life for yourself.

You have learnt from the past and day by day you are learning more. You now understand yourself and the world better and that understanding is growing. Past experiences have made you better able to build a fulfilling life for yourself now. As the days go by you feel more and more satisfied with what has happened, however difficult it may have been. You are able to see the positive side. You are able to see that you are now a better, stronger, more complete person. You are becoming happier and happier, more and more determined, clearer in your mind. You are able to get all that happened in its true perspective and to learn from it. You understand what happened. You understand yourself, and you are working on increasing your understanding.

Inside you feel whole, you feel complete, you feel warm. Feel that warmth building up behind your navel. Feel it spreading throughout your body. How good it is to feel whole, to feel that warmth, to feel that wonderful glow throughout. Feel the glow extending all over your body. You are radiant. Now, when you meet other people, that radiance will show in your smile, in your movements, in your speech. Now you are able to look on the bright side. You see the positive in all, you feel full of hope.

Above all you are now able to create a good future for yourself. You are not quite sure what this will be but you have faith that it will be good. You know that it will be good because you are now open to all the many golden opportunities that surround you. You are going to make opportunities. You are going to keep your eyes open for any opportunities there may be to expand your life. You feel confident; you are moving on.

Imagine yourself stepping out into the sunshine. You are smiling. This is such a big, wide wonderful world and you are going to make the best life possible for yourself because you know that you deserve it. Now take the time to imagine one thing that you would like to do, or to experience, imagine yourself doing it, achieving it. Really be there....

From now on this is how life will be, bringing you positive and joyful experiences, bringing you good things. And that is right. It is how it should be. It is the right way for you.

[*Usual waking-up procedure.*]

Other Scripts

The self-hypnosis scripts for self-esteem and relaxation on pages 237 and 41 will also help with the negative aspects of relationships.

four

A Feeling of Wellbeing

'O, health! Health! The blessing of the rich!
The riches of the poor! Who can buy thee at too dear
a rate, since there is no enjoying the world without thee?'

Ben Jonson, Volpone

your health

It is not uncommon for us to make great efforts to get money and love. Health, however, is rarely given the same priority. We measure it negatively, as the absence of disease. We put up with regular aches and pains, feelings of lethargy and fatigue, in the belief that these are normal. Indeed, they are normal in our culture, but that doesn't mean they are unavoidable or acceptable. Gauge the state of your health by considering whether or not the following statements apply to you.

1. It is not uncommon for you to feel so full of life you could run and jump.
2. You regularly experience surges of joy.
3. You almost always have the energy to do the things you want to.
4. You are enthusiastic about several things in life.
5. You sleep pretty well most nights.
6. You enjoy a variety of different foods and you eat heartily.
7. It is true that your weight does not cause you undue concern.
8. You drink alcohol in moderation or not at all.
9. You only smoke only occasionally, if at all.
10. As far as you are aware you have no particular allergies.
11. You have no nagging, chronic complaints.
12. Most days you do something energetic that makes your heart beat slightly faster for ten minutes.
13. After exercise your heart rate quickly returns to normal, and you feel invigorated.
14. Your sex life, or your attitude to sex, gives you pleasure and satisfaction.

Your Score

* If you agreed with twelve or more statements, your health is optimum, or close to it. Wonderful! Make sure you keep it that way!
* If you agreed with eight to eleven statements, it sounds as if your health could be improved. You could certainly enjoy life more – read on, for some hints.

✳ If you agreed with fewer than eight statements, your health is cause for concern. That certainly does not mean that you have a disease, but it may mean you are more susceptible to contracting one. Certainly you could get more out of life. You might like to give this some serious thought.

> **Top Tip**
> *Being in good health is about far more than being without disease – it means feeling great!*

Written Evidence

Did you know that health and vigour shows up in your handwriting? Graphologists believe that the way we write reveals our personality, and this idea is receiving scientific backing in some countries. Graphology is a complex study deserving detailed examination. However, for our purposes, let us look at some easy-to-spot give-aways.

Pressure Some people write so hard that they almost puncture the page while others leave a gentle scrawl. If you are not sure how much you press, lift the paper on which you have written and run the tips of your fingers over the back of it. Can you feel the indentations you have made? Then you have used very firm pressure. People with lots of energy and determination do this, and it is a very general indication of robustness, although if there is no outlet for the energies, frustration and tension may cause problems. If this is you, then you need both an active sport and a relaxation programme. If your pressure is so light as to leave only thin strokes, then you need a tonic, some TLC and something to get excited about! Uneven pressure may signify weakness or pain, or possibly temporary emotional excitement – calm down!

Upper Sections of Letters Bowed Over to the Right This may mean mental pressure and headaches. Use lavender oil for its soothing properties and off-load some of your responsibilities.

this is a testing time

a feeling of wellbeing * 99

Lines of Writing Droop Downwards If this is habitual, it indicates depression and exhaustion. Take a holiday and don't be afraid to ask for some help. Upward sloping writing indicates an optimistic nature.

Lately I have been feeling so tired

Writing Slopes Backwards If your writing was recently upright or forward-sloping but has started sloping backwards, this indicates emotional hurt and a possible need for counselling.

I prefer to keep myself to myself

Writing Slopes Forwards Lines that are increasingly sloping forwards indicate that the need for others is growing.

No man is an island!

Writing with Variable Slope Writing that slopes in more than one direction indicates that you may be currently experiencing hurt, which is making you wobbly.

At the moment I feel torn two ways

Strong Lower Loops These indicate physical vigour and a healthy sexuality.

Yesterday's match was great!

Invasive Lower Loops If the upward stroke cuts into the higher section of the writing, or if the loops are exaggerated, there may be excessive self-indulgence.

Lovely that you got top grade!

Short Sharp Downstrokes Short, sharp downstrokes can indicate repression. Be honest with yourself about your feelings and desires.

My lips are sealed

Angular Loops Angular loops may mean anger and frustration. Realise that you also have a right to fulfilment.

Yesterday is gone but not forgotten

Very Tall Upper Strokes with Detached T-Bars This may indicate someone who is not in firm contact with reality. Possessed by a compelling ideal, they may neglect sensible habits and diet. Come down out of the clouds!

totally idealistic

Signatures These need to be considered in comparison with the rest of the script. One that consistently drags below a line indicates depression, but where it slopes downwards, this may be only a mood – give yourself a treat! A signature that is deliberately placed far to the left of the page shows fear of life. This may result in behaviour that veers between aggression and self-pity – hypnotherapy is likely to help. A stroke that crosses through the signature, effectively cancelling it, denotes self-hatred, which could lay the subject open to all types of disorders, even self-harm. If this is you, do you feel it applies to you? If so you owe it to yourself to get help.

How Can You Improve Your Health?

Now that you have started to think about it, you may realise that there are elements to your health that could be improved, and that is half the battle. For instance, if you disagreed with Statement 11 in the questionnaire, then you need to clarify what the problem is and get help. One example might be if you have had a nagging pain in your back that you have ignored in the belief that it is nothing important, you may now see that it is getting you down and make an appointment with a chiropractor or osteopath. Simple. Often the only barrier between us and optimum health is the lack of belief that we can have it! If you disagreed with Statement 5, why was that? Once you have tracked down the answer you can find the remedy, whether it is a new bed or a cup of chamomile tea! Of course, during difficult periods in life it will not be easy to achieve a state in which you can agree with all 14 statements; everyone gets ill sometimes. However, when things are on an even keel, you should be able to agree with almost all the questions, unless you have a chronic illness or disability.

Finding a Remedy

Take responsibility for your own health as far as possible. If you have a disorder, become a mine of information about it. Read books, investigate on the Net, try some carefully selected remedies. It is not enough to go to your overworked GP and get a prescription. The medical model used in our culture treats the disease, not the patient, and this approach is coming under increasing fire from alternative practitioners and the countless patients who have been harmed by drugs. More people die per month in the UK alone as a result of prescribed drugs than were killed in the terrorist attack on the Twin Towers in New York. (These statistics are available from *What Doctors Don't Tell You* – see Further Reading.) Pharmaceutical companies are very big business indeed and may be sometimes suspected of putting profit before – well – everything. Not all GPs are totally au fait with the side-effects of what they prescribe – how could they be when the lists that are given on the packets are so long? Besides, if you are taking a cocktail of medication it is unlikely that the complete combination has been tested in clinical trials, and even if it has, how can anyone be sure how you, as an individual, will react? Substances designed to attack the disease often attack the patient.

This is not to denigrate all medicine; modern medicine is often a wonderful thing and none of us would wish to be without it. However, our society's reliance on drugs is felt by many informed people to be excessive. Treatments that support the whole patient – i.e. holistic treatments – may take longer to be effective, but they result in a patient who is stronger and healthier all round, rather than someone who has got rid of one malady only to have been damaged and weakened. A prime example is that of antibiotics. There is no doubt that these drugs save lives. However, in the process of curing the illness they strip the body of all its benign bacteria, which can lead to a variety of problems that spiral out of control, for instance thrush. Antibiotics, it is probably fair to say, should only be taken for serious conditions. They should also be aimed at an identified bacterium, rather than 'throwing' a broad-spectrum antibiotic at something unknown.

Antibiotics are just one example. As the list of drugs increases, so do the possible side-effects. Here is a list of simple guidelines to follow if you become ill:

* Unless your symptoms are mild or totally familiar, take them seriously and get them diagnosed to your satisfaction. Do not be fobbed off if you are at all uneasy – ask for a second opinion.
* As a patient you are in a vulnerable, dependent position. This gives power to those who attend to you. Power, sadly, is sometimes abused. So, if you feel at all afraid of being brow-beaten, don't worry about looking silly – take along a feisty friend with you when you have an appointment.
* Have private healthcare if you can. It is sad but true that you will usually get better treatment and be given more time and attention if you – or your insurance company – are paying. It will also probably mean you get seen much quicker. People are prepared to spend thousands of pounds on holidays but begrudge paying for health – which is more important?
* When you have your diagnosis, discuss the matter with your doctor and/or specialist as thoroughly as you can, so you fully understand your condition.
* Research as much as you can about your disorder – the Net is a wonderful resource.

- ✳ Seek alternative therapy if it has anything at all to offer – which it probably will. Indeed, an alternative therapist may be able to diagnose your condition. However, make sure any therapist you see is well-qualified and belongs to a professional body.
- ✳ Take responsibility for your own wellbeing by attending to your diet and other habits.

Illness as Metaphor

It is generally accepted that our mental state plays a big part in our physical health. Some diseases are attributed to a great extent to tension or anxiety – for instance migraine and irritable bowel syndrome. But if body and mind are one unit – which is the approach of holistic medicine – then does not all illness stem from or involve the mind?

We are apt to look upon the physical world as split from the spiritual – if, in fact, we believe at all in the latter. Is it not more likely that it is all linked – different rates of vibration along a spectrum? Peoples such as the Native Americans and the Australian Aborigines, with a strong traditional culture, see the material world as a metaphor for spirit. In the same way, our bodies are a metaphor for our minds, and when we get ill it means something, regardless of the illness. For instance, if you have something as simple as an in-growing toenail it can indicate fear about taking the next necessary step along your life path. If you have trouble with your gallbladder, it can mean that you are bitter about your circumstances.

These links are explored at length in Louise Hay's *You Can Heal Your Life* (see Further Reading). Of course, we should not be too simplistic about this – every case is individual. Nor – heaven forbid! – should we use this as a reason for blaming people when they are ill. however, it is very useful to be aware that our mental state does indeed closely affect our bodies, even in ways we might not imagine, and that mind and body are one organism. Are happy people healthy people? Generally they are.

Much of this book is about finding as happy a lifestyle as possible, and this is a healthy lifestyle. What can you do as a short-cut, if things just won't fall into place? Make sure you have plenty of laughter in your life, that's what!

being in control of your weight

Exercise

We all know we should take exercise, and we are all bored by being told this. Exercise is tedious, tiring and time-consuming – yes? No, actually. The 'No pain, no gain' philosophy has us believing that nothing good comes without struggle. Effort we do need to put in; struggle, no. The truth of the matter is that exercise releases endorphins into the bloodstream – these are the body's own equivalent of morphine. Exercise gives us a high! The chances are that if you agreed with the first four statements in the list on page 97, then you also agreed with Statements 12 and 13. In other words, you exercise regularly.

The key to regular exercise is firstly that you should enjoy it and secondly that it must fit in with your lifestyle. There is no point doing a form of exercise you hate, because you will probably pull a muscle and your inner resistance is sure to have an effect on your body chemistry. Plus the likelihood is that you simply will not keep it up. If you just hate all exercise, this is probably because you have done so little in the past that it has become a gargantuan effort. Start slowly and build up.

Be creative about your choice of exercise. Going to a gym may take too long and be too expensive. Ask yourself what you like doing, when you have time to do it and who you would like to do it with. It doesn't matter what – walking, playing footie with the kids, running up and down stairs – all these are proper exercise if you do them enough and regularly. Don't over-commit at first, and be prepared to change if it doesn't work out – please note, making changes does not mean abandoning all efforts to exercise! It just means you give yourself permission to re-think.

The people in many of the case studies in this chapter found ways of motivating themselves in keeping with their own individuality and lifestyle. Because of this they found it easy to keep going. Keep it simple, make it individual, break it down into bite-size pieces, and there'll be no stopping you.

Barry's Story

Barry held down a demanding job as District Manager for a pharmaceutical company. Not only did he have a team to manage, but he also had to travel hundreds of miles most days, visiting customers. He knew he was putting on weight and that the stress of his job was telling on him. His wife suggested that he go to the gym and play football on Saturdays, but to tell the truth Barry was afraid to show himself up. Besides, he was often out on the road for twelve hours at a stretch and at the end of the day all he could think about was falling into his armchair.

'Use it or lose it,' Barry thought, and when he looked in the mirror he knew the latter was happening. He transferred the dynamic, pro-active approach that had made him successful at his job to his own health. 'What would motivate me?' he asked himself. One weekend he cleared out his garage and fitted it out as a mini-gym. On the wall he fixed a large TV and took out a subscription to Sky. Now he spoils himself watching the sports channels while he pumps iron in the privacy of his own home. Mind you, he's looking so good now he may decide to strut his stuff down at the gym after all....

Carol's Story

Carol's second child had just started school. She was determined to get back the figure and the vitality that she had before she became pregnant. However, she had also just started a part-time job, and time was not as plentiful as she had expected. Her commitment to visits to the gym was becoming strained as she was finding it very hard to get back in time to pick up the children.

Carol decided to re-think her fitness regime. She admitted to herself that she found the gym strenuous and boring. She remembered that before she had the children she used to love to go clubbing and how frustrated she had always felt when there wasn't room to dance! She cancelled her subscription to the gym, bought herself some new CDs and danced on her own, in the space of her own living room, each day for about half an hour before walking up to school. Soon she felt much better and quite excited about life. The money she saved from the gym meant that she and her husband could go out clubbing together again, too, when they could get a babysitter, and Carol could show off her new moves – and sleeker figure!

Weight

Being overweight is a disease of modern times, and it is growing. In America a third of the population is obese, while in some European countries it is quarter of the population. These figures are increasing. At the same time the fashion is to be very thin – because, of course, we always want what is hardest to come by! This is a recipe for ill-health and misery.

The basic reasons for excess weight are not hard to discover. We now have more food than ever in the developed world, and this food is of unending variety. Far from waiting for hunters to come in with the kill, we can eat meat three times a day in whatever quantities we like. We do not have to wait for summer for strawberries, or Christmas for nuts. Furthermore, food is processed and packaged to make it as delightful as possible. Our lifestyles are more sedentary into the bargain. No wonder fat is on the increase. It has been suggested that another reason for being overweight is that the food we have now is less nutritious, produced from tired soil and full of additives. We overeat because we are not getting the vitamins and minerals that we need.

It is almost universally accepted that to lose weight you must eat less. Food is graded by calorie content and most diets are based on this in one way or another. The reasoning is simple – the body uses energy, food contains units of energy, eat too many units and you put on weight, eat too few and you lose it. Some allowance is made for faster/slower metabolisms, but in practice very little account is taken of individual differences, or indeed of complex body dynamics. Fewer calories = less fat; that's that.

The experiences of the last 50 years or so have proved, however, that low-calorie diets do not actually work. 'Ah!' one might exclaim, 'that is because the fatties don't stick to them!' Well, yes, that is true up to a point. It is also true that no-one is fat in a famine. However, our culture with its Judaeo-Christian tradition tends to think in terms of blame, guilt, punishment and general abasement of the body as an inferior, almost evil, thing that needs to be kept firmly in check if we are to attain any sort of virtue. Fat people can be blamed – and almost inevitably blame themselves, feel guilty and try to punish their erring bodies by more starvation. At the same time there are forces that continually invite us to all forms of indulgence. Neither approach has any true respect for the wisdom of the body, its sanctity, and its inherent harmony. We are severed from our innocent, instinctual selves and quite out of tune with our true needs.

From a purely practical point of view there are sound reasons why low-calorie diets don't work. Firstly, eating less than you need makes you very hungry and real hunger is horrible. If you accidentally press your hand on a hot pipe, no-one is going to blame you for taking it off! If the hungry person seeks to alleviate that nagging sensation in the stomach, they are only doing the same sort of thing. More important than this, low-calorie diets play hell with the metabolism. Studies on lab rats (poor things) show that when put on a low-calorie diet, at first they lose weight quickly, but when the diet stops they gain weight more quickly than they lost it. Each time they 'diet', the loss is slower and the gain quicker. People are the same – the body adapts to what it perceives as famine conditions in the same way that a starving dog will still bury its bone. Regardless of the 'shoulds' and 'oughts', how many people do you know who have lost a substantial amount of weight on a diet – say two stone or more – and who have kept it off for five years or more? Not many, I'm sure!

There are, of course, people who do not put on weight, and some who remain thin, regardless of what they eat. My own convictions as a hypnotherapist dealing with people seeking to lose weight and with an interest in nutrition are that there are many factors involved in the weight question.

Perhaps I should clarify my own position in the fattie/thinnie spectrum! I am 5'6" tall, a size 14 above the waist, and a 12 below the waist, and while I am about half a stone overweight (at a guess) my size doesn't really vary despite the fact I regularly consume far, far more than the designated number of calories for a moderately active woman! The one time in my life when I seriously dieted, determined to be a size 10, I suffered a horrendous week of ravenous bad temper – and put on two pounds! After that I threw away the scales and vowed to like myself the way I was, along with the odd chocolate bar. I had the luck, or the self-indulgence, to avoid getting onto the dieting roller-coaster. However, as the mother of active boys in a world of junk food, I also have an avid interest in nutrition. Besides, in my hypnotherapy practice I see many patients who want to lose weight.

Some Dieting Approaches

Food metabolism is a complex affair. In *Eat Yourself Slim* (see Further Reading), Michel Montignac explains the significance of the glycaemic values of food, which is the measurement of how much the food in question elevates the blood sugar after consumption. This is distinct from calorific value. If the pancreas is worn out through years of coping with too much refined sugar, insulin levels will be affected, resulting in the ready build-up of fat. So foods with a high glycaemic index will put on weight faster than those with a low one. Cooking can greatly affect the glycaemic value of food – for instance cooked carrots are much higher on the index, with a value of 85, as opposed to raw carrots, with a value of 35. Processing also tends to affect foods adversely. Montignac advocates a diet of foods low on the index, which does not specifically restrict calories and does not mean you go hungry. Cheese, chocolate (of 70 per cent cocoa solids) and wine are permitted. Montignac advises the eating of protein-lipid meals separately from carbohydrate meals because of the effect the presence of carbohydrate has on the digestion and metabolism of fat molecules – another contributory factor in weight gain. However, the entire Montignac approach seems balanced and very much gourmet class! Apparently this system has worked for many people. The point I am making is that there are other approaches than the starve yourself, calorie-controlled one.

The Slimming World system of Red Days and Green Days means that it is possible to eat your fill of rice, fruit and pasta, get slim and not go hungry. In practice, however, weight loss for those significantly overweight may slow down after a period of time. Attention is paid to the amount of water drunk, and certain foods are called 'sins' and allowed in moderation. The association of food with sin is prevalent in our society, but still unfortunate, as it leads to that bête noire – guilt. Slimming World encourages the eating of special slimmer's foods that are high in artificial additives. However, there is much that is good in this system, encouraging as it does the eating of lots of fruit and vegetables.

High fibre diets are also worth considering. One of the big differences between our diet and that of our ancestors is the fact that food today is very refined. Fibre-rich food passes more slowly through the stomach – increasing a feeling of fullness – but rapidly through the gut. This is much healthier, avoiding constipation and arguably taking more food right through the body rather than allowing it to be stored as fat. I have known people report a significant weight loss through eating wholefoods in preference to processed and refined ones.

Fat was less of a problem for our ancestors, even when famine conditions were not present. It is possible that their eating habits were healthier because – in the very distant past – they were more in contact with their natural instincts. After all, obesity is unknown in wild animals. Sugar was introduced to the West by the Crusaders but has only come to be consumed in quantities over the last 200 years. Potatoes were introduced in the sixteenth century. Countless artificial additives have been introduced over the last 50 years. In contrast, the earliest tribes, the hunter gatherers, lived off fruit, nuts and meat, after which phase grain farming was introduced. From this it may be deduced that the food to which we are best suited is the hunter gatherer diet. Needless to say, nutrition is no way that simple, and in any case we must remember that the life-expectancy of people in those days was extremely short. However, it is worth remembering, in our search for optimum nutrition, that our digestive systems are still essentially Stone Age in terms of evolution, and working from there.

Other tips for weight loss include drinking a fair amount of coffee to speed your metabolism, although more than a little coffee is not good for health. Green tea may do the same, as may eating spicy foods and, of course, doing regular exercise. Even very small changes will probably have some effect if they are given enough time. For instance, if your weight is stable and you decide to stop having sugar in your tea and walk for ten minutes each day, you will very probably lose weight, as long as you don't add something else to your diet that is as fat-inducing as the sugar.

Perhaps the best approach of all is not to interfere too much with your diet, for this may be artificial and distorting to the mechanism that has the power to keep you thin – your instinct! Instead watch the behaviour of your slender friends and learn from them. How do they know what is just the right amount to eat to remain at a good weight? In other words, what has their instinct got that yours hasn't? Everyone eats too much sometimes, but thinner people tend to check out foods before consumption by imagining how they will feel inside if they eat that food. Fatter people may not think this way – they see food, their mouth waters and their awareness may never get down as far as the stomach itself. Use the hypnotherapy script on page 125 and the Charm for Healthy Eating on page 123 to help contact your own instincts and body wisdom.

Gary's Story

Gary was a lorry-driver. On long-haul drives he often ate chocolate bars to keep him alert – and to reduce the boredom. His weight was increasing steadily and his wife insisted that he diet. For a few weeks he lost weight, but then on a family holiday in Spain he regained all the weight he had lost – and more! Then he was made redundant. While his wife worked to pay the mortgage, Gary took a temporary job as a postman while he built up his own haulage business. To his surprise, he found he lost half a stone in a month – simply through the extra walking!

The Many Meanings of Food

When we are born, one of the first things of which we are aware is needing to feed. We can't see properly and we are completely powerless. We are intensely aware of the many feelings transmitted to us with the milk we take. Is Mother relaxed or anxious? Do we have as long to feed as we would like or do we sense her impatience? Is she enjoying feeding us, or not? The impressions that we absorb will colour our attitudes to food all our lives. For instance, if we sense Mother's impatience, we will feed quickly – our survival depends on it! Not feeling confident of Mother's commitment to the business of feeding, we take down all we can as fast as we can, regardless of how much our little tummy might

a feeling of wellbeing * 111

need. It doesn't take a mastermind to understand that in later life we may well eat too quickly and too much because we are programmed to be anxious. If we develop eating disorders such as bulimia, one possible cause may be having had food thrust upon us by an over-anxious mother, one whose love was actually invasive and whose feelings were about a need to control, not to nurture. In later life we vomit the food back, as we wanted to vomit out the milk we didn't really need and the emotions which we felt were poisoning. Of course, eating disorders are very complex matters and there are many possible reasons for them. Nor is it fair to blame mothers everywhere for everything, for mothering is a demanding and scary business with a zillion different ways of getting it wrong! However, it is worth remembering that attitudes to food may be established pre-verbally and may haunt us in adulthood.

Instincts are further distorted by what we were taught as we were growing up. If food was used as a reward, then it has associations with being 'good'. If we were told to 'Waste not, want not' and 'Eat what you're given', we have internalised messages that have nothing to do with what our bodies really require. In fact we have been conditioned not to listen to our bodies, but to eat what others dictate or provide, regardless. For instance, if you have a compulsion always to clear your plate, you are hardly listening to your body.

In addition, there may be other problems, still current, that make us not want to lose weight. Women who are overweight may be avoiding the issues that their sexuality might raise – it is safer to be fat and less attractive than to cope with a relationship and its attendant emotions. Fat is something that people hide behind for a variety of reasons – it means they can postpone life and all its challenges because they are just 'too fat' for everything.

These and similar issues may need therapy to be resolved. However, you can make a start by being very honest with yourself. Take a pencil and paper and jot down your attitudes to food. Here are some questions to ask yourself.

* Do you always feel you should clear your plate?
* Do you reward or console yourself with food?
* Do you eat more when you are upset, anxious or unhappy? If so, why?

- Do you know when you are full, or could you just keep on eating?
- Do you always eat food that is available or offered, regardless of whether you need it?
- Are you aware of your body's fluctuating needs or are you always prepared to eat your favourite foods whatever?
- When food is being served up, do you feel worried that you will not get your share?
- Do you binge on 'forbidden' foods? If so, why?
- Do you look forward to times alone when you can eat your fill of delicious food? If so, why?
- Are you postponing life until you are 'thin'? What is your vested interest in staying overweight? Does it mean you can postpone dealing with other problems? Is your weight protecting you from something you fear?
- What were the attitudes to food in your family, as you were growing up? What do you recall of mealtimes? How did you feel at mealtimes?

> **Top Tip**
> *Weight loss that works will not starve you! Make changes in your diet and lifestyle that fit in with your needs.*

Think about what you have written down means for you. Have you realised anything? Would you like to change it?

Sally's Story

After having three children in quick succession, Sally knew that her figure had suffered. However, with the eldest not yet at school, she needed all the energy she had – and more! She was also aware that many women's weight problems effectively begin when they decide to diet to lose weight quickly after childbirth. Sally did not want to alter her metabolism – after all, she had never had a weight problem before. She read all she could about nutrition and decided to put the family on a diet of whole, natural foods containing very few artificial additives, cutting down on animal fat and processed sugar. When she was hungry, Sally ate nuts, dried fruit, wholemeal bread and jam sweetened with concentrated apple juice. To her satisfaction, her waistbands gradually became looser and her energy levels increased.

Weight Loss that Works

If you decide you really do want to lose weight, you will need to think and research to find the best approach for you. The following is not intended to be a weight-loss system, because that would be a book in itself. These are just a few pointers to bear in mind:

* Do not try to lose weight too quickly. This just doesn't work. If you are losing one pound a week, that is probably enough in most cases.
* Don't go hungry or go for long periods without eating.
* Keep your foods as natural, high-quality and organic as you can. There is some evidence that traditional ways have value. For instance, proper Italian espresso coffee is not as high in caffeine as may be imagined because the preparation method extracts all the flavour without the high caffeine content. More importantly from a slimmer's point of view, the body has ways of coping with food produced and prepared naturally that it may not have with processed foods.
* Eat unrefined foods such as wholemeal bread, brown rice and wholemeal pasta, and ensure that the flour used is proper whole flour, not flour that has been refined once and then had the bran re-introduced.
* Drink plenty of water. This flushes through the system and may help you to feel full. If you don't like tap water, experiment with spring water, warm water or bottled water. However, avoid artificially carbonated water.
* Remember that you also need exercise to speed up your metabolism and make you feel good. Plan to do ten to twenty minutes exercise a day.
* Remember also that your weight is not just a product of what you eat and do – it is a product of what you are. If you need to lose a lot of weight your lifestyle will probably need to alter a great deal. For instance, do you have things to be excited and passionate about?

Do you have many interests? There is more to getting a life than having a run round the block each evening and coming back to a slimmer's meal.

* Whatever you do has to work for you. There is little point in following a diet that lets you fill up with pasta if you hate the stuff.
* Stress is one of the factors that can affect your weight. Some people find that if they are really anxious, weight falls off them. Others are the opposite, because certain fat cells around the abdomen can react adversely to adrenalin. If you are one of the latter, you may need some stress-busting therapy if you are to lose weight.
* Set time aside to prepare food or do it in advance, so you are not caught out starving and reaching for junk food.
* Be aware of the flash-points in the day where you may eat more than you really need, such as when watching the telly or talking with a group of friends at lunchtime. Take steps to avoid these situations.
* Consider hypnotherapy, not as a magic way to stop you wanting food but as a way to get you in the right frame of mind to make positive choices about your food.

Becky's Story

Becky started a new office job in a new town where she didn't know anyone. She was anxious to prove herself and spent her lunch hours at her desk, eating sandwiches. Because she was stressed she found she was also eating chocolate bars between meals as a treat. At the end of the day she was too tired to do anything but phone her family and fall into bed early. Her energy levels were falling and she knew her health was suffering. After a tearful conversation with her mother, Becky realised she was not only run-down, she was also very lonely.

There was no way to avoid the demands of her job, but the money she was earning meant she had some to spare. She took a deep breath and invested in a women-only fitness club near her flat. The first few visits were a huge effort, but gradually Becky began to make new friends and relax. Soon she looked forward to going to the club after work. Although she felt tired, she told herself she would just exercise gently and then have a drink. However, she always found she did far more exercise than she had planned, because as she warmed up she became more energetic. Her fitness improved dramatically, and so did her social life.

Eating Disorders

A profusion of food, adulterated food and a pre-occupation with being slim form the background for eating disorders, which are such a common problem. In keeping with the current trend towards specialisation and compartmentalisation, the 'disorder' may be treated in isolation, as a disease. While there is no doubt that eating disorders are illnesses – and sometimes very serious ones – the factors that give rise to them are rooted within the personality. For them to be treated effectively, counselling or psychotherapy of some sort is usually necessary.

Bulimia With bulimia, the patient has a compulsive urge to eat. This is more common in cultures where it is considered an advantage to be thin. Having indulged, usually to excess, following previous starvation, the patient then induces vomiting. Bulimics can be very cunning about the buying, eating and vomiting of food, and if efforts to be sick fail they may instead resort to diuretics or laxatives. Programmes to help bulimics involve hospitalisation in extreme cases, and a strict eating programme. Bulimia is a result of low self-esteem – the person feels they must be thin to be attractive but their confidence is rock-bottom. Self-disgust follows when they do not have the control to starve themselves, and a downward spiral results. However, by no means everyone who is plump and/or lacks confidence becomes bulimic, and the deeper causes may very well lie with early experiences of feeding and emotional interchange. If a child has been forced to swallow emotional content that they cannot deal with, bulimia may result in later life. For example, if a mother forces feeds onto a baby to satisfy her own emotional needs as opposed to adopting a sensible routine or focusing on the needs of the child, the child experiences a double-whammy of unwanted food and the weight of the mother's own needs; this may form part of the background to bulimia. The bulimic person may need to unpack some of this history, and then proceed to an establishment of respect for and attunement to their body, along with some confidence that they can maintain their own boundaries and balance.

Anorexia The anorexic starves her/himself in order to reach an ideal of thinness, which is usually stick-like. Even when weight loss is achieved, the anorexic will still see her- or himself as fat. Anorexics may become bulimic. Bulimics may long to be anorexics, seeing that state as being purer and more lovable and admirable. Anorexia may have similar origins to bulimia, in early feeding patterns, but in the case of anorexia the patient is more successful in keeping out food and all it represents. They may feel responsible for their parents' emotional problems and have a wish to avoid the implications of their sexuality. Both anorexia and bulimia may be linked with an unease or even hatred of the physical body as being something unclean. This is part of our cultural heritage, which has encouraged a view of the body as unholy and 'the world, the flesh and the devil' as a reprehensible package.

There are other eating disorders, less extreme than either of the above, in which the patient obsessively avoids certain foods. In fact any excessive worry about or preoccupation with food (apart from creatively, with the gourmet or chef, of course) may be termed a disorder. Ideally humans should be able to enjoy food, eat it when they are hungry, eat enough to satisfy themselves and have no problem listening to the messages of their bodies as to when to stop.

If you (or anyone you know and love) have ever had an eating disorder, you will know how painful this is. Every body is individual and has different needs. On a practical level, to maintain health (and even life) a way has to be found to get the sufferer to eat, and that is a matter for professionals. On an emotional level, some respect and liking for one's body needs to be developed; this has to be built up slowly or it will be hard to accept. The Lovely Me charm on page 79 may be tried as a first step to boost body image. The hypnotherapy scripts for relaxation and self-esteem from Chapter 1 and Appendix 2 make a good start in building a more constructive attitude. The scripts for de-stress and coping with fears in Chapter 9 may also be appropriate.

addictions

Most cultures have drugs that are sanctioned for use. It is natural for human beings to wish to explore other levels of consciousness, and the easiest pathways to this may be offered by drugs. Even the most materialistic and least imaginative among us realise that the way you look at life is far more important than your actual circumstances, and drugs offer a quick and easy way to change our consciousness. The current use of recreational drugs may be seen not merely as escapism but also as a sign of a yearning for spiritual experience. Among many tribespeople, hallucinogenic drugs are regularly taken by those seeking to expand their minds, and these may be administered by an experienced shaman or tribal priest who has knowledge of the substances and their effects, so these drugs do not usually cause harm.

Drugs in our culture are not taken in the same aware manner. We do not approach them as explorers but as escapers – there is a difference! However, certain drugs are sanctioned by our culture as legitimate forms of fun – these include alcohol and nicotine. Despite the fact that these are arguably at least as harmful as many illegal drugs, most people at one time or another indulge in one or both. Many people find that they become addicted, dependent upon the drug to the detriment of their health, and it is beyond the power of their will to control the situation.

While there is certainly a physical component to addiction, the principal issue is a mental and emotional one. Physical addiction to nicotine only lasts a few weeks after the last cigarette. However, emotional need and habit are other matters entirely, and these may be very hard to break.

Alcohol consumption can be said to have reached an addictive level as soon as it interferes with a person's ability to run their life. It is often said that 'drink is a good servant, but a dangerous master'. The line between servant and master is a fine but definite one. It is possible to be a fairly heavy drinker without being an alcoholic. The true alcoholic will sacrifice everything for the sake of a drink – work and family included. Such addiction is a medical matter and requires specialist help beyond the scope of this book (see Useful Addresses). Many experts believe that alcohol addiction is biological and can be passed on in the genes; others feel that body and emotions are so closely linked that it isn't possible to make a distinction. One explanation for compulsive drinking may even be a quest for the Divine, a bid to lose the ego in something much greater – for the sensation induced by alcohol is that of having all boundaries dissolved. The association Alcoholics Anonymous use the concept of Higher Power, which links with this notion. In connection with this, there is a very useful saying which we can all do with bearing in mind whether we are alcoholics or not: 'God grant me the serenity to accept the things that I cannot change, the courage to change the things I can and the wisdom to know the difference.'

Hypnotherapy and counselling may support a recovering alcoholic but are not sufficient in themselves to treat the disorder. If you fear that you are drinking too much, help yourself with the Self-Hypnosis for De-stressing on page 222. Work through this list of questions to see if your drinking is getting out of hand.

* Are you regularly drinking alone?
* Do you feel you need a drink to cope with your day-to-day life?
* Are you drinking early in the morning?
* Are you lying to other people about your drinking?
* Do you gulp your alcoholic drink?
* Are you becoming disinterested in food?
* Do you drink at work?
* Do you have blackouts?
* Do you need to get tanked up before social functions?
* Do you fear being without your drink?

A 'yes' answer to any of the above may mean that you have an alcohol problem. Try to be very honest with yourself. Only you can help yourself, but you will also need support – so don't delay getting help.

Research is on-going into precisely how addictive recreational drugs such as cannabis are, and how harmful they can be. There are always political, social and economic issues involved in the greater picture. Many people assert, with some justification, that smoking pot is far less harmful than drinking alcohol. But no drug can be completely safe, and cases of teenagers who die as a result of taking just one dose of the drug ecstasy tragically make the newspapers from time to time. If you regularly take recreational drugs you are, of course, breaking the law! You need to be very aware of your own body's responses. Also be aware of how much you are doing this to impress your peers – is it really worth the abuse of your body? Use the checklist for alcoholism to decide whether you have a real problem with drugs. Again, only you can decide whether you need help.

Although there are some things to be said in favour of alcohol – for instance that moderate drinking lowers the risk of heart attack – smoking seems to have no similar benefits. Of course, getting pleasure from something is very therapeutic, and we should never underestimate how good it is for you to enjoy yourself! The problem with smoking, however, is that the 'pleasure' tends to come from the craving being answered. It feels very pleasurable to scratch an itch, for instance, but it is not the same type of pleasure as that gained from smelling a rose or looking at a sunset. Great pleasure can come from the relieving of a discomfort. Smoking is often nice because it relieves the discomfort of needing a fag! (Heavy drinking is similar, of course.) Smoking that is very light – for instance one or two cigarettes here and there and a couple more at the weekend – may possibly do us good if we enjoy it very much. Such light smoking is very rare, however, and the wish to stop smoking is one of the most frequent issues that bring people to a hypnotherapist.

In coping with any addiction, it is important to have a strategy. Although hypnotherapy is a very powerful tool, it cannot always simply and dramatically stop dead all urges to smoke and provide an instant cure. Of course, this does sometimes happen with some people who are 'good' subjects and who are particularly receptive to the particular therapist. However, it is best to approach smoking with plenty of strategies for stopping in addition to using hypnotherapy.

To give up smoking, you need to realise that it is your belief that is the challenge. Remember that although after a few days the nicotine will be out of your system, your belief that you need cigarettes takes longer to go, for it is ingrained upon the subconscious mind; you have to learn that you are fine without cigarettes.

Firstly, you need to be totally committed to giving up. This is your choice, no-one else's. Cutting down is not a good approach because it means you have to learn different habits and then different ones again as the occasions when you smoke become more restricted. You need to have decided that you will do it for yourself, not because someone else has insisted.

It will help if other family members give up at the same time because that reduces the chances of temptation in the days that follow. Certainly you need to enlist the support of your partner or family in what you are doing.

Make a list of those times in the day when you usually have a cigarette. What else could you do instead? You need something definite to occupy you, such as reading a magazine, going for a walk, chewing gum, eating fruit or chatting to a friend on the phone. What you choose to do should be pleasurable for you and something you can look forward to. List those times in 24 hours when you don't smoke and feel fine – for instance, when you are asleep. Your body can cope without cigarettes for many hours at a stretch. There is no reason why you should not be fine at all times without nicotine. List also the many good things there will be to reward you when you don't smoke, such as breathing clean air, being able to taste food, running without getting out of breath, etc.

When you are clear exactly how you will manage your time, throw away your cigarettes, start your self-hypnosis (see Appendix 2, page 239), and never look back.

visualisation and meditation for wellbeing

A Visualisation for Feeling Healthier

Sit in your auditorium and watch the curtains on the stage swing apart, revealing a beautiful beach. Walk up onto the stage and enter the scene.

Here there is gentle warmth, as the sun plays on your skin. The breeze lifts your hair, bringing with it the fresh tang of the ocean. Beneath your feet, the sand is smooth. Ahead of you the ocean stretches in

a feeling of wellbeing * 121

shades of blue and emerald. The sun glints on the dancing waves and the sky above is clear. You hear the rhythmic swish-swish of the tide and the wild cry of seagulls.

Walk down to the edge of the water, so that the waves ripple close to your feet. Bend down so that you are close to the level of the swelling tide. You are aware of the vastness and the power of the waters, of their unfathomable depths, their overwhelming strength and their mystery. Watch as the waves break onto the shore, bringing with them multi-coloured pebbles and fragments of driftwood.

Look out over the waters. Out at sea you see a round shape bobbing up and down on the waves, catching the sunlight with a brilliant gleam. Closer and closer it floats until you are able to make out that it is a bottle. You watch as the tide brings the bottle in, slowly, until it lies at your feet.

You pick the bottle up and see that inside it there is a piece of paper, folded into a scroll. You pull out the stopper and tip up the bottle. The scroll slips out easily onto your palm. Step back from the water and unfold the scroll. What does it say? This is an important message for your deepest wellbeing.

Taking your scroll with you, walk back up the beach to where the sand is smooth and level. Placing your scroll safely underneath a large pebble, lie down and make yourself comfortable on the sand.

The sun falls on you with delicious warmth. Feel it caressing you. Feel the warmth of the sun bathing your limbs, enveloping you in a golden glow. Enjoy this. Feel the glow penetrating your skin so that it fills your body. Your entire body is suffused with this wonderful radiance. Feel it especially strongly in any part of your body that has been less than well.

You are growing stronger, healthier, full of joy. Feel this sensation for as long as you can; feel the warmth, the wellbeing filling you up. Enjoy it for as long as you can.

When you are ready, get up. Look out to sea and breathe deeply. Pick up your scroll and make your way back off the beach and find yourself on the stage.

Walk down into the auditorium and place your scroll somewhere safe, for it is precious. Come back to everyday awareness.

charms for wellbeing

A Charm for Good Health

Poppets, or voodoo dolls, have been used in magic for thousands of years. Making an image of a person in wax, cloth or any other substance is a powerful way to fix your will upon them, for good or ill. The history of folk magic is full of the sinister use of poppets, but as with most things there is another side to poppets and they can be very effective in beneficial charms. Your poppet is going to represent and help you in a very positive way.

You will need a piece of green felt or other non-fraying fabric large enough to make two outlines of a human figure 15–23 cm (6–9 in) tall. You will also need scissors, a needle and green thread, a green candle, a strand of your own hair, some of your nail-clippings and some dried eucalyptus leaves. If you cannot get the leaves, stuff the poppet with organic cotton wool and anoint it with eucalyptus essential oil.

Draw two identical outlines of a human figure on your felt, cut them out and sew them together, leaving the shoulders and head open. Stuff the poppet with the herbs or cotton wool, plus your hair and nail-clippings, then sew up the entire figure. If you like you can add further little touches that connect you to the poppet – for instance if you always wear a necklace, place something similar on the poppet. Be very gentle and careful with your poppet as it represents you.

Light your candle and hold the poppet between your palms. Pour all your will and intentions for healing into the poppet. Imagine it glowing with a healing energy. Place your poppet beside the candle while you imagine how you will feel when you are brimming with health. Repeat this on successive evenings until the candle is burnt out. This charm is best done on a waxing moon. When the charm has taken effect, give thanks. Remove your hair and nail-clippings and dispose of them. Strongly affirm that the poppet no longer represents your essence, pull it apart and bury what bits you can, saying, 'I plant the seeds of health. May they grow hearty and strong.'

This charm can be for the healing of major and minor illnesses and also for inducing and maintaining optimum health. You can vary this charm according to the effect desired. Eucalyptus is for healing generally, and especially for colds, flu, etc. It can also help maintain good health. Try St John's wort for optimism and an end to depression; dried oak leaves for strength; thyme for energy and inner purity (good if you are giving up a bad habit such as smoking); nutmeg for rheumatism, neuralgia and sores; bay for athletic prowess; and lavender to heal stress.

Charm for Energy

Energy is deep within you and you can find ways to motivate and inspire yourself. The symbolism of this charm should give you a kick-start. Anyway, it'll be fun!

You will need a firework (preferably a rocket but please note the safety advice at the start of this book whatever you use), a red candle, some powdered ginger, a small red egg-cup or pot, a piece of red paper and a pen.

Light your candle and imagine yourself full of energy. Think of all the things you will do, how you will feel and what you will accomplish. Write a special message to yourself on the paper and burn it in the candle-flame. Now that energy has been released into the ether and will come back to you, for your use.

Hold the palm of your active hand (the one you write with) over the powdered ginger in the little red pot and imagine a stream of energy going into it. This ginger is super-charged to conduct all the energy you need in your direction.

Now light the rocket safely outside in celebration of your charm and your coming energy. Keep the ginger in a safe place and put just a very tiny bit in your shoes or pocket when you need that extra oomph.

Charm for Healthy Eating

This charm first appeared in *Spellbound!*, one of my earlier books. It will help you to give up eating foods that are not good for you, for whatever reason. However, please be careful. You should only be intending to get rid of foods that really are of no nutritional value or are harmful to you. If there is any possibility that you may have an eating disorder, please do not use this charm as it will make it worse. If you have acquired a talent for creating your own charms, do not be tempted to make one up to lose weight! With all charms, it is important to be very careful about the messages you are sending out, whether you see this as being into your subconscious, into the ether or both. Weight loss can come in a variety of ways, many of them very unpleasant. Always aim for health.

All you need for this charm is a piece of the food you want to stop eating (there can be several foods if you wish, and the pieces can be very small); a plant pot; some soil, sand or compost and seven cloves of garlic. It is best to do this charm when the moon is waning. This charm has two parts.

Firstly lie down and relax. Take your time over this. You might like to listen to some soothing music or record some instructions onto a tape – the Self-Hypnosis for Healthy Eating on page 125 is ideal. If you don't like your own voice, get the help of sweetly spoken friend. Make sure you are deeply relaxed and comfortable. Now imagine there is a table laid with all the foods you know are harmful to you (Mars bars, sticky toffees, cream cakes, fizzy drinks, etc). Really see all the foods. Now imagine all these things being bundled up in the tablecloth and thrown out. Then visualise the cloth spread back on the table and imagine all sorts of good food – vegetables, wholemeal bread, fruit, yoghurt, etc. Make sure that you like the foods that you are putting on the table; nothing should go there that you don't find delicious. Tell yourself that you eat to satisfy your body; that you may leave food on your plate if you wish; that you eat slowly, whatever you are doing; that you only take a small portion of foods that are not healthy and then you have had enough; that you eat sensibly of the good foods and you feel good. Repeat to yourself that you eat sensibly and you feel good.

When you are ready, get up. Put a little of the soil in the pot. Now put the pieces of food in the pot and cover them with the rest of the soil. Place the seven garlic cloves into the top of the soil. Put the pot in a corner of your garden and enjoy your healthy meals. Whether the garlic grows or not, it will cleanse you of the wish to eat these foods, for they have been returned to the earth to be neutralised and the garlic is the seal.

This charm can be adapted for smoking by burying a cigarette in the pot and altering the visualisation to the one in the Self-Hypnosis for Stopping Smoking on page 239 – namely throwing the cigarette packet away on the breeze.

self-hypnosis for wellbeing

Self-Hypnosis for Healthy Eating

[Usual induction.]

You are beautifully relaxed, and because you are so very deeply relaxed you know deep inside you that you can achieve the things you want. You know that you can be the best weight for your own body structure. You know that you can be fit, look good and be correctly nourished. You can learn new habits and keep to them, because you know they are good for you. You have chosen them. You know you can be the weight you want to be. Imagine yourself at that weight. Really see the new you. You eat healthily and you are keeping to your great new shape. You are fitter, happier, shapelier. Really see yourself as you would like to be. Imagine the wonderful new you as you look in the mirror. How much better you feel! You allow yourself to become like that, to be like that. You are now so relaxed that that image is a reality to your mind and you are creating it.

Eating habits that are not good for you are now changing into healthy ones. You allow this to happen easily and naturally. You know this is best for you, you know that is what your body truly wants and needs. Now imagine in front of you a table laid with all sorts of foods that you have decided are not good for you. *[Name these, along with their negative properties, such as 'fatty,' 'greasy', 'sticky'.]* Junk foods, processed foods, fast foods with low nutritional value. Really see all these foods – foods that make you feel physically under par, foods that interfere with your moods, foods that do not make you happy. Imagine all these foods laid out in front of you. These foods are not good for your body; they do not support your health. You choose not to eat these foods. If you do eat them, you have just a very small amount and you feel satisfied, full. You can only manage a tiny portion and it is enough. See yourself wrapping all these foods up in an old tablecloth and throwing them into the rubbish bin, where they belong. They are gone, and you are glad. You feel free, happy, positive.

Now imagine the same table laden with foods you have chosen to eat – luscious fruit, fresh vegetables, natural foods that keep your body healthy. *[Elaborate with foods you like that you have chosen as part of*

126 * a charmed life

your new way of eating.] Mmmm... these foods are not only delicious, but they are good for you; they make you feel energetic, clear-headed and optimistic. Eat these foods slowly, enjoying them and eating your fill. As you eat, you are aware of how your stomach feels at all times. You are aware of how your body feels. Whether you are talking to someone, watching television or reading, you remain in touch with how your body feels. When you have had enough to eat, you simply stop. You feel full; there is no pleasure now in eating any more. You feel full, you feel satisfied, you push away your plate and you stop eating. You may leave food on your plate if you wish; that is good, that is a great thing to do. You take just the right amount of food for your body at all times. You feel in tune with your body. Whenever and wherever you eat, you have just the right amount to satisfy you and then you stop. And you feel wonderful, you feel great and you have a sense of everything being right.

Let yourself feel really pleased with yourself. How well you have done! How well you are doing! Other things in your life are so much more important than food – you do not think about food except at mealtimes. You reflect on all the good things you have achieved in your life. *[Here you can insert some reminders of your achievements.]* And you know that you are now achieving a trim, healthy body. Take another look at yourself in the mirror. How good you look now you are eating healthily! You know this is within your grasp. You feel confident, relaxed and peaceful. You feel in touch with your needs so you know that at all times you will eat the correct amount of food for your body. You feel tranquil, optimistic and positive about life and about your own ability to eat healthily and look good. You have new habits in your life *[describe these]* that suit you and what you want to achieve. You feel confident, positive and relaxed. You reflect on your good points, your talents and achievements and you know that you can build on these to have the healthy, trim body that you desire. And you continue to be beautifully relaxed.

[Wake-up procedure.]

Note The above script can be used for any eating regime, not just for weight loss, with just a few minor adaptations. It is inspired by the excellent book *Hypnosis for Change* (see Further Reading).

Colin's Story

Colin was promoted to the position of Regional Manager in his firm. Two months after he started his new job, his mother died. Being of the stiff-upper-lip type, Colin soldiered on, making sure he let no-one down. A year later he was successful at his job, but had developed irritable bowel syndrome and was very stressed and anxious. His GP prescribed Prozac, but Colin felt no better and his IBS did not improve. At this point his GP suggested hypnotherapy. With his therapist, Colin was able to discuss all his feelings about his mother, plus many other issues. He received hypnotherapy for stress and for IBS. In six weeks all his symptoms had disappeared.

five

Making Friends, Staying Friends

'A Friend may well be reckoned the masterpiece of Nature....
The only way to have a friend is to be one.'
Ralph Waldo Emerson

'A friend in need is a friend indeed.'
Latin proverb

the place for friendships

Many of us put a lot of effort and energy into our relationships and our jobs, but we expect friendships just to 'happen'. While this may seem to be indeed the case with some people, this is usually more apparent than real. Extrovert people, because they are natural interactors, seem to attract company effortlessly. Actually they are putting in bags of effort, time and energy but because they are 'people people' this just seems normal to them.

> **Top Tip**
> *Putting in effort to make friends doesn't mean you are needy or sad – it means you have a great sense of priorities.*

Polly's Story

For many years Polly was a person who just thought friendships came about in a haphazard, relaxed kind of way, imagining people were like iron filings, sort of attracted together by subtle magnetism, never doing anything so contrived as to plan, to think to themselves, 'I need more friends and I'm going to try to make them – where can I go, how can I do it?' In fact she thought that to behave like that was rather sad, and meant you weren't basically likeable. She was very preoccupied with her relationships and moved around a lot from town to town, mostly influenced by the men she met. She wanted more friends, but found a lot of the people she met casually were not very interesting to her. She wanted to interact at greater depth; she wanted rapport, shared interests, wicked humour and honesty. Her situation didn't improve much when she had children for what she wanted wasn't to be found at the school gate, and she often felt lonely.

Her family life being more settled, she began to yearn for adult company. After thinking about this, she realised that it was okay to put in effort for friendships. She started to join societies related to the things she liked, so meeting kindred spirits. As she began to relax more with people, so they relaxed more with her, but at the same time she had more motivation to put out formal invitations: 'Come round for lunch!' 'Why don't we go to the theatre?' She also realised that because she had been very busy and quite preoccupied with sorting out parts of her life that were giving her problems, she had often shied away from company, feeling she didn't have enough time. So she started to accept invitations, because whatever they were they could lead to other things – and at the very least she could have a gossip! She added matters to do with friends to her 'to do' list each day and soon found she had lots of friends, several of them the sort that she could call at 3.00 am if she really wanted to. Although there was nothing forced about her friendships, she found that effort and organisation paid off in this as in other areas of life.

How Good Are your Friendships?

How do you really feel about your circle of friends? Do they provide you with what you need? Answer yes or no to the following statements to find out.

1 If you need a chat, there is always someone you can phone.
2 If you have a problem, there is almost always someone who will listen and talk it through.
3 You have at least two people you could call in the small hours for help if you were desperate.
4 If there is something you want to do, such as see a film or go to a lecture, there is usually a selection of people you can ask to accompany you.
5 You have friends you can have a good laugh with.
6 You have friends you can have a good cry with.
7 You have more than one friend you have known for five years or more.
8 You always help a friend if you possibly can.
9 You always make time to chat to a friend if you possibly can.
10 If a good friend was in great distress, you would drop everything (within reason) to help them.
11 You always have someone with whom you can discuss issues that you consider deep and important.

12 You feel your friends are honest with you about important things.
13 You feel you can trust your friends.
14 Your friends make your life seem richer.

If you disagreed with more than a couple of these, the chances are that you could improve your circle of friends and feel happier about this aspect of your life. Of course, people's requirements vary enormously. For instance, someone who is very extrovert will need a lot more friendships and a lot more activities within these friendships than the introvert who likes his or her own company. However, the introvert may be choosier about associates and actually have deeper friendships. If you are very introverted, a wide circle of friends will probably seem irrelevant to you. However, you will still need two or three really close friends with whom you can feel comfortable.

improving your friendships

You can work to improve your friendships – don't believe, like Polly, that it all just has to happen on its own! Here are some pointers.

Things to do

- Be organised! Keep a note of birthdays and important dates – send a card, make a call.
- Make a note of things friends say they like so you can buy a small gift that's spot on.
- Don't be afraid of being too formal – a thank-you card to say you appreciated someone's company and meal they prepared is a delight to most people who receive one.
- Follow interests that you can share with other people; join societies and groups.
- Go to a show that you both find funny with a friend – laughter is a great relaxer.
- Be an organiser – don't be afraid to arrange outings and get-togethers. Other people appreciate it, and they can always say no.

- Keep in contact. If your circle of friends is fairly wide, keep a list of people you need to keep in contact with and, if your memory is bad, the date you last did so. After a couple of weeks, give them a call.
- Keep a note even of people you meet casually. Keep their address, telephone number and email address so you can contact them if/when you like.

Things to Remember

- Find the things in people that you really enjoy and warm to – be positive about people.
- Remember, carelessness is not 'caring-lessness'. Some people are just more casual in the way they behave. Does this mean they cannot be good company for you? Hardly!
- Be honest and true to yourself. People sense this and like you better for it – and it's the only way to be happy.
- Make time for friends whenever they call. If you *really* are too busy, then keep it to five minutes and/or arrange a later time to phone or get together. Remember that even if this person is a right nuisance at the time, in the scheme of things friends matter.
- Don't be afraid to take small risks and let people into your confidence – that makes them feel they can open out to you too.
- Anyone can feel a little on edge when meeting new people, but do your best to keep your body language open. Smile, open your hands, make eye contact.
- Take a genuine interest and be a good listener.
- Bear in mind that making friends takes time. Some people take longer to warm up than others and will want to be sure of you before responding. This is no reflection on you.
- Do remember that having several – or even many – friendships can give you more to bring to each friendship, as in 'So-and-so suggested…' 'I want to…, you might like it too.' 'Let me introduce you to so-and-so – you'll get on great!'
- Jealousy does exist in friendships – you don't have to be a little girl or boy to feel it. If you have several good friends you will be less likely

to get jealous, however, because it spreads the load. Generally, people love you more for introducing them to other people – you cannot lose a good friend as you can a lover!

There are ways in which you may find yourself reacting that aren't going to help you make the friends you need or keep a good rapport with the ones you have. If you feel lonely, it may be harder to be relaxed about making friends – try to give it time.

Things to Avoid

* Don't take things seriously or personally – people are people, they aren't all the same, and they aren't all like you.
* Don't flog a dead horse – if you felt someone was your sort but they haven't responded after two or three overtures from you, forget it and look elsewhere. If this happens, don't try to analyse where you went wrong. Probably this has nothing to do with you. They may just be too busy, too preoccupied or too hard up.
* Don't make heavy weather out of social occasions – they are supposed to be fun! So when entertaining, choose an easy menu that will leave you time to be with your guests – they have come to see you, not assess your cuisine.
* Don't force yourself to be with people you dislike just to expand your social circle – it won't work.
* Don't judge people – they may not have your standards. If they forget appointments and leave you to do the arranging, does this matter if you enjoy each other's company?
* Distinguish between carelessness and callousness – if you feel bad around someone, don't bother again.
* Don't be a doormat. Helping people and supporting them does not mean you have to sacrifice yourself. Be a friend to yourself too!
* Don't do all the giving. If you are feeling resentful, it's time to ask yourself some hard questions.
* Don't ignore your intuition. If you feel at all uneasy, back off and don't take this person into your confidence until you have worked out why you feel that way.

- Don't expect friends to be always there with open arms and a box of tissues – that's a mum! If you never got that from your mum it is natural to yearn for it, so realise that's what's happening and don't let it ruin good friendships. Yes, some friends are like that a lot of the time – and that's great. But if you have a continual need for that sort of treatment and that sort of friend you may need some therapy to sort out what you did not receive in your earlier life.
- Don't expect one friend to be perfect or to give you everything. And think carefully before letting one friend tie up all your time. Best friends are great, but where the intimacy is too intense you risk the same kind of issues that you have with a partner, without similar commitment. This could be a recipe for emotional upsets.
- Your friend's partner is out when it comes to anything apart from the most superficial, innocent flirting – unless it is Grande Passion. Then, of course, you will in all probability lose your friend (see page 135).

difficult issues

Ideally a friendship is about shared laughter, enjoyment, company, understanding, support and help where needed. Although each party may bring very different things to the friendship, generally there is a feeling of equality, in value placed upon each other, in effort put into the friendship and benefit received. However, as we know, things don't always work out like that, and some far less desirable emotions can enter the picture.

Envy can become an issue – yours or your friend's. If your friendship is close enough, you may find it helps to tell your friend you are envious – and you may learn, to your surprise, that they are also envious of you! Being envious is a perfectly natural human emotion and not one to feel ashamed of. What you *do* with your envy is the important thing. Are you going to let it colour your outlook, affect your actions, make you nasty? Or are you going to say to yourself, 'There is a part of me that is envious, but there is also a big part that is not. I choose to deal with this.' Being envious of a friend can cause you to improve yourself, using him/her as an inspiration.

Envy may be defined as involving only two people – you envy your friend their possessions, their looks or their money. Jealousy is when a third party enters the picture, and this can be a bit tricky. If you really fancy your friend's partner, what do you do about it? Who means more to you? If you know the true meaning of friendship, the chances are you will choose not to betray your friend. The exception to this is what the French call 'Grande Passion' – if your friend's partner is the love of your life then it is understandable if you are not able to walk away. Being swept up by powerful emotion is different from just wanting what someone else has.

> **Top Tip**
> *We all have negative emotions. The important thing is not to feel ashamed of these or deny them, but to realise that they are only part of the picture and that we do not have to be controlled by them.*

Dependency may be an issue in close friendships. Of course we are all dependent on our friends for their company, etc. Also most of us go through times in our lives when we need to be rescued. However, where one party is very dependent on the other and this goes on beyond a few months then something less healthy is entering the scene. Very needy people may manipulate others through guilt or pity. The hard thing is that this can happen within a friendship that also has good elements.

The other side of the coin is that some people feel their function as a friend is to be a rescuer. This may be because they have such low self-esteem that they assume no-one would want to be their friend unless they have something extra to offer. It may also be because they feel guilty about the good things in life that they have, or because rescuing makes them feel powerful and in control. If you are part of such a dynamic, your first task is to decide exactly what it is within you that is keeping you involved in this way. Then try to create a little distance. Do not always be available. Arrange fun things that you can both do, rather than getting drawn into heavy scenarios. Insist on drawing the friendship back onto even and enjoyable ground.

Usually it is the 'saviour' half of the duo that finds the situation onerous. The 'saved' one may just feel cherished (or, in a worst case scenario, may be quite aware that they are using their helpful friend). But it is possible that they feel kept in a dependent position by a mate who insists on always sorting everything out! If you are the dependent one and can recognise this, then you are one step towards sorting the situation out. Friendship is, in fact, an unspoken contract. There is such a thing as fairness, and while no-one is keeping a balance sheet it is reasonable that both people should feel they are getting out about the same as they are putting in. It isn't selfish, calculating or in any way unreasonable to take that attitude.

Sometimes issues arise in friendships that are more unpleasant. These may be similar to the matters covered in the section on abusive relationships. If your 'friend' regularly tries to control you, manipulate you, put you down, make you feel bad about yourself or in any other way leave you feeling unhappy, then he or she is not a friend. However envious, competitive, bossy or unreliable – or in any other way less than perfect – your friend may be, basically, if they are a true friend, they want to see you thrive. While a true friend may be careless, ill-mannered and unreliable, they do not have a hidden agenda of use and control, and deep inside they value you. Your intuition will tell you this.

using astrology

Even if you do not really believe in astrology, the chances are that you know your sun sign. An interesting exercise is to find out the sun signs of your friends and see if there is a pattern. This often emerges in respect of the Elements – for each of the signs of the Zodiac belongs to one of the four Elements, as follows:

FIRE: Aries, Leo, Sagittarius
EARTH: Taurus, Virgo, Capricorn
AIR: Gemini, Libra, Aquarius
WATER: Cancer, Scorpio, Pisces

Which Element are you? Are your friends predominantly of the same Element or pair of Elements? Then ask yourself what you most prize from friendships. Is it:

- **A** Entertainment, fun, stimulation, admiration and maybe a little competition?
- **B** Practical help, sound advice, someone who you know is always there, people you have known for a long time, people you do things with?
- **C** Lots of discussion, going to cultural events together, entertaining, social intercourse, gossip?
- **D** Support, understanding, closeness, empathy, loyalty, love?

Group A qualities relate to the Fire signs, group B to the Earth signs, group C to the Air signs and group D to the Water signs. Of course, we are all complex creatures and for astrology to work properly the entire chart for the moment of birth needs to be considered in detail. However, this little rule of thumb applies very often.

If there are things you are looking for that you are not quite finding with your circle of friends, consider whether this is down to Elemental considerations and whether you could develop friendships with folk of the Element that carries the attribute you want – for instance if you want extra sympathy, seek out a Water person. Needless to say, you should not make radical changes and commitments merely on the strength of someone's birthday, but it is worth bearing the Element in mind.

Sometimes as things change in life we find we are attracting friends of a different Element, and that can be an interesting reflection on the changes that are occurring within us.

visualisation and meditation for friendship

A Visualisation to Meet New People

For this visualisation it is a good idea to first create the rose quartz Friendship Charm (page 139). Then begin your visualisation as usual.

Wait in the auditorium of your theatre and watch as the curtains smoothly part, showing you a lakeside scene. Go up the steps and onto the stage, finding yourself now surrounded by the new scene on every side. You have entered the peace of Otherworld. *[Pause.]*

Walk quietly by the side of the lake, looking at all the plants and the emerald green of the clear water. This is a wonderful place, so peaceful and possessing a deep beauty. As you walk, you glimpse beings that occupy the place – ethereal, exquisite creatures, playing, carrying gifts and garlands, tending the trees and the waterside. Your walk is shaded and secluded and there is a pleasant, fresh mossy scent in the air. *[Pause.]*

Ahead of you, you see a faint pink glow among the greenery. You go ahead to investigate this. As you come close there is a sound of sweet music playing very softly. Closer and closer you come, until you see that the glow is emanating from a smooth throne made of polished rose quartz, gently radiating light and love. *[Pause]*

Slowly you approach and sit yourself comfortably on the smooth stone chair. It fits you so well – you never would have thought that stone could be so comfortable! It feels as if it was made for you. It feels cool, but not cold, and there is a feeling of such ease and peace as you sit in it that you feel as if you will never want to leave. *[Pause.]*

All around you there is a landscape of tranquillity and beauty. You look about you feeling utterly at peace. As you sit in the chair you become aware that trails are radiating out from it, like the spokes of a wheel. Gradually they become more and more obvious until they are shimmering pathways of soft pink, extending out into the countryside that surrounds you. Right into the distance the pathways stretch and you look out along them, feeling a sense of being at the heart of something important. *[Pause.]*

Now you see figures coming towards you along these pathways. As they approach, you see they are pleasant, likeable people with smiles on their faces. Wait for these people to come up to you. Speak with them, take the time to get to know them. Maybe there is one that seems special, maybe several. Make conversation for as long as you like – these people have come to see you. *[Pause.]*

When you are ready, take your leave of your new friends. Promise

making friends, staying friends • 139

that you will meet again and thank them for coming. Make your way back alongside the lake to the place where you entered the scene. As you get to the correct spot you notice that you are once more on the stage. Walk down from the stage, out into the auditorium and sit down to watch the curtains close on your friendly world.

Make a note of the experiences and conversations that you have had.

charms for friendship

Friendship Charm

Acquire a piece of rose quartz; some jasmine, rose or sweet pea oil; a soft pink cloth; and a pink candle. Although we used rose quartz earlier in a Love Charm, this gentle stone also serves for friendship if that is what you wish. If you are using rose quartz for a Love Charm and a Friendship Charm, you will need two separate stones, in different shapes, to signify the two purposes.

Cleanse your stone in a running stream and leave it out in the light of the full moon. As you look at it, allow feelings of warmth and welcome to arise in you and imagine you see the stone glow softly in response. Anoint the stone with a little of the oil of jasmine, rose or sweet pea and wrap it in the soft pink cloth. Whenever you are going out where you may meet people, light a pink candle and place your piece of rose quartz before it, on its opened cloth, affirming that friendship is coming your way. You may take your rose quartz charm with you if you wish, in your handbag or pocket.

Charm for Growing Friendships

This spell is useful to create new friendships and to strengthen existing ones. Flowers are often given by friends, and this spell makes use of a flower's gentle energy. Hyacinth is a good choice because of its fragrance and the colour varieties available, but you could also use a chrysanthemum, miniature rose or cyclamen – in fact anything that takes your fancy. A pink flower signifies warmth and sympathy; white, purity and clarity;

blue, peace; orange fun and shared creative pastimes; purple religion and spirituality; and yellow, mental stimulation. Red is a bit too 'hot' for friendship, strictly speaking, unless perhaps you share sporting interests.

Choose a large bowl to pot your flowers and obtain some good quality, soft compost – organic products are best for charms. Place the compost in the bowl and add some little tokens to the soil if you wish. For instance, if you long for a friend who shares your love of theatre, a piece cut from a theatre programme could go in the soil. Visualise what you would like from the friendship as you play with the soil.

Lovingly place the bulbs in the soil or re-pot your plant. Be very careful not to disturb the soil around the roots. You may also place crystals or semi-precious stones in the soil to intensify the message from the flowers – choose them to co-ordinate with the colour of the flowers. Place your plant on the windowsill and water it carefully, but don't overwater it. Imagine that the message of the plant is being amplified by the crystals, sending out an irresistible invitation to anyone suitable. Every so often, when you make yourself a cuppa or pour yourself something stronger, make one also for your friend-to-be and place this near the plant. Later pour the drink away onto the ground outside.

Needless to say, you will know what to get that new friend as a present when they come into your life – a pot-plant!

Tribe Charm

We may imagine that in times gone by the women of the tribe stuck together. Understanding what each was going through, the others would have been there with a helping hand with children, food preparation, home-building, and so on. These days, people – especially women – are very isolated. This is particularly difficult for women with small children who are, arguably, put in quite an unnatural position bringing up their children between four walls, largely alone.

It isn't possible to change the structure of society overnight and in any case most of us have some vested interests in leaving things the way they are. However, actually having a project with friends may lead to a greater sense of bonding than just having coffee at each other's houses.

making friends, staying friends * 141

A good charm for this bonding is to do something practical together like making a patchwork quilt. By doing this, time is created for chats, for interacting with each other's children and for being productive. At an instinctual level a sense of bonding takes place. When the quilt is complete, it can be given to charity and another one begun. Another possibility would be to share an allotment or have tree-planting sessions. Making meals works similarly, and taking it in turns to make a meal at each other's houses might be an idea. The point is that by doing something 'earthy' together the tribal instincts come to the fore.

These ideas only have relevance if you are at home for the greater part of the week. They will not appeal to everyone, and that is fine. But if you wish to create a community of women you might like to consider them – or evolve ones of your own. Men often bond by playing sport or doing similar activities and while they tend, very generally, not to evolve emotional bonds at the depth women do, the tradition of huntin' and fishin' together remains less broken.

self-hypnosis for friendship

Self-Hypnosis for Relaxing with New Friends

[Usual induction.]

As you are lying there so wonderfully relaxed, you know that you are open and receptive towards friendships. There are no barriers between you and pleasant relationships with suitable others. You are attracting friendships simply by being. You are open, positive and pleasant to others and you know that you are attracting the right sort of person into your life. With every day that passes, you feel more and more able to get close to the right people to be friends with you. With each day that passes, you are more at ease in company. With every day that passes, you feel a greater sense of warmth between yourself and others.

Feel how relaxed your body is, how pleasantly warm it feels. When you are with other people, your body language is open and welcoming. You feel relaxed and content in the company of others. You feel at ease when talking to others; you project an interest in them. You are able to forget your own concerns and be deeply interested in the other person. You are open to appreciating the good in other people. You enjoy the company of others and it is a good feeling to be able to forget your own concerns for a while and give attention to other people. This is nourishing, diverting and supportive for you. You enjoy it, you remain relaxed and your body language is open. It is a good feeling, a warm feeling.

The people you meet are interesting. Of course, some people are more interesting to you than others – that is only natural. But there is something to interest you in every person you meet. You see the good in people, you are receptive to the things that you have in common with others and you are positive and appreciative of other people. Of course, at times you may meet people about whom you do not feel so good and at these times it is wise to take note of your instincts. But the great majority of people are essentially good; they have something good to give you, however small that may be, and you focus on all the positive things in the people you meet.

You are relaxed and smiling, you feel contented and happy and you radiate this. Feel how relaxed and contented you are, how open and pleasant. You radiate warmth and welcome. You radiate pleasure in company with others. People are drawn to your warmth – it is only natural that people should be drawn to you, for you are pleasant to be with. It is simple to be pleasant – it is so very, very simple. All that you need to have is a genuine interest in the other person, and you *are* interested in people. You are truly interested in people. You find something interesting in so very many people. You respond to them and you make an effort to understand them.

When you go into company, you are surrounded by a wonderful glow of warmth, pleasantness and magnetism. As you lie there, so beautifully relaxed, feel yourself surrounded by this glow. Feel the warmth within and around your body. Feel yourself radiating welcome and approachability. You are radiant, attractive, open. You have a glow of welcome, acceptance, a positive attitude. You project an aura of gentle magnetism, serenity and welcome. Feel this subtle glow around you. How good it feels to know you are likeable and that there is so much pleasure to be had in the company of others.

making friends, staying friends * 143

You have a balanced attitude to others. You like their company, you enjoy it, you welcome it. But you are also happy to be alone at times. You know that this does not have to last if you do not want it to. You are relaxed about being alone, relaxed about the needs that other people have to be in their own space, too. You know that when the time is right you will have all the company you wish for. You know that this will be good company, the company of like-minded people, the company of pleasant people, because you are a pleasant, relaxed person and you are drawing to you people of the same type as yourself. You are a magnet for the right sort of friend; you have so much to offer and so much to enjoy.

Feel yourself once more surrounded by a welcoming glow, feeling so relaxed, so at ease. When you are with other people you are relaxed and open, you are calm and quietly confident. Feel yourself glowing with confidence and welcome. Feel that gentle radiance around you, feel your body glowing with it, feel that magnetism emanating from you.

Now imagine yourself in a social situation. Imagine going into the room, imagine what it looks like, imagine the people you meet and how they speak and act. Feel that radiance around you, that calm, relaxed, confident glow. You have nothing to prove. All you are here for is to enjoy pleasant interaction. Imagine meeting people, people you like, taking an interest in them. Imagine them reacting pleasantly to you. The conversation is flowing, your body language is open, you are smiling, responding in a calm and relaxed way. You are attracting people and enjoying the feeling.

Continue imagining this social scene until it has concluded to your satisfaction. Then you may come back to everyday awareness, bringing with you relaxation, confidence and a certainty that you are soon going to meet the kind of people with whom you can be good friends.

[Waking-up procedure.]

SIX

Family Fortunes

'All happy families resemble one another,
each unhappy family is unhappy in its own way.'
Leo Tolstoy, Anna Karenina

happy families

A happy family, with loving parents and two healthy, smiling children, is our cultural ideal. The fact that there are not as many 'happy families' around as there might be perhaps hints at the fact that human beings do not as easily gel into such units as we might like to think. The modern family is very insular – often there are few uncles, aunties, grannies and cousins within striking distance. This is a fairly recent shift. A hundred or so years ago people often lived and died within walking distance of where they were born, surrounded by an extended family network. Centuries before, humans lived in tribes – as is still the case in some remote areas of the world. Tribal living means that the childcare is more a communal concern. The current idea of the sheltered family unit is only one way for human beings to arrange themselves, and it may not necessarily be the best way. Nonetheless, there are many blessings to family life and it is up to us to make the best of it.

Family life has many stresses. Parenthood is particularly taxing – everything is laid at the door of a parent, especially the mother. Little credit is given when things are good and heaps of blame are given when things are bad. The modern trend towards psychotherapy and self-knowledge usually leads back to the mother as being the source of all one's problems! But how can we really have any idea whether our family is 'happy'? Certainly the individuals in our family are not always happy! We have no idea what goes on behind the closed doors of our neighbours, so we have no yardstick to measure how happy we really are.

Start by seeing how many of the following statements you agree with to get an initial idea about how happy a family yours is. If you live with flatmates or in some other family type situation, adapt the questions as necessary (alternative suggestions are given for some questions).

> **Top Tip**
> *A happy family is not one with 'never a cross word'; it is one in which the cross words are listened to and followed by laughter.*

1. There is a lot of laughter in the house.
2. Family members feel free to express negative feelings such as anger without things getting out of hand.
3. Everyone has their own space, physically and emotionally.
4. The parents have fun on their own, regularly, without the children. (If you live with housemates, consider whether each person is free to enjoy themselves on their own with their own friends.)
5. There are certain activities the family enjoy doing together.
6. In general, family members are honest with each other.
7. No-one has to pretend to be/feel something that is not genuine in order to be accepted.
8. Love (or acceptance, if in a shared house) is not conditional upon any type of behaviour, achievement or religious belief.
9. Efforts are made for you all to eat together several times a week.
10. You have 'occasions' and celebrations together.
11. Important issues are talked through, with younger family members also being heard.
12. Everyone has jobs to do or a part to play in family life, according to age and ability. (Or in a shared house, everyone pulls their weight.)
13. There is a comfortable interaction with the wider community.
14. Family members respect one another.
15. Everyone's achievements are appreciated and displayed.
16. Family members support one another if there is any trouble from outside.
17. Despite understandable rivalries, family members are proud of each other's achievements.
18. Family members consider each other's comfort and happiness at most times.

If you agreed with 15 or more statements, your family is probably a happy one. Ten to 14 agreements means that there is something to work towards. Fewer than ten agreements implies that it would be best to get the family together to discuss how you can improve things, right away!

What a Happy Family Is Not

A happy family is not one where there is never a cross word, where everyone is always smiling and agreeable, where everyone is very polite at all times, where everyone is successful, enjoying optimum health, having every material possession they want – or where there are necessarily two parents! A 'perfect' surface may often hide some of the most disturbing and unhappy matters. Where parental expectations are high and very specific or where a child feels the parent has a great need for certain behaviour, then the identity of the child may be compromised. A child may realise at a very deep and instinctual level that in fact they have to live up to an ideal, not only to be accepted, but also to prevent their mother or father from falling apart. Such a child cannot possess their own identity – they exist for someone else, and while on the surface all may seem very rosy, there may be emptiness and fear within. A happy family can only be composed of reasonably contented individuals who are accepted – and accept themselves – for what they are.

Happy Families Start with Happy Parents

The children will usually be happy if their parents are happy. There is possibly some truth behind the idea that big families tend to be happier, but only because if there is significant pathology in the parents, there is at least 'safety in numbers' for the children, who will usually support each other, and, as they get older, have some effect on the way the parents behave through ganging up on them! Let's hope that isn't the case in your family! Here are some suggestions for parents for a happier family life.

* Make sure you have goals in life that are unconnected with your children.
* Have fun without your children – this may be especially hard if you are a single parent, but it is even more essential. It is burdensome for children to be responsible for a parent's enjoyment of life, despite complaints when you go out! So don't feel guilty about having a good time – it's essential for their health as well as yours.
* Never, ever live through your children. Wish you'd travelled the world,

got a degree or learnt to play guitar? Well, there's still time to do it, but not if you waste energy trying to get Junior to do it instead!

* Try to delight in your children simply as they are, for that is how they teach us, their parents, things we never knew about the world and about values.
* Be as self-aware as possible, for that way you are less likely to fall into unconscious, manipulative patterns.
* Accept your own failings – there's nothing more daunting than a paragon of virtue!
* Remember this wonderful phrase (coined by the pioneering psychotherapist D. W. Winnicott, see Further Reading) – 'The Good Enough Mother'. You don't have to be perfect – just good enough. You should be good enough to give a general feeling of security, nurture and encouragement, but allowed to be sometimes bad-tempered, impatient, busy, absent or critical. You are not like this all the time, and the times when you are not outweigh the times when you fall down a bit on the job. Who could blame you?
* Avoid the trap of trying so hard to avoid your parents' failings that you go completely to the other extreme.
* Remember that a happy family can contain an individual who is, at least temporarily, very unhappy! You cannot be responsible for cheering everyone up, all the time.
* Remember that wanting a happy family can in itself be a form of coercion if it gets out of hand. It is not the veneer that matters, and the discontent of family members has to be accepted as part of the picture you are working with.

> **Top Tip**
> *Remember that you do not have to be perfect – being a 'good enough' mum, dad, or housemate is fine!*

Some Practical Pointers

A home, as well as being a place to feel safe and comfortable, is also an institution. Time-planning and the practical matters that keep it running need to be dealt with. Here are a few practical pointers to bear in mind.

- Have a list of daily jobs and weekly jobs.
- Keep a running list of shopping pinned to the fridge. Everyone in the family who can write has the responsibility to note any stocks that are running short, before they run out.
- Enlist the help of the children in a way suitable to their age – they usually enjoy this! You could have a reward system, or extra pocket money if you like (but no-one pays Mum for doing the shopping and cooking, do they?).
- Give children clear boundaries and stick to them, unless there is a clear reason for changing them on a particular occasion.
- As your children get older, be prepared to talk through rules with them. Children are often very logical – don't be afraid to re-think if you really do not have a good answer to their questions or challenges!
- Schedule time to spend with your child and always stick to this, unless you have a very good reason not to. Then you need to explain and make it up to the child at another time.
- Praise children's good behaviour as often as you possibly can.
- Display achievements on a family notice-board, shelf, etc.
- Decide the level of tidiness and organisation you feel is necessary and stick to it – it is less stressful and time-consuming that way.

Helen's Story

Helen was brought up with three brothers by old-fashioned parents who believed that woman's place was in the home. While her brothers were encouraged to do well at school, Helen often had no time to do her homework after she had done the ironing and helped her mother get the tea. The older she became, the more resentful Helen felt. Having been made to leave school early to get a menial job to help support her brothers through university, Helen ran away from home and went to live with her aunt. She was then able to go to university herself and forge ahead with a career. In her mid-thirties Helen had a daughter and because of her successful track record she was able to spend a significant amount of time with her child, leaving her business largely in the hands of people she had trained. Helen made sure that her daughter had everything she could want, that she never had to cook or go anywhere near the laundry – she even bought her Lego and a train set, feeling determined that her daughter should not be set in any predetermined role. She was amazed and deeply upset when her daughter, at the age of 16, had a blazing row with her because she was not letting her 'be a woman'. Helen came to realise that just as her mother had stifled her potential, she was doing the same, albeit in a totally different way, with her daughter! Determined that she would *really* avoid her parents' pitfalls, Helen made changes with her daughter and began to validate her femininity as she seemed to want. Now they are the best of friends!

the pain of infertility

More and more people are choosing not to have children, or at least to have children later. Leaving children until later in life increases the risk of not being able to have them. Infertility, due to pollution and lifestyle, is itself on the increase. Like many things in life, one doesn't always appreciate children until one cannot have them. For a woman who cannot have children, life may seem tragic. Here are some points for consideration.

- If you are sure you want children, do not leave it too late. While things are more difficult with children around, they are not impossible. Many women have successful careers, a lively social life and the experience of travel – all with children.
- If you put off having children because you feel other things are more important, please give this serious thought. Do not assume that at 37 or 38 your biological clock will cry 'Cuckoo!' and lay an egg just on time for you! However regular your periods, however healthy you are, you can have no idea about your fertility. This starts to decline during the late twenties anyway, and if you were sub-fertile beforehand, by the time you reach your mid-thirties you may have serious problems. Then there is the possibility of early menopause, which some women start to experience before the age of 40. There are very few things for which it is 'too late' at any time in life, but for women there certainly does come a time when it is too late to have your own child.

- If you are very sure you do not want children, try to find out why this is. If the answer is satisfactory – i.e. based on the fact you want to devote more time to your creativity or just don't like the idea (as opposed to being afraid, carrying issues over from your own childhood, etc) – then do not let anyone make you feel guilty or inadequate. You have made a choice that is right and valid for you and is enabling you to explore parts of yourself and contribute different things to society.
- If you want children, look after your health, especially when trying to become pregnant. Stop smoking, cut back on alcohol to just the occasional glass, check your intake of minerals and vitamins, especially folic acid (but be careful about taking supplements, especially of the fat-soluble vitamins and always check with your doctor), and try to get as much relaxation and contact with nature as you can.
- If you are not pregnant within a year, get medical advice. Insist on tests, especially if you are over 30.
- If there are problems, ask yourself how much you want a baby. If it is very, very much, then leave no stone unturned in the way of medical techniques (and there are many, improving all the time) to get what you want.
- This is a life-fundamental, urgent biological call for which response time is not unlimited. Give it your best shot. It is said, 'Better to regret what you have done than what you have not done' – in the case of baby-making, very few people have ever regretted what they have done, but many what they have not.

Coping with Infertility

If you cannot, despite all efforts, have your own baby, you will probably feel quite dreadful – for a while. You may feel worthless, life may not seem worth living, everything may seem empty and you may feel that you are shut out of normal life. Everything that is warm and cosy, sweet and lovely seems to be on the other side of a thick pane of glass against which you have your nose eternally pressed, never to break through. You may look at young mums with their push-chairs and feel as if your heart will break and your chest explode. This is a true mourning period, for essentially what you have suffered – and are suffering – is a bereavement. This bereavement is all the harder to bear because it is not widely acknowledged. There is no funeral, nothing to mark your loss, and many people may not understand, including your partner.

At this time, look after yourself as if you were really ill – treat yourself gently. Do anything, see anyone that makes you feel better, even for a little while, as long as you don't damage your health. Try to believe that although you cannot now imagine it, life will get better and you will get over this. There will be other things to live for – promise! Naturally you will consider other options, such as adoption and fostering, and to many people it can be the answer to give a loving home to a child who has no other haven. Older children and children from overseas may be easier to adopt. You do not need to rush into such a decision.

Find something else in life to be passionate about, to be devoted to. Become a little self-analytical. What, for you, is the worst thing about not having a child? Is there more here than a biological call? Many people yearn for children so they can in some way put right their own childhood, give someone else what they did not have – essentially re-parent themselves. If this is the case, is there some other way that you can achieve this?

Many couples go through a very challenging time when they discover they are infertile. Men and women cope with emotional issues differently on the whole, and few circumstances are more guaranteed to highlight these differences than childlessness. In the majority of cases, the man is considerably less affected than the woman and he may struggle to understand her extremes of emotion, although he may well feel inadequate in some way because of the infertility. (This will be especially the case, of course, if he is infertile.) He may also feel that his partner can't love him that much if she so desperately needs a baby as well. Counselling, talking to friends who have had similar experiences and giving each other plenty of time to talk and explore feelings can keep the closeness between a couple intact.

As the dust settles a little, it will be possible to have formal contact with other childless couples through agencies and support groups. Explore how other people have coped. What does life hold for them? It might help to spend time with other similar couples. At first it may feel uninviting to associate with the childless – after all, you do not want to think of yourself that way and it only rubs it in. But childlessness is not the same for everyone; it does not make people the same. It may, in effect, be 'childfree-ness' and offer a life with many other options.

Nothing anyone can say will convince you of the advantages of not having children until you eventually find them out for yourself through a positive approach to life. Try to remember that the happiness children bring is precarious. Rather than relieving heartache, they bring a life that is endlessly full of it, with anxiety and identification with all their sufferings. Babies grow all too quickly into human beings who may be very incompatible with their parents and who offer them no companionship, even in adulthood. A life devoted to a family may be a life that is, in the end, rather lonely, if friends and career have been neglected in favour of children who emigrate in their twenties. All this is the other side of the coin. It is possible for a life without children to be full, creative, peaceful and contented.

step-families

In fairy-tales it is often the wicked step-mother who is the villain of the piece. Stories and myths often contain truths about life, and they help us to process what actually goes on. There is no subtle allegory involved when the Babes in the Wood are sent out to die in the grim forest by their father's new wife – the destructive potential in such relationships is graphically portrayed.

There have always been step-families. Decades ago, when life expectancy was less than it is now, people often died before mid-life. Women particularly were more likely to die in childbirth, leaving the children they already had motherless – and ready for the tender care of a step-mother. These days it is much more frequently divorce that leads to step-parenting, with the added complication and stress of access, maintenance, and so on.

There is a reality to the myth of the wicked step-parent figure. Children are challenging enough when they are one's own flesh and blood. When they are someone else's, the challenges are much greater. Step-children may represent much that you dislike, fear, envy or resent about your partner's ex – and they may play up to this, in full knowledge of the power they have to upset. In addition, it is far easier to feel jealous of the attention your partner gives to a child when it is not your own. Step-brothers and -sisters in particular may deeply resent each other, somehow linking the new sibling/s with the heartache of the split of the original family unit and seeing them as usurpers.

In these situations, it is important not to pretend to feel what you don't feel, either to yourself or to others. What you feel is understandable and may even be connected with survival at a biological level. A child that is not your own even smells different and feels different in many ways! So give yourself permission to feel quite evil at times! However, the rational, adult part of you can deal with this more primitive part and choose not to display it. Don't let fear of appearing the wicked step-parent prevent you from addressing issues of unfairness in a rational manner. Try to have special times with your partner totally without your step-children. Make sure you have a full enough life to be able to cope with jealousy. Best of all, try to find common ground with step-children, not necessarily as a parent figure but as a person.

Of course, there are plenty of step-families that work really well. While it may be hard to love someone else's children, it may also be very easy, and step-parents are often very enriching to the lives of their partners' kids. Step-siblings can make life more fun – the picture does not have to be negative, or remain negative. Try the Step-Families Charm on page 161 to ease the situation, if necessary.

visualisation and meditation for happy families

Co-operative Family Visualisation

Find yourself in your familiar auditorium. Walk towards the stage. The curtains swing open onto a woodland scene. Walk up and enter this.

Now you are walking along a forest path. All around you it is green and peaceful. Notice all the trees, the grass, the stones, the patchwork of sky between the leaves. Breathe in all the scents of the woodland. Birdsong is echoing all around and the dappled sunlight falls upon your path.

Ahead of you there is a sapling lying beside the path, its roots exposed. It looks strong and healthy. Its leaves are bright green. You are aware that it needs to be put back into the earth. You take it up and find a spade lying beside it. You take this up, also. Carrying both of these, you continue walking through the woodland.

Now the trees are thinning and you are coming out onto a plain. Ahead of you there is a stone circle. You walk towards the circle of stones, still carefully carrying the tree and the spade.

You are getting closer to the stones. How solid, weathered and majestic they are! There they have stood for century upon century. You feel warmth and welcome emanating from them. They represent all that is worthwhile and enduring.

Passing between two of the stones, you walk towards the centre of the circle. There you see that a circular patch of fresh earth has been dug – this is just right for your tree. You approach this patch of earth, put down the sapling and start to dig.

Now you realise that all the members of your family are approaching, coming through the gaps in the stones, each one bringing their own shovel and bag of compost. You take it in turns to make the hole bigger until it is the right size.

It is time to plant the tree. You place it lovingly in the earth and you and your family members take it in turns to add compost and fill in the earth around the tree. You pat the earth flat.

Standing around the tree, you all hold hands for a moment. How beautiful and strong the tree looks, its branches reaching up towards the sky! You thank everybody for their part in planting the tree. Does anybody have anything to say? Listen carefully. Do you have anything to say? It is your turn to be heard. After a while your family members turn around and walk away, back outside the circle of stones.

It is time for you also to leave. You touch the bark of the sapling in farewell. Turning, you go back the way you came. As you enter the woodland, a gentle rain begins to fall. You turn back to see the circle of stones and your tree, just visible between two of the stones, its grateful branches glistening with the welcome rainfall.

Under cover of the trees you make your way back to where your journey began. You find yourself on the stage and you step down into the auditorium with a feeling of satisfaction and peace.

Come back to everyday awareness when you are ready.

charms for family fortunes

Charm for a Happy Family

Every time you and your family share a meal or celebration, you are in fact creating a charm for co-operation and harmony.

It is said that 'the family that prays together stays together'. Of course, unfortunately that does not mean that all families who stay together because of their religion (or any other reason) are happy, because fear and guilt can also make people stick together. However, there is much to be said for some shared spirituality, because it does create a link on another, powerful level.

You certainly do not have to subscribe to conventional forms of religion in order to have a spiritual approach. More and more people are discovering the value of ancient spiritual practices that honour the cycles of Nature, seeing our poor, mistreated natural world as essentially holy and a showing forth of Deity.

So a very simple charm or prayer could be merely to say at the start of a meal 'Thank you for giving your lives to feed ours.' This applies to a cabbage as well as a cow! Lighting a candle in the middle of the table is also a powerful little ritual. You might say, 'I light this candle in honour of....' on important occasions. Family members can be invited to raise toasts – the little ones can often be very inventive when they are the centre of everyone's attention! Try to make mealtimes pleasant, considerate and an opportunity for people to air their views, give their news and have a giggle. Resist the temptation (to which I all too often succumb) to take advantage of the fact everyone's together to give them a lecture about putting their washing in the linen bin!

If you have teenagers who scoff at anything spiritual, you might be best to keep your charms to yourself until the years have given them at least a portion of the sense they think they have! Why not turn your cooking into a charm by simply stirring a saucepan of food sun-wise (clockwise in the Northern hemisphere, anti-clockwise in the Southern hemisphere) and visualising the results you want for your family being stirred into the pot? If you need more harmony, drop in some Venus-ruled thyme (all herbs are ruled by a planet and connect to the themes that the planet represents) and, as you watch the tiny leaves go round, affirm that you are stirring in love and co-operation. If you need more communication, stir in Mercury-ruled mint or dill. If some success, inspiration or joy is called for, add some sun-ruled rosemary; for healing, empathy and a sense of family, add moon-ruled lemon balm; and if you all need energy, add some Martian ginger – but watch out for arguments!

You could continue working your charm into the table decorations – for Venus, using soft pink or blue; for Mercury, yellow; for the sun, gold or orange; for the moon, white or silver; and for Mars red. Use these colours in candles, napkins and flowers. If you do not choose to tell them, no-one will know they are being served up a little magic with their meal!

Observing the Seasons

We are all aware of the magic of Christmas and how this binds families – albeit sometimes reluctantly! There are many charms associated with Christmas (or Yule, as it used to be known). For instance, kissing under the mistletoe is an old charm for fertility – of mind as well as body – and putting coins in the plum pudding is another.

There are eight traditional festivals which were celebrated by the people of old and which are being rediscovered by more and more people today. Of these eight festivals, Yule, or the Winter Solstice, is but one and together they act as staging posts in the sacred round of the seasons that frame all our lives. This is why reconnecting with them can be a grounding and also a magical experience. The birthday of Christ was moved to

Yule so that it would coincide with far more ancient celebrations in honour of the rebirth of the Sun God. We know of many ways to celebrate Yule – why not unite the family in observing the other festivals also? Space does not permit detailed descriptions of the festivals – for more information see Further Reading. However, the following are some simple descriptions. Why not use them as the basis of a themed family meal, with seasonal greenery or flowers, candles of the appropriate colour, a specially iced cake, decorated napkins or anything you fancy?

Imbolc – at the Start of February 'Imbolc' means 'in the belly', for now in the earth's belly life stirs. It is the feast of whiteness, brightness, creativity, cleansing and new starts, and its colour is white. It is the time when the lambs are first born. Ideas could be to have snowdrops as a centre-piece; serve white food such as milk, cheese or white grapes; feature family creativity in poems; and make new starts.

Spring Equinox – around March 20 This is a feast of vegetation fertility, and joy at the increasing light and strength of the sun. Days are now longer than nights. The festival's colours are spring green and gold. Ideas could be to display daffodils, and serve marzipaned cake and eggs. (Easter is always on the first Sunday after the first full moon after the Spring Equinox.) Now is the time to talk about summer plans – what are you 'hatching'?

Beltane – at the End of April and Beginning of May This is the feast of animal fertility. This is traditionally a very sexy festival, with Greenwood marriages and bringing home the May, which was sacred to the Goddess. Its colour is deep rose. Days are warmer, and evenings have a heady, sensual quality. Ideas include displaying scented flowers and serving chocolate, wine and everyone's favourite food. Talk about what you most enjoy. Get the kids to bed early and have the evening to yourselves.

Summer Solstice – around June 21 This is the feast of light at its greatest. Now the earth is luxuriant, and flowers are everywhere. Colours are deep reds and bright blues. Now is the time to eat outdoors, have a barbecue and play games. Stay up late to savour the endless day, sleep in a tent in the garden or have a midnight swim.

Lammas – End of July This is the first harvest festival – the feast of the bounty of the land. The air is heavy and the fields are golden. Its colour is honey-gold. Bread should be featured as a table-centre, e.g. poppy-seed plait, together with honey and local produce. Ears of wheat can be placed on the table. Consider what is the family's 'harvest' this year, both personally and collectively. Ideas for celebrations could be a picnic in a cornfield, or making corn-dollies to hang over the cooker to keep the summer luck in the kitchen.

Autumn Equinox – around September 21 This is the second harvest festival. Nights are drawing in, and blackberries are in the hedgerows. The colour is purple. Blackberry pie, chutneys, preserves and locally grown apples can be placed on the table. Consider how everyone feels about the new term and the start back to work after the holidays. What are you going to do to make this a positive time? What, if anything, are you sad about? How might that change?

Hallowe'en – October 31 (All Souls) This is the eerie, scary time of year. In the old days it would have been a bit sombre, involving the laying in of stores for the winter, but also lots of feasting to keep cheerful! The colour is black. Hollow out a pumpkin for the table and serve hot-dogs, tomato soup and liquorice cakes that look like spiders! Tell ghost stories and talk about your ancestors (as did the Celts) by firelight. Tell jokes. Let off fireworks.

Yule/Christmas Yule is actually on (or around) December 21, but it is by Christmas Day that the sun can actually be seen to be returning. Colours are red, green and gold. There are plenty of Christmas themes and ideas, all about abundance, joy and rebirth. You can use these with an awareness of the cycle of Nature. For instance, the evergreen tree is a symbol of enduring life, and although brought to Britain in the time of Queen Victoria, it is based on older customs. Talk about your experiences of love. What is the best you've ever given or received? If you had one gift to give the world, what would it be?

Full Moons

It is fun to celebrate these as a family. The moon is linked to fertility and especially rules families and home. A nice idea is for Mum to be celebrated in her own right, but it is more likely that she will have to do the organising! Light a big silver candle, tell fairy stories, eat white food (as at Imbolc), and have a party. Full moon is often a high energy time, but accidents are also more likely, so take care. Make or buy a silver coronet and take it in turns to wear it and say a party-piece. Say a prayer to the Moon Goddess, who is, after all, the representation of the Great Mother – compose your own words, e.g. 'Hail to the shining Goddess; may her light fill our nights, our homes and our hearts.' Dress up and hunt for fairies in the moonlit garden!

A Fertility Charm

If your fertility needs a boost, a good charm may have a powerful effect. No-one knows all the answers to baby-making. Doctors have been surprised countless times by pregnancies that occurred against all the odds. This is where the magic of Nature comes into the picture, and you can play your part. A charm may have a potent effect on your subconscious and on the secret places within your body when your mind acts as conjuror.

When you do your charm, make sure you are as peaceful as you can be. Take walks in the sunshine, let the rain fall on your face and become aware of the cycles of Nature and the moon. Touch trees and feel yourself become in harmony with them if possible. All this is attuning your body to the cycle of life.

Try to find a lovely peace lily growing in a pot. If this isn't possible, some fragrant lily stems in a vase can take its place. You will also need a white feather, a green egg-cup, some essential oil of patchouli and three white candles. A small muslin cover for the egg-cup is also necessary – if you can, choose a lace one, weighted at the edges with small crystals.

When the moon is waxing, place your peace lily or lily flowers on a windowsill that catches the sun. For three mornings and three evenings in succession, very gently stroke off a little lily pollen with the feather and catch it in the egg-cup. Just a tiny bit will do, and it doesn't matter if you spill some.

After gathering the pollen on the third evening, anoint your candles with patchouli oil and light them, placing your egg-cup between them. Imagine your fertility coming into being. Light the third candle and place it behind the egg-cup. Imagine the light from the candle streaming into your womb, glowing there and growing into a child. Hold this image for as long as you feel comfortable.

Cover your egg-cup and place it underneath your bed. Bury the lilies outside when they die, or tend your peace lily. Light the candles at successive full moons, placing them round the peace lily if that is what you have used, until they burn down.

Step-Families Charm

This charm is good for 'ordinary' families, too, but it can be especially beneficial in addressing tensions within step-families.

In old tribal cultures there existed the tradition of the Talking Stick – a special stick that was passed around the assembled community in order to designate who was speaking and to help them command attention. The Talking Stick is a symbol of authority and importance and a kind of wizard's staff that transforms the holder into a powerful voice. Find yourself a Talking Stick for your family – this could be Grandad's walking stick, a special staff you have bought or just some wood you've picked up. Sending the children to look for a Talking Stick can engage them in the matter. You can decorate the Stick with ribbons if you like, and it is a nice idea for everyone to have their own ribbon tied to the Stick.

Every so often, hold a pow-wow. Set aside an hour or so for everyone to talk and raise important issues and elect someone as scribe. The agreement is that everyone has their say, that the person holding the Stick is listened to and no-one runs out of the room in a tantrum. If it is hard to keep a boundary, use an egg-timer for the length of time any one person speaks. Pass the Stick around the circle and make it a rule that the one who holds it commands attention. Things that are agreed, and things that still have to be resolved are written up by the scribe and pinned to the family notice-board.

After the pow-wow, have a nice meal together – something everyone likes – followed by a pudding, preferably a steamed one, home-made, with yummy custard or ice-cream. Conceal symbols in the pudding – little charms such as you would attach to a charm bracelet, or anything you can find that feels suitable. These might be a heart, a star, a key and a cat. They might be self-explanatory or they might have symbolic meanings that are agreed beforehand. The symbol each person finds in their pudding defines what they should put into the family until the next pow-wow. For instance, the person who finds the heart can try to be especially warm and loving within the family, a cat might mean feeding the pets, a key could signify making an effort to be communicative, and a star might mean being called upon to find entertainment and fun – whatever the family needs can be put in the pudding and served up 'by luck' to the participants. The element of chance and fun is likely to elicit co-operation. When you make the pudding, mix into it what you feel the family needs (see the choice of herbs and spices in the Charm for a Happy Family on page 156). Visualise a happy outcome as your own private input to the charm. It's your secret!

Charm for Single Parenthood

Today, many children are brought up in single-parent homes. If you are a single parent you are likely to face many of the same issues as you would if you had a partner, but some may be different. You might lack what every reasonable two-parent family should have – support in the care of the children. If you do, this charm is for you.

You will need a square lace scarf (preferably silver coloured), a green ribbon and a small symbol to represent you and each of your children. These symbols can be crystals, initials or something that seems particularly appropriate, such as a toy car for a little boy. You will also need a symbol to represent the specific sort of help that you're looking for, or, alternatively, just write down what you want on a piece of paper.

Try to do this spell when the moon is waxing. Light your candle and spread out the scarf (making sure it won't accidentally catch fire). Place the symbols representing yourself and your children on top of it. Close

family fortunes * 163

your eyes and imagine help coming to you. Open your eyes and place the 'help' symbol on the scarf. Then, anoint each corner of the scarf with patchouli oil and tie the corners tightly together with the green ribbon. Keep this bundle near the family notice board, the telephone or other dynamic and useful spot. Repeat the charm as necessary.

self-hypnosis for family fortunes

Self-Hypnosis for a Happy Family

Obviously you can't make your whole family happy just like that, so this bit of self-hypnosis will help you to set up a healthy boundary in a family situation that might be invasive, manipulative or just fraught, as all families can be!

[Usual induction.]

You are beautifully relaxed, and as you are lying here beautifully relaxed you are aware of the boundaries of your own body. Yes, you are aware of the extent of your body. You can feel your feet, so beautifully relaxed, and you can feel the top of your head. Wonderfully relaxed. And you can feel your arms, your sides. You can feel the bed *[or chair]* supporting you. The bed *[or chair]* is not your body; your body is separate.

Around you, you are aware of an egg of light. *[Choose a warm colour to imagine for this egg, but not red.]* You can feel this egg. You can see it with your mind's eye. It keeps you safe, it keeps you calm, it keeps you in place. You radiate love and acceptance with the glowing egg around you, but you also keep yourself contained and safe. *[Repeat this message in several different ways if you wish.]*

You are part of your family, but you also exist on your own, safe within your egg. Your existence does not depend on your family; it is your own, just as your body and its boundaries are your own. Your feelings do not solely depend on your family – they are your own. Your happiness does not solely depend on your family – it is your own. You have your own life path, your own destiny to fulfil. You are aware of yourself as a separate, happy entity, safe within your egg.

In family situations you remain calm, you remain relaxed, you keep things in perspective. In the presence of your family you are serene and able to think clearly. You are calm within your family, you are perfectly relaxed, because although you love your family, they do not control how you feel. At times your family may affect you, yet you recover your serenity quickly because you know that you are safe within your egg. You find balanced ways to cope with family situations; you remain serene and collected; you remain in touch with your own feelings and needs and able to balance these with the feelings and needs of other family members.

You radiate warmth, light and love with the glowing egg that is around you. You send love out to your family. You send warmth out to your family. You send understanding out to your family. *[Repeat this three times in all.]* You value your family for the good things they have given you and continue to give you. But you do not lose sight of any negative feelings you have, such as anger. You do not repress these feelings. However, it is your choice whether or not you wish to show these feelings to others. You exercise your judgement about what you need to express and what you wish to keep private.

You can feel the warmth and light around you that forms your protective egg. Whenever you need your egg to become stronger, it does so, and you feel its protection and its radiance. You can choose whether or not to let anyone through the boundary of your egg. You can also radiate special love and understanding with your egg of light.

You are now imagining a family situation in which you have felt challenged. You are imagining it in every detail. You remember how it feels. You remember what happened and what was said. You now imagine this situation coming out well, for the good of all. You imagine your part in it being sensible and loving. You imagine your part in it respecting yourself as well as others. You imagine a good outcome for everyone.

When you have imagined a good outcome for everyone, you will awaken, feeling calm, wide awake, refreshed and relaxed and bringing with you all the instructions and suggestions you have been given, and being able to put them into practice.

seven

Making Your Work Work for You

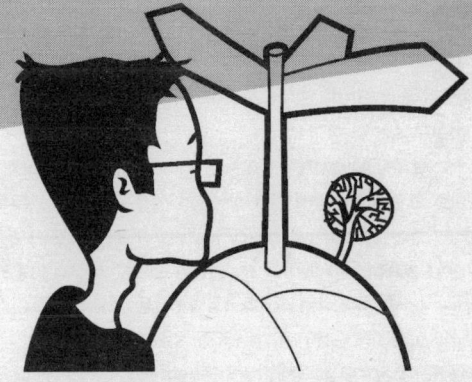

'No man is born into the world, whose work
Is not born with him; there is always work,
And tools to work withal, for those who will:
And blessed are the horny hands of toil!'
James Russell Lowell, 'A Glance Behind the Curtain'

'Work is the curse of the drinking classes.'
Oscar Wilde (attributed)

'Laborare est orare – To work is to pray.'
Latin Proverb

Many people assume that work, by definition, cannot be pleasant. The main purpose of life, they feel, is to get work behind you, so you can play. Others endure jobs they detest, and even more are simply bored and unfulfilled. That really is not good enough! Life is too short to be spent wishing it away.

Ah, you may say, that's all very well, but I have to work for the money – I can't live on air. Of course not – but the truth of the matter is that it is quite hard to make real dosh doing something you resent. Nothing flows, nothing gels – you're always going against the grain and doing violence to something deep within. Contrary to what you may assume, things can and do come easily. That is not to say that you will not have to work very hard – the chances are that if you want to be successful you will certainly have to be prepared to work very hard indeed. However, there is a difference between the effort you put into something you like doing and the drudgery of something you hate. One of life's greatest joys, in fact, is working, being productive and creative, making a difference.

Luckily, in work as with all other things, we are not all alike! One person's meat is another's poison. Some people like doing accounts, some need to be artistic, and some feel that what they are doing is worthwhile and satisfying when they are emptying dustbins or working with sewage – and they are right! It's 'horses for courses', and there is no reason why you should not find the right one for you.

If you are not happy at work you have several choices. You can:

* Carry on moaning and enduring until you get ill or retire – whichever comes first!
* Change your attitude to your work.
* Change your job.

Before we examine these alternatives, first let's find out a little more about what you need from your job. Read through the following list of statements and note whether or not you agree with them.

* You hate to be interrupted while doing your work.

- You look forward to times when you can read a book or watch telly.
- The office party is a nightmare!
- You wouldn't mind being in an office all on your own.
- You generally avoid socialising with colleagues.
- The jobs you've had have tended to come through making applications rather than networking.
- You wouldn't say you were a team player.
- You often wish the telephone had never been invented.
- The people you work with are often more of a challenge than the work itself.
- You often get lost in your own thoughts.
- You work much better when left to yourself. This includes all your work. For instance a sales person may feel they get on with the form-filling better alone, but the main purpose of their job is in fact making sales, which cannot be done without people present.
- People who chatter a lot make you irritable or uneasy.
- When you wake up in the morning your primary concern is your state of mind rather than who are you going to meet and what you are going to do.

The more statements you agreed with, the greater your degree of introversion. The more you disagreed with, the more of an extrovert you are. Scores for introversion and extroversion can vary somewhat day by day and year by year, and it is possible to have a more introverted attitude to work than to pleasure. If you are very introverted there is no point in entertaining a job working with people or as a salesperson – you need to get stuck in to something on your own. If you are very extroverted, don't even contemplate being holed up with a computer for company because it will drive you mad, even if the salary is fabulous. This may seem obvious, but the world is full of square pegs trying to ram themselves into round holes without taking into account some very basic facts about themselves. It's okay to be you, whatever that may be, and while a salesman's hefty commission may not be for you if you are not an extrovert, you are in great company because they don't apparently come more introverted than Howard Hughes!

168 ✳ a charmed life

Now try the following quiz. Of the four alternatives offered, choose the one that applies most to you, most of the time. Don't think too hard about your answers.

1 You prefer pictures on your wall to be:
   a) of nature and familiar scenes,
   b) fantasy and abstract subjects,
   c) light, minimalist or possibly maps and diagrams,
   d) family photos, furry animals or lovey-dovey images.

2 You feel best when:
   a) secure,
   b) inspired,
   c) free,
   d) protected.

3 You would like to be known most for your:
   a) practicality,
   b) creativity,
   c) intelligence,
   d) kindness.

4 The main purpose of life is:
   a) to make a living,
   b) to find a sense of meaning,
   c) to improve one's mind,
   d) to care for others.

5 When you look into a room for the first time, you are mostly aware of:
   a) what's there, of course!
   b) its general appearance and potential,
   c) its order and layout,
   d) its atmosphere.

6 Your favourite films are:
   a) a good, basic story,
   b) fantasy, sci-fi,
   c) something with a clever plot,
   d) romantic, human interest.

7 You feel best in clothes that are:
   a) serviceable, comfortable, good quality,
   b) stylish, a bit different,
   c) smart and fashionable,
   d) clothes your friends like.

8 Imagine your birthday is coming up – you would like to spend it:
   a) somewhere familiar, where you know you'll be comfortable and get value for money,
   b) swept off to somewhere exotic,
   c) in a pleasant gathering with interesting people to talk to,
   d) with your family and close friends – it doesn't matter where.

9 Your friends are mostly:
   a) people you've known for ages,
   b) people who are interesting and unusual,
   c) intelligent people that know how to have a conversation,
   d) people who understand you deeply, and whom you understand.

10 You would describe your ideal home as:
   a) one on which the mortgage is paid,
   b) something big, rambling and preferably impressive,
   c) a smart town house within easy reach of the cultural centre,
   d) a cosy cottage.

Your Score

Mostly A: You are an essentially down-to-earth, practical person. You have a healthy regard for your own welfare and like to see that the basics in life are taken care of before anything else. You can't be bothered with too much speculation and you can be a bit impatient of imagination – you like to see solid results and you may be quite good at hands-on stuff. You are very identified with the evidence of your five senses and do not readily get carried away or fired up. Of all the four types listed here, you are the most able to put up with a job for the money. In fact, you can derive real satisfaction from your earnings and may even 'enjoy' a dull job for what you know it is bringing in.

Mostly B: You are looking for much more in life than just to jog along.

Your job needs to have promise, originality and variety and be full of possibilities. There needs to be scope for creativity and imagination – you really cannot bear to have your day – or, God help us, your year – mapped out ahead of time. You cannot function at your best if you are chained to routine. You may have loads of ideas but you aren't always wonderful at carrying things through to a conclusion. Often you get hunches and if you are left to yourself your attitude to life is quite playful – after all, there is so much to experience! Being tied to a dull job is anathema to you, and may even make you ill.

Mostly C: You need to be able to use your brain in your work. This doesn't necessarily mean that you are an intellectual – just that what you do needs to be rational, well thought out and subject to review. It is important to you to be able to talk through what you are doing and to feel that your point of view is heard. You believe that everyone should say what they mean and that an answer can always be found if all concerned are civilised. You would find it especially hard to cope at work if you thought there were too many things that didn't make sense about the way the place was run, if your colleagues weren't reasonable and efficient, and if you did not have a degree of freedom to choose how your day went.

Mostly D: Who you work with probably matters more to you than what you do. You probably like working with people or animals and may well feel best when you are in a caring role. You'll fall in with the way others want things done if it means keeping the peace, but if your colleagues are getting upset then you have to speak out. One thing you cannot tolerate at work is a bad atmosphere! You are probably the one who makes the tea and remembers birthdays, and you may be able to put up with doing boring and repetitive things as long as you can chat to your friends while you do it. You like your work to be part of the community, or to fit in with your role in the community. Your family is likely to be of prime importance and you may put up with work you do not enjoy and even gain fulfilment from it if it fits in with domestic requirements and benefits your nearest and dearest.

We all have several sides to us and we may do many different things in life that express these sides. Our hobbies may contrast markedly with our working lives, as in the case of the high-flying executive who likes to do a little woodwork in his spare time. However, when it comes to working life, it is very important that our work should be an expression of the greater part of the personality.

changing things

On page 166 we looked at three possible courses of action if you are not satisfied with your job. Let us hope that the first alternative of carrying on complaining isn't your choice! In the light of what we have uncovered about your personality, let's look at how you might put the second option – changing your attitude to work – into effect.

You've decided that for some reason you cannot, at present, physically change your job. Changing your attitude to it might be a temporary ploy until your situation changes, or it may be more long-term. Changing your attitude is not going to work if you find your job really dreadful – this is an approach for you if there are bits of your job you do like.

If you scored high on introversion in your responses to the list of statements on page 166, look at ways you can keep yourself to yourself more. For instance, if your job involves some dealing with people, can you create boundaries so there are times when you are not interrupted? Can you switch off the phone for periods? Can you work flexi-time and come in when the office is empty? Could you ask for an office on your own or work from home sometimes? Might you explain to others that you really need to be quiet, and perhaps make up on your popularity by making a special effort to chat at lunchtime? Remember that if you accept yourself there is much more chance of getting others to accept you. What ways are there to create space for yourself?

If you scored high on extroversion you will need to take the opposite route. In what way can you get more involved? Maybe your boss will consent to you taking on a more interactive role when s/he understands that you function better with people around. Ask to be moved if your desk is in a corner or you have an office alone. Offer to be the one to man the phones when other people want to get their heads down. Be the person who shows visitors round, who makes everyone laugh, who is always brimming with the latest news. If this is 'you', the chances are that you are doing most of these things anyway, but do them with greater application and conviction. This isn't about self-indulgence, it is actually about you functioning more efficiently, because you will, despite the chatter!

Now look at your answers to the quiz on page 168. If they were mainly 'A's, then your emphasis is on the practical. Can you ask for more money? Could you transfer to a branch where there is less travelling involved? Could your day be better planned, your lunch better provided? Are there ways in which you could change your routine and your surroundings so both are more under your control? For instance, do you need more desk space? Could you function better if other employees respected your schedule? Do you feel the workplace is too disorganised? Are there some basic, commonsense things that aren't being done? It is quite possible that if you approach the management in the right way they will be pleased that you want to improve things. However, if you feel this is not likely to be the case then concentrate on things that are within your control. Make sure that where you sit is comfortable. Remain very grounded and keep in mind the reasons why you are doing this at all times. It's a means to an end. Count what you have achieved.

If your answers were mostly 'B's, is there some way you can introduce a challenge into your work? If you have stamps to stick on or boxes to pack, be the quickest sticker or packer the world has ever seen! Turn your work into a game – how can you do it better, differently? Play games also in respect of your fellow employees – imagine them in other roles, from other times in history. How might they behave? Pretend they aren't real people but characters in a play you are writing – how can you get them to behave differently? (Common sense, of course, dictates that this should not go too far!) Pretend you are researching for a bestseller you're going to write and that you won't be in the job very long (probably you won't!). Make a list of all the things you are doing in your job that are actually worthwhile and that are leading somewhere for the greater good – see how it all fits into the big picture. Investigate the possibility of changing roles with other employees. Let your imagination range over ways to do things better – then offer them to your boss if you feel this will be welcome. Imagine also how much worse life could be – really fill out this scenario in your mind, and then feel relieved that it isn't true! Try to work where there is a view out of the window. See how many jokes you can memorise to tell your colleagues.

If your answers were mostly 'C's, is there some way you can get more mental stimulation from what you do? Can you ask for this? Is there a course you could go on? Is there some way you could be involved in talking through what you have to do and finding more efficient ways to do it? Can you get more discussion going at work? Are there people's views that need to be heard? Are there other ways you could get more co-operation? Improve your charm and your people skills and see what happens. What is there about what you have to do that doesn't seem logical and reasonable – and would it improve things generally if this were changed? Occupy your mind drawing up plans for changes, even if you feel you have to keep these to yourself. Set yourself mental challenges such as finding out more about your job and the company. Develop aspects of your work that really interest you, even if this sometimes extends outside work hours, because this may make the entire job more attractive. Can you improve spreadsheets or databases? Can you network more extensively? If you were the boss, how would you do things differently? Turn this into a mental exercise, because one day it may actually stand you in good stead.

If your answers were mostly 'D's, is there some way you can feel better about the people you work with? Can you make friends with them more? Are there things you could do to make everyone feel more comfortable? Would it lighten the atmosphere if you brought in a box of chocolates to share or some fruit? Is there someone in the place that you haven't yet spoken to? Why not start up a conversation? Could you get a friend to come and work close to you? Why not start up a joint venture such as a Christmas club or all doing the lottery together? Like the 'B' category people, you might enjoy memorising jokes to tell your colleagues. Make a special occasion of birthdays. Try to get people to talk if something is bothering them. Make sure that you find a way to talk if something is bothering you. Try to find common ground such as a soap opera you all enjoy watching. If someone is being unpleasant, choose a time and a place to ask them what's on their mind. Think about the community values of your job – how does it fit in? Can you feel that it is worthwhile? How many people can you get to smile at you today?

bullying and office politics

The sad fact is that people are not always nice and being in a working environment often brings out the worst in them. In a way an office is a family and unresolved issues from childhood may emerge as competitive behaviour, bullying, jealousy, telling tales and generally behaving like a spiteful child in a situation where one would be expected to be at one's most adult!

Bullying is harder to deal with in a work situation than it is in school, where one is, after all, a child and entitled to seek protection, and where one can always appeal to responsible adults. At work one feels one should be grown up enough to deal with the situation. Besides, adult bullies may be cleverer and they may have real power over your future opportunities. However, there are ways of dealing with this, so do not let a bully immobilise you – you are not a mouse being hypnotised by a cat! Here are some tips.

* Enlist support from colleagues – the chances are you are not the only target and the last thing you should do is suffer in silence.
* If you are a junior being bullied by a group of more senior people, tell your boss.
* Decide on a firm, multi-purpose response and keep saying it, like a broken record.
* Don't let pride paralyse you – it is okay to feel scared, confused and powerless, and some people have a talent for stirring this up in others. Recognise your emotions and deal with them rather than being controlled by them.
* Ask yourself what part of you the bully is hooking into – were you bullied as a child? Remember that now you are adult and take decisions with your mind, not your emotions.

- ✻ Don't allow your fears to show in your body language. Keep your shoulders straight and your head high, and take care of your appearance.
- ✻ Remember that the worst thing this bully – or bullies – can do is to lose you your job. If you let them also take your peace of mind and self-respect then you have given that away yourself.
- ✻ Spend a little time imagining what awful thing must have happened to the bully to make them so crippled and malevolent.
- ✻ Spend a little time imagining what they look like on the loo, picking their nose or some other undignified position.
- ✻ Finally, there are no Brownie points for sticking at it. Who wants to go daily into a hellish situation? Get out – anything is better than working in such conditions.

Office politics are more subtle than bullying but the simple answer to this is not to get drawn in. Never say anything about anyone that you would not be prepared to say to their face. Refuse to take things personally – after all, your job does not have to involve your social life or any relationships you have. Concentrate on what is positive and remain detached. Avoid getting a reputation for being aloof by developing a sense of humour – if you can regale your colleagues with a funny story or two then there will be less time and energy left over for bitching. Make sure you do not reveal any personal vulnerabilities in situations where you are not absolutely sure you can trust those involved.

Try the Charm to Feel Safe at Work on page 187, for bullying or any fraught working situation.

✻ changing your job

It is possible that going through the above options has given you one or two ideas to improve your job satisfaction. However, it is also possible that it has served to highlight just how awful your job is! If you decide you want to change your job, start looking! This sounds so obvious but it is amazing how many people are too apathetic to do this, or too negative about their ability to find anything else.

Make sure you have a good CV prepared and circulate it to as many agencies and companies as you can think of. Turn finding a job into a hobby. Keep a diary and chase up contacts every three months. Network – ask anyone and everyone if they know of anything that might suit you, and keep asking. Strike up conversations with employees in places you might like to work – find out what the work entails. Look up old friends and acquaintances and ask them. Follow up every lead, however vague it appears.

When going for interviews, take each one very seriously, role-playing with friends, listing questions you may be asked, etc. Always make sure you look your very best. Treat each interview as an opportunity to learn. Even if you do not get this job, what you learn about being interviewed is going to help you when you eventually do find something – which you will. If you do not get a job, always ask for feedback and explanation – why did you not get the job? Often the reason will be something as simple as location. Don't take anything personally – different people will see different things in you and even the most successful people have been criticised for some amazing things, such as beautiful actresses being told they were too ugly!

Please do not be afraid to take a completely different type of job if you fancy this. I know at least three people who have embarked on totally different careers at the age of 50. One of the principal reasons people put forward for not looking for new work is 'I am too old'. That was never true, and is now less of a problem than ever, as companies are developing respect for the 'grey fox' who has a wealth of experience and a proven track-record. Always consider acquiring new skills, going on a course and updating your abilities. Keep an Achievements Book in which you record everything, large and small, from the friend's party that you helped organise through to your qualifications and job record. List here any skills that you have, even 'keeping the house tidy', 'working late at night' and 'getting the gang together' –

> **Top Tip**
> *If you need to find a new job, turn your job-search into a hobby that you try to enjoy.*

anything is relevant. Support this with cheerful photographic reminders, certificates, letters of praise and anything you can think of – it all counts. This Achievements Book will keep you positive and focused on your abilities as you market yourself.

unemployment

Being unemployed can be the most severe blow to self-esteem and can be quite terrifying. Feelings of worthlessness and despair can be overwhelming. At this time it is important to keep positive and to have an action plan. Here are some pointers:

* Try the Self-Hypnosis for Self-Esteem given on page 237.
* Start an Achievements Book, described above, as well as putting into practice the other hints in this section.
* Turn looking for a job into a job in itself, keeping folders and notes, a follow-up diary, a job-hunting schedule, etc.
* Try the hints on pages 29–31 for maximising your luck.
* Use the free time that you have as a gift, not a burden. Start a new hobby, help a charity, catch up on reading, see friends, take up a sport, get fit, do DIY and get the garden sorted.
* Use this opportunity to find out what you really want to do – try the Vocation Visualisation on page 184.
* Use the Charm to Get that Job (page 186) when you have an interview.
* Be positive! This is very hard and you may feel trapped and hopeless if rejection after rejection lands on your mat, but this is normal. Read success stories. Hang out with people who are hopeful, up-beat and have encouraging things to say. Remember that the Chinese character for crisis also means opportunity.
* What have you always wanted to do? Keep on asking yourself this – it might take a while to dredge up ambitions and yearnings that you surrendered years ago. Make a note of them, however stupid they may seem. Take the first steps towards them.

Bob's Story

Bob had worked in insurance all of his life. He regarded himself as a basically contented fellow who got on with life, and liked his drink and cigarettes. He was a family man with a mortgage. When at the age of 45 he was made redundant, this seemed like the end of the world. For a few months Bob went virtually into a state of breakdown, smoking even more and regularly getting drunk. His relationship was in jeopardy, and, as he had expected, his losing his job meant he was losing everything.

Bob saw a counsellor who pointed out to him that he was in fact creating the end of the world reality that he feared, and that if he stepped back from the situation there were many things he could do. Bob was encouraged to write down all the things he wanted to do in life that he had never been able to do while working and all the good things about being out of work. This exercise was the beginning of seeing things just a bit differently.

Bob identified a wish to work with wood. Having brought himself to the point where he could admit this to himself, he realised that one of the reasons he had never risen further in his profession was that he had never liked pen-pushing. Now he knew what he wanted to do, it was possible to explore avenues for approaching it. He feared discussion with his partner, but she was so pleased to see him being positive again that she was supportive. They found a way to send Bob to college to learn how to make furniture, as he had always desired.

Eighteen months later Bob had stopped smoking (it is hard to enjoy this while you are wood-working and in any case Bob no longer felt such a pressing need for it) and was beginning to produce some fine pieces. Two years further down the line he was making a reasonable amount of money selling exquisite articles in top-market hotels and galleries. Bob is grateful for the redundancy because it enabled him, for the first time, to focus on what he really wanted to do.

finding your vocation

While everyone can expect to get some satisfaction and pleasure from their job, not everyone has a vocation. A vocation is a calling – it is something you feel guided to, almost by an inner voice. Sometimes this can happen literally by an inner voice. A vocation truly does involve input from the centre of your personality. It means that a part of you – and sometimes a very big part of you – goes into your work. It means that you feel enlarged by your work. Often it feels as if your personality cannot grow and develop without following that vocation.

Perhaps more people have a vocation at some level than may be obvious; it is just that not everyone expresses this in their working life – or at least not in their paid working life. For many women, it is a home and family that is the vocation. For some people, what they do in their spare time may feel like a vocation – such as charity work or painting pictures. Some people feel no particular vocation, or need for one – they are content simply to jog along from day to day. Fortunate souls have found their vocation, while others have that sneaking feeling that they should have one, that something is trying to attract their attention but they aren't sure what.

Probably all of us were aware of a vocation quite early in life. It will have been something we did well, or something we were drawn to. Family expectations and pressures may have affected our pursuit of our vocation. These may have caused us to believe, at least superficially, that our vocation was elsewhere. However, when we finally find it, it is like coming home.

Often the vocation is quite obvious! In my case I devoured books from an early age and was always busy writing poetry and bits and pieces. I even compiled a weekly 'newspaper' for which I extorted money from family members. I passionately loved books and was always very good at English – it was all so easy! I missed the fact that my place was with books partly because of this. I had an idea that somehow things should be harder. This was fostered by family assumptions that I would do other things, such as become a doctor or do something altogether more high-flying. After many, many years, several false starts and lots of time bringing up children, I found again what had always been so pleasant! I feel very fortunate in that I love what I do and find it very easy. Of course, I work very hard, often long into the night, but it flows and it feels right, and so that is okay.

If you look back at your childhood you may well recall something you simply loved that came easily and that you did repeatedly. It is such a shame that often what we do easily we do not regard as a talent. If no pressure is applied, often people are able to flow, like water, into the course that was meant for them. Both of my older boys found their vocation by being left to it. Being typical boys, all my efforts to get them to work failed and I settled for having them happy. At the age of 11 the eldest decided he wanted to be a policeman – a career I would never have dreamt of. He just found his own way, and has recently been accepted into the force. His younger brother is dyslexic and I could not imagine what he might do as everything seemed such a struggle, but he showed an interest in the theatre, followed that and is now at Bristol Old Vic Theatre School. This has shown me what I already knew but was afraid to trust – that things just happen naturally. A sense of vocation is more likely to be thwarted if we are pushed in any way (by ourselves or others) or try to bring too much that is rational into the frame.

The pressures of life are such that we do not always let things happen naturally. In fact, as we grow up it is all too easy to lose ourselves, to see ourselves as others would like us to be rather than as what we are. But always inside us there is that 'still, small voice', however muffled it may be. If you need to contact that lost, wise part of you to help you find your vocation, try the Vocation Visualisation on page 184. You might also like to use the Self-Hypnosis for Relaxation on page 41, which can remove the barriers to inspiration.

> **Top Tip**
> *Prize the things that you can do easily. They are a gift to be used.*

Colour Me Clever – An Interesting Exercise

Colour can be used as a means to self-knowledge and also as a simple charm – for colours have meanings and effects. This is no surprise – after all, colour is a vibration. Vibrations are experienced either as harmonious or not, so not only will your colour preference give a hint about your vibe, but colours can also be used to make specific impressions. While some of these may be obvious, others are less direct. Obviously fashion and cultural norms need to be borne in mind – for instance, it is rarely the done thing for men to wear a bright red shirt under a business suit. If a man likes red it will usually show itself in his choice of tie, etc.

Black Black is a smart, popular and practical choice for many clothes, from working daywear to glamorous evening kit. If you like black you are probably self-contained, strong-willed and quite adaptable. You notice and absorb more than you betray. Your self-discipline is probably good and you may be a touch mysterious. Actually you are probably quite sensitive and lacking in confidence but you are great at hiding this. Wearing black can create many impressions but will generally mean you are seen as serious, authoritative and maybe a dark horse. Black has an intriguing yet efficient vibration.

Red Red is energetic and demanding. People who wear red love to be noticed and are often ambitious and forceful. If you love wearing red you like to project yourself and may also want your sexuality to be registered. Sometimes you may be aggressive – usually you are assertive. Darker shades of red are more subtle, but all convey passion and warmth. Wearing red can impress everyone that you are a force to be reckoned with and that you are going to shake things up. Be careful that you are prepared to back this up because sometimes your red garb may make people compete or argue with you – or come on to you!

Orange This is a creative and cheerful colour. If this is your choice, you like to be seen as a little ray of sunshine. You have a light-hearted and enthusiastic approach and you are creative and optimistic. You like to be the centre of attention, too, but you are less demanding than the red personality. Wearing orange can mean you bring a smile to people's faces and enhance their faith in life – and in you! Be careful, however, in jobs where you need to be taken seriously – wearing too much orange may give the impression that you are very playful. Shades of peach and ginger have some of the orange vibe but are more subtle.

Yellow This is the colour of mental freedom and creative change. Yellow stimulates thoughts and endows mental energy. It is a good colour to have somewhere in a study. If you like to wear yellow you are probably a bright person with lots of ideas. Some traditions link yellow with practicality and earthiness. Wearing yellow can be inspiring to those around you. Like orange, it needs to be chosen with care in situations were you need to create a serious impression. Yellow shows you are capable of independent thought and that you can adapt, apply and think laterally. It also signifies creativity.

Green This is the colour of the natural world, the peace and beauty of trees, grass and plants. If you like wearing green you are probably a cautious, reliable person who likes to be quiet and tranquil. You may even have a conscious link with nature or a job that is involved with the natural world. Generally you are laid-back and optimistic. Wearing green will impress people with your groundedness, your reliability and your calm. They are likely to feel reassured by your presence. Green may have a healing effect. Be careful of wearing too much green in situations where you need to be seen as dynamic, creative and original.

Blue This is a wonderfully serene and calm colour. If you like wearing blue you are probably creative, but in a less flamboyant fashion than the wearers of orange and yellow. Blue denotes intelligence, sensitivity, gentleness and healing. There is also a quiet determination about you and you may gently achieve all you wish without others noticing. Wearing blue will impress people with your harmonious and tactful nature and you will make people feel soothed by your presence. Be careful of too much blue where you need to be warm, responsive and ardent – blue can be a little cold at times. Dark blue or navy also have some of the characteristics of black and are very cool and efficient.

Purple This is the colour of intuition and spirituality. Deep shades may also be quite regal and sumptuous. If your choice is purple, you are a deep-seeing, possibly psychic, person with a philosophical side, and your emotions are very profound. Shades of lilac and mauve are similar, conveying more sensitivity and less strength. Wearing purple will get you respected in certain circles – say, if you were lecturing on a metaphysical topic or counselling people. In a busy workplace it might give the impression that you had your mind on higher things and weren't willing to get your hands dirty with the day-to-day. However, it might also give the hint that you have several answers up your sleeve!

Pink This is a gentle colour and if you like wearing pink you are probably affectionate and want to be taken care of. You are sociable and understanding. Possibly you want people to know you are vulnerable and to be gentle with you. You aren't too worried about seeming dependent and you don't like to cause offence. If you wear pink, you are giving the message that you are approachable, pleasant and friendly. What you are not doing is projecting strength, dynamism, decisiveness and strong individuality. Pink is not a good choice if you want to be seen as a force to be reckoned with, although it would be great for a receptionist, for instance. Pink worn by men is slightly different and can accentuate their masculinity, as though they are stating that they have enough testosterone so are prepared to tone it down! The stronger and deeper the pink, the more it partakes of the passion and flair of red. Fuschia and magenta also bring in some of the meanings of purple.

Brown This is a practical, down-to-earth colour, showing that you prefer to keep your feet on the ground and to know where you stand. You like to take your time and adapt to circumstances. Brown has similar meanings to green and shows an attunement to nature and a need for security. It also indicates you are something of a builder and an establisher, a putter-down of roots. Wearing brown gives people the impression they know where they are with you. They are likely to see you as a person of common sense, warm-hearted, but maybe lacking in imagination and drive. Beige, stone and natural colours partake of yellow and brown vibrations. However, fashion must always be taken into account and any trendy colour will give a sharp impression. For instance, wearing beige with brown boots will not get you taken for a slow soul!

White If you like to wear white you are confident, uncomplicated and open. There may be a childlike innocence and simplicity to your personality, but you are also capable of the ultimate in professionalism. White is crisp, bright and coping. Wearing white lets people know you are efficient. It is a great choice if you want to create a professional image, and white coats are the uniform of doctors and many therapists. However, in some settings white can have a clinical and cold vibe and it is best to avoid too much white if you want to be seen as vibrant, original and ardent.

visualisation and meditation for your working life

Vocation Visualisation

Find yourself in your auditorium, looking at the curtained stage. Walk towards it and see the curtains swing wide upon a wonderful city that looks rather Grecian in character. Walk up the steps – now you are in the city, walking along one of its wide, tree-lined roads.

Look around this place. All you see fills you with wonderment. The streets are wide and the buildings immense, not so much in height but in breadth, like cathedrals. And like cathedrals they are carved with a beauty and intricacy that you could never have imagined. Everywhere there is subtle colour, beautiful shapes, statues, frescoes, murals and impressive architecture. Some of the buildings are seats of learning, some offices, some hospitals and medical centres. There are many trees, shrubs and parklands within the city precincts and all is light and airy.

Although the city reminds you of Classical times, it is very modern. More than modern – it is futuristic. For the vehicles glide without a sound; there are no fumes, no pollution, and there is absolute safety, for all seem to be guided by remote control and sensors that detect pedestrians.

The people you see are wearing robes, and are smiling and talking. They seem pleased to see you, as if they know you. You are surrounded by cultured faces, people carrying books and scrolls, sitting on park benches for deep and animated discussions. Under awnings, artists,

making your work work for you * 185

sculptors, potters and so on are calmly working. Across a wide parkland there is building going on. Further off you are aware of agriculture, clean industry and other matters that support the life of the city. Everywhere there is an atmosphere of peace, culture and order.

You find yourself before an especially imposing building with great carved oak doors. As you look at these doors they swing open of their own accord and you enter a dim hallway, fragrant with wood polish and the scent of ancient stone. You see row upon row of shoes before you, so you take off your own and walk barefoot on the strangely warm, smooth stone until you come to another doorway. This also swings wide.

Before you there is a low platform with a desk, and behind the desk sits a kindly and wise teacher. She or he may come in any guise. They are here to help you and are at your disposal for as long as you like. Step up onto the platform and take a seat beside the teacher. Talk freely about your feelings in regard to your vocation. What have you always liked doing? What are you good at? What do you feel you should be doing? What pressures have there been or are there on you to take a direction? How do you feel about this direction? What are your fears and hopes? Lay anything that is on your mind before this being.

Now the teacher pulls a cord and a screen on the wall is revealed. On it you see yourself as a child, doing something. What are you doing? Take a note of this. The screen is again covered.

Again the teacher pulls a cord and a picture is shown relating to your education and experience. What is this? Take a note of this. The screen is again covered.

For a third time the teacher pulls a cord and this time a new scene is revealed. This relates to your future. What is this? Take a note of it. The screen is covered over for the last time.

Now you may speak some more with your teacher, discussing what you have seen. When you are ready, thank this being and take your leave. Go back through the hallway, putting on your shoes as you go. Follow the street back, through the rows of glorious buildings until you see a modest building with a door opening out onto the street. Open this door and find yourself on the stage, before your familiar auditorium.

Step down into the auditorium. The curtains close behind you. Come back to everyday awareness and make a note of anything that seemed important.

You can repeat this visualisation as often as you want, going back to ask for clarification until you feel you have achieved it.

charms for a working life

Charm to Get that Job

This little charm will get you very focused on landing that special job. You will need a dark green candle, some oil of patchouli, a pin, a small piece of malachite and a dark green drawstring bag. In addition you will need a symbol of the job you want, such as a brochure, badge, picture or letter-head.

Do this charm with a waxing moon if you can. Write your name and the job on the candle with the pin, e.g. Joe Bloggs, Chairman of the Board, or Annie Apple, Successful Artist. Then anoint the candle with eight drops of patchouli oil. As you rub this in, imagine yourself in the position you want, as vividly and in as much detail as possible. Anoint also the piece of malachite with a little oil, plus the bag and job symbol. Light your candle and repeat the message you scratched onto the candle as many times as you like while you watch the flame. When you feel ready, place your piece of malachite and job symbol into the bag. Light your candle and chant your name and job title for five minutes every evening until full moon and again on the night before your interview. Take your malachite (and also the drawstring bag if it is sufficiently small) to the interview with you.

Charm for Making a Change

If you are fed up to the back teeth with the same old, same old... but aren't quite sure how to take that first step out of the situation, try this charm to help you on your way to lateral thinking.

You will need a selection of socks in outrageous colours, any other strange clothing that you fancy (it should be something you do not usually wear), a crazy hat, a rainbow candle, some oil of orange (alternatively you may use an incense or joss-stick that has a lively, fruity aroma), a party-popper, a sparkler and a lump of self-hardening clay. Heat the oil or light the incense or joss-stick. Light the candle and dress up in the clothes – put them on inside-out, put on odd socks and sit in a position that you do not usually adopt – stand on your head for a few moments if you can! Think about the situation that you feel must change. Let off the party popper.

Now tidy up the popper streamers and re-arrange your clothes in any way that makes you feel more comfortable – change completely if you like. Sit comfortably in front of the candle and form the clay into any shape you like. Light the sparkler from the candle and write any message you like with it in the air. Stick it into the clay shape and watch while it burns out. Bury the cooled sparkler-stick in the garden and put your clay shape in the place you have set aside for your charms. Light your candle each evening and bring small offerings such as flowers to your clay shape until the desired change has come into your life.

If you have the time and the skill, instead of a clay shape you may make a mobile out of thread, wire and cardboard shapes. Cut out shapes of things you want to attract: general good luck symbols such as horse-shoes and cats and more specific things such as keys, tools and badges that might represent individual things you would like, such as a job or the chance to go on a course. Place a little oil of orange on your mobile and hang it near your window where it can pick up the winds of change.

Charm to Feel Safe at Work

People aren't always nice – it's a fact. Of course, there are ways to bring out the best in most people, but sometimes you don't have the time or the inclination to schmooze. Try this spell for the times and the places when you need to keep a pleasant atmosphere about yourself.

For this you will need a white or crystal stone, preferably about the size of a paperweight, although smaller will suffice. In fact, you may use a paperweight if you find one that appeals to you. Failing this, you will be able to find a suitable stone in a New Age shop. You also need access to a stream or bottled spring water, a white cloth (preferably cotton), soap (preferably lavender) or salt, a little oil of rosemary, a broom and a white candle.

Take your stone out to a running stream and let the fresh water wash all over it for a few seconds. (Alternatively, wash it at home with bottled spring water.) Dry it with the clean, white cloth and keep it wrapped in the cloth. Take it home and place it on your working area, next to the white candle. Wash your hands carefully, with the lavender soap or salt. Now sweep the room or working area, repeating, 'Begone, begone, begone – all that is bad, begone!' Imagine any negativity in you or your surroundings being swept away in clouds of grey. Do this until you feel the cleansing is complete and then do it for a little longer.

Light the candle. Take up the oil and anoint the stone with it, saying, 'I dedicate this stone as a protective force. May it always keep me safe from negative influence. So may it be.' Say this three times. You may baptise the stone, giving it a suitable name, if you wish, for instance the name of an archangel, or a god, or a character from myth – anyone who is pure and true, e.g. Galahad, Aragorn or Gabriel, or anyone/anything you see as strong and protective. Visualise this as your Spirit of the Stone. Or simply see the stone as having a powerful aura.

Position your stone so the fire of the candle is reflected in it. Imagine the stone absorbing the fire and becoming very powerful. Now the stone is able to project a force-field around you, keeping you from any harmful influences, botheration, criticism and harassment. Take a while to imagine that you are inside an egg of light projected by the stone. If you wish, imagine your guardian spirit there also.

When you feel ready, blow out the candle and wrap your stone up in the white cloth. Take it to work with you and place it on your desk; leave it to do its work. If you do not work at a desk, you will need a stone that you can wear or carry in your pocket.

Every so often – perhaps during a holiday or long weekend – you can repeat the process, cleansing your stone and re-charging it. You can adapt this charm to give you some insulation and privacy if you are introverted. Instead of 'negative influence', say 'intrusion'. But be careful that you don't end up more isolated than you wish!

Charm for an Interview

This charm is designed specifically for an interview situation, so that you will feel prepared from the top of your pinstripe suit down to the bottom of your subconscious! It will help you with the three important factors – clear thought, a relaxed and pleasant manner and some good luck.

You will need one yellow candle, one purple candle and one green one. You will also need a silver bracelet and three charms to hang on it – a horseshoe or star, a bird and a flower. If you can obtain these in silver, so much the better. You can find symbols like these in shops that sell decorations for special occasion cakes.

Place all your objects on your working area. First light the yellow candle and hold your bird symbol in your hand. Think of the clear sky, fresh winds and a feeling of scope and expansion. Say, 'During my interview may my mind be clear as the sunlit sky.' Now light the green candle, take up the flower symbol in the same way and say, 'During my interview may I be pleasant and charming and may all be impressed with my personality.' Last of all, light the purple candle and take up your star or horseshoe. Say, 'Luck, be with me and stand beside me during my interview so all goes smoothly.'

Wear or keep your charm with you, and just before you go into the interview room, touch each of the symbols one at a time.

self-hypnosis for work

Self-Hypnosis for a Balanced Attitude

This script is mainly for the type of job that means you have to be in a closed environment with the same people all or most days, probably doing a job that you do not feel is your vocation. If your situation is different, then you may adapt the words somewhat to suit.

[Usual induction.]

Now you are so pleasantly relaxed, so beautifully relaxed, all your cares have fallen away and your mind is clear. Your whole body is relaxed and your mind is open. You can see things from a fresh perspective. You want to see things from a new perspective. You want to get things in proportion, and to keep them that way. You know, because you are so relaxed, that you can be detached, that you will be detached and that everything will fall into place for you.

You remember that your job is just a job. It is not your whole life. It is something that you do for a purpose. It may not be perfect, but there is a reason why you do it and that is a good reason. It does not have to be perfect. You do not have to be perfect. You do your job to the best of your ability and you keep matters to do with it in perspective.

What happens to you at work is not a reflection on you personally. You do not evaluate your worth by what is said to you and about you at work. You realise that your true worth is not just about work. Only a very small part of you may be expressed at work. You do not take seriously things that are said to you at work. These things are said to the 'working you', not the entire you, not the complete person that is really you. Whatever is said or done at work, you keep a balanced attitude to everything and everyone concerned. Many, many factors are involved when you are at work. People have their own reasons, bosses have their own reasons, companies have their own reasons. The great majority of what is said and done has nothing to do with your place in the scheme of things. Instead it is a combination of many factors. You realise this and you do not take things seriously. What happens to you at work is like water off a duck's back – you simply do not take it too seriously. You do not let it affect you deeply. You realise that it is not about you personally, but simply about the 'you' that goes through the working day.

While you are at work you feel as if you are surrounded by a golden bubble. This bubble goes with you wherever you go, whatever you do, whoever you happen to be speaking with. It doesn't matter where you are at work or what you are doing; your glowing golden bubble is always in place. It keeps you protected from all that is negative, all that may be unpleasant in any way. Nothing can touch you. Your golden bubble radiates pleasantness to others. It is warm, welcoming and inviting. However, at all times it keeps you safe, it keeps you insulated, it keeps you secure and protected from anything that is negative or harmful.

You do your job to the best of your ability. You find ways of enjoying what you do more. You make the best of the tasks you have. It gives you pleasure to do well, to complete things, to be efficient. At all times, whatever you may be involved in at work, you do it to the best of your ability. At all times, you look for the positive aspects of the things you do, at the pleasant nature of what you have to accomplish. You feel pleased with yourself when you get to the end of the day and you know that you have put in some solid, worthwhile work. You feel good about your productivity and your positive attitude to what you do.

At all times you look for ways to improve your working life. You look for ways to do your job more efficiently. You look for ways to make your work more enjoyable for you and for your colleagues. You look for ways to be more comfortable at work. At all times you try to make the best of what you do and where you are because you know that will make life more pleasant for you.

Your working life is going so much more smoothly, so wonderfully smoothly. You have everything in its right perspective. Everything and everyone is met by you in a positive way. Everything and everyone is easier. You have everything in a balanced perspective and it feels good, it feels right, it feels very, very pleasant for you.

[Waking up procedure.]

Other Self-Hypnosis Approaches

If you feel you need more self-esteem, consider the Self-Hypnosis for Self-Esteem on page 237. If you want to maximise your luck, try the Self-Hypnosis for Luck on page 236. For increased calm, use the Self-Hypnosis for Relaxation on page 41. These may be suitable for your situation.

eight

Money Matters

'He that wants money, means and
content is without three good friends.'
Shakespeare, As You Like It

'Money is a good servant, but a bad master.'
Seventeenth-century proverb

attitudes to money

There is a lot of double-think in our culture, on the subject of money. On the one hand, most of us are preoccupied with acquiring it, but on the other we tend to be shame-faced about it, rarely divulging what we earn and hating to be thought too money-minded. Attitudes to money are very much affected by the matter/spirit split in our society. If we are at all religious, we tend to regard the material world as being inferior and potentially evil compared to the spiritual realms; we feel there is something not quite nice about 'filthy lucre' and that really good people don't bother about money. Meanwhile we are bombarded on every side by images that encourage us to concentrate on all the good things money can buy, as being what life is all about.

But what if matter and spirit are not split? What if they are on the same spectrum? Occultists believe that this is so and that this is one of the reasons charms work – by a system of harmonics. Thus roses on the material plane harmonise with love on the spiritual and so can be used in love charms. What if matter is as much a manifestation of the Divine as anything we might call spiritual? There is a growing trend today towards nature-based spiritual paths collectively called 'paganism' or 'nature worship'. Such people may worship the Goddess of Nature and believe that the earth is a showing forth of Her essence and Her body. If this is the case, then money, too, is part of this blessing. Even if you have no spiritual beliefs, it is quite possible to see money as energy – for that is, in effect, what it is.

Money is energy, money is power and money is freedom. Money is not the only important thing, or even the most important thing in life, but it is very important indeed. Being miserable is not so bad if you are rich! Money has a hand in almost everything in life, and while it is true that money cannot buy you love – and to the very rich love may be extra-elusive – it can buy you many things that make it easier to look good, get out and meet people and generally do the things that can put you in the way of love. Money may not buy you health precisely, but it is a known fact that the better-off are healthier and live longer, partly because they can afford the best food and lifestyle.

Never be shamefaced about anything to do with money. Like other forms of 'selfishness', getting money puts you in a better position to help others. It may free up time to spend with those who need you, allow you the means of transport to get to them and even the means for giving a helping hand, if you wish. But most of all, having enough money makes you feel good, and that good feeling spills out on others that you meet. After all, there is plenty to go round.

> **Top Tip**
> *Money is energy, money is power. Acquire it without shame. Use it with wisdom.*

Do you See Money as Energy?

Try this quiz to help you understand your attitude towards money.

1 **You always know exactly what is in your bank account:**
   a) yes, almost to the penny,
   b) you'd rather not contemplate your overdraft so you don't think about it if you can help it,
   c) you've got a rough idea and you know you can pay your bills.
2 **A bill comes through the door:**
   a) you feel grumpy – you don't like paying bills,
   b) oh no! – you kick it under the mat and try to forget about it,
   c) hmm – you knew it had to be paid and there is a funny kind of satisfaction in getting it sorted.
3 **It's your special friend's birthday and you are choosing a present:**
   a) you wear out yourself and your shoes walking around trying to get a bargain,
   b) you splash out on something you can't afford – that is if you remember the birthday at all,
   c) you love going round finding just the right thing to bring a big smile to the birthday face!
4 **You have a special date coming up and you see just the garment you want but it is twice the price you planned to pay. Do you buy it?**

money matters * 195

  a) no way – you never pay through the nose,

  b) you get out the magic plastic – you've got to have it!

  c) you try it on and if it looks great you figure it's worth it.

5 Here come the charity raffle tickets again!

  a) you shuffle around and pretend you've got no cash,

  b) you empty your purse or pockets – it's in a good cause after all,

  c) lovely! Two gifts in one, a chance to win and feel virtuous at the same time. You buy as many as you can afford.

6 You have the chance for the holiday of a lifetime, but you don't have enough cash and the only way you could manage to go would be by going a month in arrears with your mortgage:

  a) of course you wouldn't go – it would keep you awake at night if you were in arrears,

  b) you hope you're never put in that position because you're already badly in arrears,

  c) you'd go into arrears for something mega-special – life's too short not to.

7 The time has come to reckon up your accounts:

  a) you spend ages doing this and you've got everything set out in spreadsheets on your PC,

  b) what accounts?

  c) you do them as quickly as possible.

8 You took a risk and got caught out and now you have a parking ticket to pay:

  a) it keeps you awake at night – you can't bear to chuck money away like that,

  b) you write a long letter begging to be let off – it just isn't fair,

  c) you chalk it up to experience.

9 A wealthy relative gives you a large sum of money as a present:

  a) you insist on giving the money back – it doesn't feel right,

  b) you rush out and buy them an extravagant gift as a thank you,

  c) you accept with an obvious show of great pleasure – they can afford it, and you will enjoy it.

10 You are short-changed in a shop so you:

  a) point out the discrepancy and make sure you get every penny,

b) you've never been short-changed – or, more to the point, you probably didn't notice when you were,

c) you would notice if the amount was substantial and would ask for it to be put right.

Your Score

Mostly A: Your attitude to money is very 'bricks and mortar'. To you money is solid and finite. You need it round you for safety, and you need to know where you are with it and exactly how much there is available. You are practical and efficient up to a point, although you may waste time on details and energy on worrying. Sometimes money weighs heavily on you and that secure haven is more of a prison. Try to have faith that 'the Universe will provide' – you will feel happier.

Mostly B: To you money is like air – it flows around you and slips through your fingers. You just can't seem to keep track of it. Sometimes you panic, as it feels as if everything has been blown. Money seems to have a life of its own and to haemorrhage out at every opportunity. Truth to tell, you can't be bothered with money – sometimes you feel it's all a bit too mundane. But then it's the pits when you try to buy something you want and the cashier hangs on to your credit card. You would feel happier if you faced what's happening – it won't be as bad as you fear.

Mostly C: You do see money as energy for the most part – or at least you would be quite ready to with a bit of tweaking! As far as you are concerned you use it, it doesn't use you. You are aware that the value of money is relative – you bless what comes to you and you let go of what you need to. Actually 'let go' isn't really the phrase because all you give comes back to you and you are aware of this at some level. To you, money is a means to an end, but a valued and respected one. Continue to enjoy!

Tips for Money Self-Awareness

* If you feel guilty about money, be very aware of this. Unconsciously such guily can block you from using money sensibly and keeping

track of it. It may subtly lead you into bad decisions, unwise loans and investments, or simply into losing your purse!

* If you tell yourself you don't care about money, why are you saying this? Do you like to project a scatty image? Is this worth the price you may be paying – literally? (If this image is important to you, dress yourself in hippy gear and a vague smile, and stash the cash as well.)
* Do you feel you cannot make money? Do you find yourself saying, 'I never have any money; I'm not destined to be rich' etc? If so, these assumptions need to be dismantled – now! There is no reason why you should not have money – it's just a life map that you have drawn, a life script you have taught yourself. Change it.
* If your family never had money, do you feel that you come from a poor background and therefore will never be wealthy? In fact this just means you are not used to managing larger sums, but you can learn.
* One of the ways we can change our attitudes to just about anything is by directed day-dreaming. If you find yourself entering a dreamy mood, tell yourself to day-dream about making a lot of money – in as much detail as possible! Research shows that this type of practice does pay off, for instance top athletes first daydream that they are winners.

Money-Handling Tips

* While contemplating re-adjustments to your money attitude, consider your personality as a whole. Are you really a happy-go-lucky type who prefers to live for today? Or do you prefer to proceed in an orderly fashion from birth to death? There is no point telling yourself you ought to be one way, while behaving in the other, and living continually with the feeling you are missing something. What is 'you'? What makes you feel really okay? Follow that.
* If your attitude to money needs to change, buy a different purse. Take your time over this, see what appeals to you and ask yourself why. Is this going to be a secure and pleasant receptacle for your money? A purse that you like and feel comfortable with can have a subtle but far-reaching effect on your handling of money.
* Shield yourself from any advertising you know will have an effect on

you. In my case I find television advertising ludicrous and often irritating, but I am sometimes tempted by brochures that come through the door, which I may leaf through while having a cuppa! Mostly this is a mistake – if you want something, you don't need a leaflet to let you know! The remedy? For me it is to 'file' the brochures in the recycling immediately. What is your weak spot? Keep it covered!

* Work out a budget! I know this is stating the obvious, but unless you balance your outgoings and incomings, how can you manage? If you have the sort of personality that hates such constraints (and feels immediately compelled to spend when confronted by them!), one way round this may be to 'trick' yourself into thinking you have less money than you do by always knocking more off your balance than you have spent, by setting up a savings standing order and 'forgetting' about it, or by putting aside all your 20p coins for a rainy day.
* Somewhere inside you there is a talent that can make you money. This may not be mega-bucks, but a comfortable amount – believe it!
* Save a little – it's a strange thing but money in the bank has a magnetic quality; it seems to draw more to it, and I'm not just talking about the interest! There is something about knowing you have a nest-egg that makes you feel powerful, and powerful people make money.
* Set up a standing order into a savings account. Savings come in several categories – saving so you simply have money in the bank, saving a safety-net in case the roof falls in or the car blows up, saving to pay tax and bills. Your standing order should cover all these.
* If you are self-employed, you must have a separate account where you save for tax. Tax is inevitable. Console yourself by the fact that you will earn a little interest on the sum you save!
* Never be afraid to speak up for your money rights. Check your change, check your salary, ask for what is yours – because it is!
* Give to charity. This will make you feel good and is part of the flow of the Universe. You are making a valuable contribution; your self-worth will grow; your money will do good – it's a win-win situation.
* Be able to say 'no' with money as with all else. If you can't say 'no', say 'maybe' and play for time. If you don't want to give to repair the church roof, then don't – maybe you prefer to support Amnesty

International, and that is your choice.

> **Top Tip**
> *When money issues are faced, they always become more manageable. Take things in bite-sized pieces and reward yourself for your achievements.*

* Handle credit cards like Semtex – very carefully! They are the easiest way to get into overwhelming debt: the interest is phenomenal and they spell financial mayhem. Many people at the age of 40 have spent so much on credit card interest that they could have bought a second house with it – don't go there! If you really are tragic with the plastic, restrict yourself to only one credit card and leave this at home when you are window shopping.

* If your debts are worrying you, confront this. Never, ever leave bills unopened – once you have started to face up to things they become more manageable. This is common sense. If you are too scared to cope, ask a friend to help. Talk to your creditors, find ways to make debts manageable, and consult the Citizen's Advice Bureau. Be very careful about taking on another debt to pay off what you owe – is this really a step in the right direction? Never borrow to make payments, only to rearrange the balance. Prioritise debts so that the most important are covered first – i.e. the ones that could result in loss of home or property – and do not take on more debt.

keeping accounts

If you are self-employed, you will have to keep accounts and do your tax (groan!). For me this is the worst job ever, bar none. Here are some ways to make it bearable (almost!).

* Keep things simple – get yourself a large ring-binder or expandable book, create an 'In' column and an 'Out' column and write everything in about once a week. Keep receipts and confirmations of income in separate transparent envelopes in the ring-binder beside the relevant

month. Keep all receipts in a separate compartment in your purse/wallet until you decant them into your accounts.
* Create filing space (or buy a home-file, the size of a very large brief-case) for all the other relevant paperwork, such as bank statements, past tax returns, record of National Insurance contributions, etc. Even if you don't file things properly, you will know they are there somewhere.
* If you just find it all so boring, then make it nicer by having a special pen and putting some pretty stickers on your ring-binder, and dabbing it with lavender oil so it smells nice. Or stick a special photo on the inside of the cover to cheer you up.
* Promise yourself a small treat every time you do your accounts.
* Promise yourself a very large treat every time you sort out your tax return.
* Please do not delay filling in your tax return. Set aside a date in your diary, with the date of the arranged treat, and regard this as signed in blood.
* Consider asking a friend or relative who is good at this sort of thing to sort out your accounts for you.
* Consider getting an accountant – it is worth every penny to have the anxiety removed, at least in part.
* If you have never kept accounts and are all at sea, just make a start, now. Get the ring-binder and start keeping records. When you have done this for a month or two, it will seem more possible to get an idea of the pattern of your income and expenses and put something together.

cash in hand

Experts in palmistry tell us that our character shows in the shape of our hands and fingers and in the lines and mounts on the hand. Like all such systems, this is subtle and complex and it takes study and practice to read a palm accurately. However, there are clues about a person's money-management skills that can be gleaned with just a glance at the general proportions of the hand. Does this mean that we are fated by the shape of our hands to have a certain attitude to money? I believe we always have choices. Hand and finger shapes may be a useful clue fpr self-awareness, but if you wish to change your 'fate', work towards this!

Long, Thin Fingers These show an idealistic nature and someone who thinks before they act. This person may be a canny investor if they bring their mind to bear upon it, but they may be too high-minded to bother about money and so either abstractedly stash it away or spend it without due thought.

Short Fingers These show an impulsive character, and if the fingers are smooth this is accentuated. Here we potentially have the last of the big spenders, but hopefully the short-fingered person finds lots of other things to throw themselves into besides shopping!

Small Hands Hands that are small in proportion to the rest of the body show someone with big ideas. This person may have long-term financial strategies, but they are also quite acquisitive and may be very tasteful.

Large Hands These show a person who is concerned with detail. They may keep their accounts neatly, but the big picture could be lost and they may be over-cautious. Large hands often denote practicality.

Fat, Fleshy Hands These denote a life of ease – hardly surprising! But possessors of these hands are generally in love with life, so others find them pleasant to be with. This tends to attract good fortune. These people are self-indulgent, but they are also kind to others, and their creativity makes money.

Bony Hands and Fingers This person tends to philosophise about life and may be slow to think things through and even slower to take action. They may erect their own obstacles. They may find it hard to be motivated and may not readily part with what they have earned.

retail therapy

'Retail therapy' is a familiar phrase – most of us realise that buying something nice really is therapy in that it makes us feel good and may pick us up when we're down. Like most things in life, this is fine in moderation. However, if you find you compulsively buy things you never wear or use, or if you often splash out on stuff you cannot afford, then you need to ask yourself what it is you are really 'buying'. Are you buying love? This might be the case, for instance, for the woman who regularly shops for clothes to make her seductive, looks at herself in her bedroom mirror, decides this hasn't worked and goes out to buy some more. Are you buying beauty? However many lovely ornaments and pictures you have, seeing them every day makes them commonplace – so, more are needed. Are you buying time? One woman whose sister died of cancer found that she started going on regular shopping sprees, to try to 'buy' herself more life once she realised how finite it was.

If your shopaholicism is a major addiction and you aren't quite sure you understand it, take some time to commune with yourself. Light a green candle and heat some lavender oil so the scent calms and uplifts you. Imagine that you are sitting beside a clear stream – imagine the scene in detail, including sights, sounds, smells and sensations. When you feel truly calm, imagine a robed figure coming towards you along the bank of the stream. Hold out your hands, with a smile. What would you like this being to place in them? This may be something abstract or symbolic – in fact a symbol is most likely. If this exercise helps to reveal to you what else you want in life, do your best to get it, or a reasonable substitute – because a new frock or new car will not, in the end, fulfil you.

If you decide that your retail therapy is quite moderate but your cash is tight, then you can get lots of satisfaction rummaging for bargains at car boot sales or in charity shops. The good thing is this can take lots of time, so when you've finished the other shops will be closing! Some Internet sites offer cut-price options and second-hand clothes sales. Another cheap kind of retail therapy is to collect something inexpensive – one person I knew collected souvenir spoons wherever she went. I have started to collect fridge magnets. For less than a fiver you can come home with a little something in a bag. Sad? Not so! These are some of the many little blessings of life!

Try to remember that wanting is not the same as needing. There may be no limit to the things we want, and this can make for continual frustration. When overcome by a want, try looking around you at some of the nice things you already have and are taking for granted. Try also looking at pictures of life in the Third World, really imagining it and appreciating how fortunate you are by comparison. Wait for a while – if you really, really need that object you will still feel the same next week, and then you can take it from there. And if you can't resist that expensive purchase, keep the receipt and leave the label attached – having satisfied the urge to splurge you may later feel better if you take it back.

If your retail therapy is landing you with worrying debts then it is *not* therapy any more, but something that is adding to your stress. Try to take this on board. Shield yourself from advertising. Throw catalogues and junk mail in the recycling box – without looking! Get busy with something creative to take your mind off compulsive spending – you can do it!

being a miser – the anal retentive

If you really find it hard to part with money then it could be that there are elements of the anal retentive in you. This expression derives from psychoanalysis, in which toilet training is regarded as being one of the (many) things that affect our development. If in some way we were made to feel ashamed of our bowel movements, this can make us uptight in many ways. An excessively tidy person may be 'anal' – symbolically retaining their own mess! Money may be subconsciously regarded in the same way. (Recall the phrases 'filthy lucre', 'where there's muck, there's brass', etc.) Money, this 'root of all evil', this manifestation of the material world at its grossest, needs to be kept in. This is also simply about keeping tight control on all that is ours.

If you detect an element of the anal within your personality (and we all have this somewhere), take some time to commune with yourself (as for 'retail therapy' on page 202). Light a candle and oil, relax and imagine that you are in the same spot, by the stream. The robed figure comes towards you carrying a box. He or she stands some way away from you, downstream. In the box is your fear – it may be abstract or symbolic. The kindly being takes the fear out of the box, holds it up so you can see it, makes it shrivel and then drops it into the stream, where it is taken away from you, out of your life.

If you decide that you are hardly Scrooge but still like to save, then make sure your money works well for you. Invest it wisely in long-term accounts. Maybe you will enjoy studying the financial news and maximising your assets. If you feel your thriftiness is getting out of hand, then try to imagine how you will feel at the age of 90 with a pile of money in the bank and lacking the vigour to enjoy it. What will you wish you had spent it on? Remember that other old money cliché – 'you can't take it with you'!

Phoebe's Story

Phoebe could never make head nor tail of money. When her marriage split up and she was left to manage on her own with her two children, she was very quickly in extreme debt. The bailiffs were threatening her and her fridge was always empty – she was convinced she did not have enough money to get by. When a helpful friend intervened, giving her advice about claims she could make and bringing her finances up to date, Phoebe realised, to her surprise, that her yearly income was actually quite good. Why then was she not managing?

Phoebe saw that there was more at work here than lack of money and sought counselling. Through it she realised that for her, being 'skint' was a cry for help. She was actually afraid that if she was seen to be 'managing', her friends would not be so keen to rally round. She became aware that the only way she had ever received attention as a little girl was by creating a fuss, having an accident or getting into trouble. Although the attention she did get at those times was often unpleasant, at least it was attention. If she was well-behaved, she was usually ignored.

So it seemed that being bad with money was Phoebe's way of ensuring no-one forgot about her. Although it felt very scary at first, Phoebe took determined steps to sort out her life. She tidied her house and had an 'American supper' to which all her friends brought a contributory dish and she made sure that she didn't once mention any of her problems during the evening. She arranged meetings with friends for walks or to do sport and was soon happily reassured that far from reducing her social circle, she was more popular than ever. Furthermore everyone was full of admiration for the way she had 'got sorted'.

During difficult times Phoebe is aware that she is prone to relapse into being helpless and chaotic, but now she picks herself up sooner rather than later. She realises that she never really enjoyed being in a mess and that it never had the pay-off she imagined.

visualisation and meditation for money matters

Visualisation to Tune into the Bounty of the Universe

Watch as the curtains swing open on a green and gold land – the trees and the grass are in every shade of bright green to deep, rich green. In the damp shadows the moisture hangs like pearls. Where the sun touches the tops of the trees and the edges of the leaves it bestows a patina of gold. Walk up the steps and onto the stage and let this world take you into its embrace. *[Pause.]*

You find yourself close to a smoothly running stream. The water is tinged with gold and you realise that this is not just a gift of the sunlight – the water itself is radiating this golden glow. Within the water, great gold fishes swim lazily. You follow upstream, all the while admiring the brilliance of the scenery. Multi-coloured birds swoop and sing, luxuriant flowers bloom everywhere, and the glow of green, tinged with gold, pervades all. *[Pause.]*

Now, ahead of you, you see a waterfall, tumbling in a cascade of gold. Beyond the waterfall the green country disappears and all you can see is a mist. Fascinated by the waterfall, you decide to get into the water. It is warm and smooth. You splash over to the waterfall and stand beneath it. To your amazement you see that the water droplets are liquid coins of gold – as you catch them in your hands they condense, and when you let them go again, they are once more water. You stand beneath the flow for a while, admiring the beauty. *[Pause.]*

You notice that the eddying pool in which you are standing is bounded by rocks and that there are dry channels on the other side, extending into the mist. These channels appear grey and lifeless, not at all like the wonderful countryside you walked through in order to get here. You decide that you will move one of the boulders to see what happens. To your surprise it moves easily when you push it. Delighted, you watch as the golden liquid pours into the channel. *[Pause.]*

A wonderful thing is happening – along the channel where the water is pouring, the mist is clearing and brilliant greenery is rising up on either side. You decide to move another boulder and another, until all the dry channels are awash with the rich liquid. Ahead the vista is clearing in every direction and a bright landscape is revealing itself. *[Pause.]*

On a branch overhanging the pool you see a large green velvet bag. Gently you take the bag and walk with it to where the water falls in its golden cascade. You hold the bag under the flow and find it fills with heavy gold coins. You take it out from under the waterfall and find that it is completely dry and filled with coins. *[Pause.]*

You decide to follow one of the channels that you have opened, taking your bag of coins with you. Again, you walk through luxuriant countryside, until you come to a cave. Across the mouth of the cave hang fronds of emerald greenery. There is an atmosphere of great peace. Gently you part the strands and unveil the cave within. The walls appear to glow with their own light and everywhere you see the glint of precious stones set into the rock. On the smooth floor of the cave sits a shining being, radiating love and welcome. *[Pause.]*

You lay down your bag of gold before this being and ask what is the most important thing you should spend it on. Listen for the answer. When you are ready, give thanks and take your leave, taking one gold piece from the bag and leaving it behind you. Walk back past the waterfall and the pool until you arrive at the place where you entered this world.

Come down from the stage and see the curtains shut behind you. You are back in the auditorium. Place your bag here safely and come back to everyday awareness.

Write down what the being in the cave said to you. You do not have to make sense of it immediately if it seems obscure – just bear it in mind.

charms for money matters

A Charm for a Sum of Money

Choose a waxing moon to do this charm. You will need a nut to represent each pound, or each £10, or each £100, or £1,000, depending where you want to draw your limit. Cashews are a good choice but you can use any nut that you like the taste of. You will also require a large green candle and some oil of bergamot, plus some paper and a pen, and a glass of wine or juice.

Taking your time, rub some oil into the candle and as you do so imagine the money coming to you from a lucky source and what you will do with it. You do not have to imagine where the money is coming from in any detail – just its arrival. Don't rush this; enjoy it and savour every detail. Imagine holding the cheque or cheques; imagine making plans, shopping and enjoying.

When you are ready, light your candle and place the nuts close to it. Watch the flame and eat the nuts, one by one, still imagining the money coming your way. Write yourself a 'cheque' or a promissory note for the amount you need.

Pledge also a gift for charity or a needy friend that you will fulfil when the money comes to you. Drink a toast in your favourite tipple and pour a little out onto the earth afterwards.

Place your 'cheque' securely in your purse or wallet until its real-life equivalent arrives. The money may come from more than one place.

Quickie Money Charms

* Carry pieces of cedarwood or ears of wheat in your purse.

* Leave a bank note – the largest you can afford to be without – under your doormat during the waxing moon. Remove it while the moon wanes and replace it when you see the first crescent in the sky.
* When you see the first sliver of the new moon in the sky, turn over the money in your purse, pocket or wallet and say, 'As the moon swells, so will my finances.'
* Keep a pine-cone next to your account books and bank statements.

Charm to Be Rid of too Much Need for Retail Therapy

For this charm you will need some pretty wrapping paper or a box; some ribbon; green or gold paper and a pen to write on it; a joss-stick containing cedar or lemon; matches; a heat-proof dish or ashtray; leaflets, brochures or pictures representing the cravings you wish to be rid of (for instance, if you keep buying clothes, then you will need pictures of the kind of clothes that tempt you; if CDs, pictures of the kind of CDs you like, etc); and some tongs.

Light the joss-stick. Take up the pictures representing the cravings you want to be rid of, one by one, saying:

> 'I rid myself of empty cravings –
> In their place are healthy savings.
> By the power of my will,
> My earthly cup with joy I fill.'

Set light to the pictures and watch them burn to ashes in the ashtray.

Now take up the pen and paper and write on it something wonderful that you have in life that money cannot buy, such as a child, a talent for painting pictures, health, good friends, etc. You must write at least one thing for all the pictures or types of picture you burn.

When you have finished, wrap up your list of blessings in the wrapping paper or place it in the gift-box. Bind it happily with the ribbon. Throw the ashes away carefully outside.

Whenever you feel plagued by the urge to splurge, open your gift-box and savour your true riches.

A Charm for Orderly Accounts

If you just can't seem to keep track of your money, obtain a jigsaw of a beautiful scene in nature such as a cornfield, a magnificent tree, etc. The picture should be mainly green and/or gold. Find a small jigsaw if you can, or this charm will be too lengthy. You will also need a lavender joss-stick and your favourite drink.

Prepare for this charm by having a leisurely, relaxing bath. Light your joss-stick and settle down to do the jigsaw. Take sips from your drink if you wish and start to do the jigsaw, slowly, in a relaxed fashion. With each piece you put into place repeat the phrase:

> *'A place for all, all in place,*
> *All my money, keeping trace.'*

When the jigsaw is complete, celebrate by enjoying the rest of your drink. Put the finished article somewhere visible to inspire you.

Should you let things slip, break the jigsaw up, give it away and do another!

self-hypnosis for money matters

Self-Hypnosis for Money Management

[Usual induction.]

You are wonderfully relaxed – so gently, peacefully relaxed. Everything feels so safe, so comfortable, so balanced. In this relaxed state you can see that everything in the Universe has its place and that everything is beautiful. You are beautiful, the world is beautiful and money is beautiful.

Money is energy and it flows round and through all your plans for life. Money is a means to an end, money is there to be valued and managed. You value your money, you have a balanced attitude to your money, and you manage your money from a position of wisdom and detachment.

You are in control of your money – calm, controlled and sensible. You manage your money as a wise farmer manages his field. Of course, for the farmer there are always elements that cannot be controlled, such as the weather. In the same way there will always be elements in life that you cannot control. But these do not matter. To these you adapt, you adjust, you make sensible shifts in what you do according to what is necessary. The wise farmer selects seeds according to his needs and sows them according to the quality of his land. He applies fertiliser and irrigation where needed. He harvests in accordance with the weather. The wise farmer's fields are always fertile. Some yields are better than others, but they are always fertile.

Your life, too, is fertile. Money will always come to you because you are in tune with your abilities, your assets and your needs. You have the ability to make money and to manage money and that ability is growing with every day that passes. With every day that passes you are becoming more sensible, wiser, more resourceful in the way you deal with your money, until you acquire the state you wish to acquire, until all your money matters are constructive, orderly and a source of joy.

The wise farmer stores his harvest sensibly. If rain threatens, his crop is covered. If the wind blows, his crop is shielded and secure. If his neighbour is hungry, he has enough to help him out. You are like that wise farmer with your money. You know how to guard it, how to make it secure and when and where to release it. As the farmer relies on the soil and the cycles of Nature to produce what he needs, so you also rely on the powers of Nature, knowing that they also are at work in your life and that your money will be produced and will grow.

Like the wise farmer, your efforts bring forth fruit because you know just how to direct them. You direct your working efforts to the best financial result for you and all concerned. You use your energies sensibly and productively in earning money. At all times you keep things in perspective, not working too hard or too little and gaining as great an enjoyment from your working life as possible. At all times and in all places you remain aware of the value of your money, you husband it well, you arrange it well, and just like the wise farmer, you have enough for your own needs and those of others.

And you trust in the bounty of the Universe. While continuing all sensible efforts to make and manage money, you trust that the Universe shall provide. The Universe does provide. You trust, you believe, you know that there will always be enough money for you and your needs.

Now imagine that you are in the middle of a field. Around you, the soil is empty and brown, and the sun shines down. Now imagine that you have a pouch full of seeds in your hand. These are the seeds of all the ideas and plans you have for making money, managing money and using money. Walk slowly round the field, feeling the gentle warmth of the sun on your back and the firm earth beneath your feet, and smelling the scent of the soil as you scatter your seeds.

Now find shelter under a tree as the soft rain begins to fall upon the field. The rain is the water of life, the attention you bring and the blessing of the Universe. See how the seeds are sprouting and tiny shoots of green are appearing everywhere. The brown field is turning green.

And now the sun comes out again and the green shoots rise higher and higher until you are surrounded by luxuriant growth. Look around at the bounty you have grown. How wonderful this is! How blessed you are!

Spend some time simply looking around the field and know that you will always be able to create what you need in life. The field is yours to tend and harvest. And you manage your money sensibly; you manage it in a balanced way, a joyful way, a constructive way. And you keep this in mind with every day that passes.

[Waking-up procedure.]

nine

Problem Areas

'Don't meet troubles half way.'
Sixteenth-century proverb

'Laugh and the world laughs with you
Weep, and you weep alone
For the sad old earth must borrow its mirth
But has trouble enough of its own.'
Ella Wheeler Wilcox, 'Solitude'

identifying problems

Life is full of challenges and much of this book has been devoted to coping with them better. But what to do if the challenges are coming from within? What approach should we take when our minds in some way turn against us, making nightmares of simple things?

The sort of problems we may meet in this respect range from tension and stress – which are partially caused by external conditions – to fears, phobias, sleeplessness, anxiety and psychosomatic physical symptoms. We all get anxious, we all feel tense at times and we all get headaches and upset stomachs – how can we know when these problems are excessive and we need help? The answer is when they significantly interfere with our lives and/or when our responses are out of the range we may call normal. For instance, a fear of spiders that makes you jump and feel uneasy about a large one behind your chair is one thing; a fear so bad that you have to shake out all your clothes before putting them on and get hysterical over even a tiny spider being in the room is another.

We all have our 'funny little ways' and most of us have an irrational fear of something. Most of us have at some time lost sleep because we were worried about something or felt so tense we could snap. If we are sensible, we do something about this – have an early night, a long chat to a friend or a holiday. If things are getting out of hand, however, we may need a little bit more help, and the first step – as with so many things – is to be honest with ourselves.

Work through this list of statements to get an idea of whether your problem is getting out of hand. How many do you agree with?

* It interferes with normal life, e.g. going out with your friends, going on holiday, getting to work.
* You find you are often preoccupied by the problem – in other words, worrying about worrying.
* Your problem is making you miserable a lot of the time.
* You fear other people will not understand your problem.
* You often feel tired and hopeless.
* Your problem is steadily getting worse.

- Your future is to some extent on hold – you cannot see beyond your problem.
- You lie or evade issues to conceal your problem from others.

If you agreed with any of these statements, the chances are that your problem needs addressing – if you answered 'yes' to two or more then this is almost definitely the case. Here are some ways to address your problem area.

- Check out any rational component. For instance, if you cannot sleep, is your bed comfortable; if you fear being burgled, do you have good cause and can you take steps to prevent it?
- Eliminate the possibility of physical causes if this is relevant (e.g. in the case of irritable bowel) by checking with your doctor.
- Admit that you need help. This sounds obvious, but it is what stands in the way of so many people who feel they are being weak or stupid if they cannot overcome an issue themselves.
- Talk to friends – this can be enormously helpful and may make you realise you are not alone.
- Investigate books or the Net for more information.
- Be prepared to make changes in life. This does not mean that you have to give up your job because you have developed a phobia about going on the tube! It does mean being prepared to change your habits, approach and lifestyle. For instance, if you are a victim of stress, you need to be prepared to give up some time in order to learn to relax – whatever the pressures on you may be.
- Be prepared to examine yourself with an open mind and very honestly. You need to find out what has given rise to this problem. It may not be what it seems – in fact it is most unlikely to be what it seems. Most problems have their roots in childhood, cliché though this may be, and are linked to denied emotions, however unlikely this may seem. For instance, if your fear of heights became bad enough five years ago to prevent you going into high buildings, what happened around that time? And in what way might this have been triggered by some buried trauma from the past? (See Babs' Story on page 218.)

✷ Seek therapy. If your problem does not yield to any of the above approaches, don't hesitate to get professional help.

✷ some common problems

When you have a problem it can feel as if you are the only person in the world to suffer in this way, and the resulting feelings of isolation can make things worse. Being able to put a name to the problem can make it seem more manageable.

Phobia

A phobia is an irrational fear and can range from exaggerated terror of things which may be potentially dangerous, such as heights, to a fear of something apparently benign, such as bananas or balloons. A deeply repressed emotion or experience lies underneath the fear, but the nature of this can vary from person to person, and may be complex. It may be necessary to unpack the fear with a therapist, or possibly by yourself – although for deep-rooted matters there is no substitute for the supportive presence of someone who is used to exploring mental recesses. In the case of a fear of balloons, for instance, the balloon could represent some kind of forced gaiety that concealed very disturbing feelings at some point in life. Or it could be linked to loss of breath, as with one man whose mother had died while out at dinner, simply through choking. Or the anticipation of the balloon bursting with a bang might trigger memories of explosions – there is any number of reasons why a person might have a phobia about simple balloons. If you have a phobia, you may be quite resistant to probing, feeling that you just want the 'stupid fear' dealt with and not to examine the reasons. This is probably part of the mechanism that put the phobia there in the first place – in other words, when we have a phobia, at some unconscious level we choose that thing to fear because the real fear is more unbearable. A phobia is also more manageable. For instance, a fear of spiders has been linked to a negative mother complex. When we are children it is much, much easier to fear spiders, which someone can come and dispose of for us, than to deal with fears of any unbalanced or invasive aspect of Mother. Phobias may be helped by gently uncovering their roots and by hypnotherapy.

Obsessions and Compulsions

These too are a defence against unwanted feelings, but in this case the feeling aspect is even more repressed. Whereas in the case of a phobia fear is present, although not directed at its original cause, with obsessions there may be little feeling component at all, apart from frustration and a desperation to be rid of the debilitating compulsion. Obsessions can range from a compulsive need to wash one's hands every half-hour to highly complex and lengthy rituals that make it hard for the sufferer to live everyday life. Sometimes fear may indeed be present, as in 'If I step on the cracks something awful will happen to me.' Obsessions and compulsions are quite resistant to treatment because they rear up in the face of intervention – for instance, a patient with obsessive/compulsive disorder may find the need for ritual intensifies in connection with the appointment with the therapist. The pay-off for having the disorder is an illusion of control – 'If I do this, this and this, then nothing nasty can happen.' It is important to get as near as possible to the root of the fears and to use hypnotherapy firstly to help the patient relax.

Anxiety

This problem is very common – and life is a scary business. When we get run down, tired and overwhelmed, we may get into a state of mind where everything seems too threatening and worry surrounds us on all sides. Yes, there are always things to fear, and the state of anxiety has probably been triggered by a present event that reminds us of past trauma. For instance, losing a life partner is a very stressful event, but if it triggers a buried memory of infantile terror at out mother leaving us then life can become quite overwhelming. Hypnotherapy can soothe this fear and create more positive images.

Stress

Modern life is stressful and we all know this. If we are stressed to an unhealthy degree, this may be because we are trying to control too many things, hanging on to an illusion that we can indeed manage things that cannot be managed. Our culture gives us messages about the importance of coping, about all things being possible to the right person, all problems solvable, all targets achievable if we are good enough. Hypnotherapy is very helpful with this problem as it helps us not only to relax, but also to make contact with what we might call an internal core, a centre of eternal stillness within. It takes us out of the maelstrom, into a quiet space where we can re-orientate ourselves.

Sleeplessness

Sleeplessness may start as a result of anxiety keeping us awake and then becomes a condition in itself. The sufferer grows to expect not to be able to sleep, tenses up and then cannot sleep. Worry about not sleeping takes over from whatever worry caused the initial sleeplessness and a downward spiral begins. Possibly there could be another, more deep-seated concern – it is easier to come to a therapist, for instance, for treatment for sleeplessness than it is to address the fact that we want to leave our partner, are afraid we can't do our job or do not want to face the possibility that we are gay. Sleeplessness can be a displacement although it is more usually simply a result of continuing stress.

Depression

Often spoken about, true depression is a state of utter bleakness and is desperately unpleasant. Here the level of consciousness is, in effect, lowered. If we are truly depressed we are hardly conscious of a beautiful spring day, but only of our internal demons or our all-encompassing lassitude. Depression may be caused by repressed emotion, for instance anger, which is too scary or potentially destructive to be faced and so eats up the sufferer from inside. Another aspect of depression is that it may be a prelude to a breakthrough, when the unconscious literally breaks through and a period of creativity may follow. Hypnotherapy can help with depression because in the relaxed hypnotic state there are fewer barriers to expression of the true self and there is an ability to connect with the wellsprings of life within, with which the depressed person has lost contact.

Irritable Bowel and other Physical Manifestations

There is a school of thought that attributes all illness to the mind, because mind and body are an interconnected system. While I agree with this in theory, it is not always a useful approach in practice and may sometimes sound horribly like blaming the victim! Some physical ills are treated brilliantly by modern medicine, such as with hip replacement surgery for arthritis, while others yield better to a mixture of conventional, alternative and psychological approaches, e.g. cancer. Yet others are principally helped by the psychological method. Among these irritable bowel is a prime example. Again, the irritable bowel is in all probability flagging up an emotional problem – for instance, a woman who has lost her husband may express her fear of being alone in the world by having her 'stomach turn to water' in inconvenient places such as in the bank or on a bus. Hypnotherapy helps by soothing the fear and re-building faith in our ability to cope, besides fostering relaxation in those circumstances in which the problem might be expected to rear its head.

> **Top Tip**
> *Sometimes we need to let go of the idea that we can control everything and just concentrate on being 'okay' as we are.*

Babs' Story

Babs came to me for hypnotherapy because she was afraid of enclosed spaces, especially lifts. As far as she could remember, this had always been the case but it had started to become unmanageable about ten years earlier. When she came to see me, she had reached a point where she could not even manage to take the lift to her office, on the tenth floor! When she needed – but was unable to face – a total body scan for suspected gall-bladder problems, she sought help. Babs was a practical woman and wanted this debility 'fixed'. She could not see how it related in any way to her past life and was quite resistant to answering questions about her past until I explained to her that although it didn't feel that way to her, the likelihood was that some past trauma lay beneath her fear. It transpired that Babs' father had died suddenly in a car accident when she was eight. Dad never came home that night and was never again spoken about. The family rallied round and Babs continued to have a happy childhood – as far as she could recall. The death of her mother, ten years ago, coincided with an increase in her claustrophobia.

I explained to Babs that, strange though it might sound, there were likely to have been feelings within her at the time she lost her father, that were too awful even to be felt. These would have gone into her unconscious. When her mother died, these feelings were reactivated to some extent, but still not recognised. People may experience a sensation of panic when traumatised, as if trapped in an unbearable reality. Babs, focused on coping, had not experienced this as such – instead her feelings had attached themselves to something quasi-reasonable, i.e. lifts, which do indeed sometimes malfunction.

With this understanding in place, Babs was more enthusiastic about the therapy. Understanding that talking about her feelings might be therapeutic in itself, she opened out. By a mixture of counselling and hypnotherapy to address the fear, Babs recovered to the point where her fear did not interfere with her life.

visualisation and meditation for coping with problems

Visualisation to Cope with Fear

You may use this visualisation exercise for any fear, depression or problem that seems appropriate. Use it in conjunction with charms and/or self-

hypnosis for the best results. Make sure that you are as relaxed and contented as possible before you begin.

Find yourself in your familiar auditorium and watch the curtains open on a countryside scene. Walk up onto the stage and find yourself walking along a sunlit path in the country. Look around you and notice all the details, the sun dappling the fields, the greenery, the blue sky, the animals and plants. Feel the sun on your face and the breeze rippling your hair. Smell the scents of plant, earth and stone. Hear the many country sounds – insects buzzing, animals making their noises, the breeze in the trees, a tractor, an aeroplane.

Walk along the country lane until you find a place that you really like. This place is special to you – it is particularly to your taste. It may be a shady spot beside a tinkling stream or by a lake. It might be a sunny, sheltered place or one that offers wide, rolling views. Whatever it is, it should feel right to you. If you wish, you may have with you a friend – either someone from real life or completely imaginary – to walk and talk with you

Settle yourself in your special place (with your companion beside you, if you so wish) and look around you. Take in every detail – the colours, the sounds, the scents, dwelling especially on anything that you find particularly lovely. Feel yourself drawing strength from your surroundings so that you are radiant with power – see this power shimmering around you.

When you are ready, imagine your fear in front of you. Turn it into an animal, a plant or an object – or group of objects. Talk to your companion about it if you like. See it in every detail, through the shining aura of power that surrounds you. How ugly it is! And how weak, how stupid, how irrelevant! It is an unimportant, trivial, nasty little thing! See, it is shrinking, getting smaller and smaller. How weak it is growing, how puny! – it is getting tinier and tinier. Now it vanishes – pop! – and the air is clear.

Congratulate yourself on the way you have disposed of your fear, on the way you have faced it and taken away its power. If you wish, talk to your friend about this.

When you are ready, look again towards the place where your fear was standing. And now see that in its place is a shining crystal of a colour you find especially beautiful.

Pick up the crystal and walk back along the path with it in your hand. Bid farewell and thank you to your friend at the place where you met.

Make your way back to the stage and walk down into the auditorium, still holding your crystal, as the curtains swish shut in your wake.

Place your crystal somewhere safe in the auditorium and come back to everyday awareness. If you wish, you could seek out a crystal to keep with you in the everyday world to remind you of your experience.

charms for coping with problems

Two Charms for Coping with Fears, Phobias and Other Miseries

These simple charms will help you to reconnect with the natural world and to return your fear or problem to the Cosmos. You may feel very isolated but the symbolism of the charms will help, at an unconscious level, to dispel that feeling and to give you some measure of connection.

Charm One For this you will simply need a black stone. Wander around your locality and pick up a stone that seems to fit your fear or depression. Preferably when the moon is waning, carry your stone to a peaceful site beside a river or stream. Hold the stone in your left palm and pour into it all your misery, your fear, your depression or your anxiety. When you are ready, hurl the stone as far downstream as you can. Say:

> 'With this stone
> My fear [anxiety, stress or whatever] has flown.
> Sufferings cease;
> I am at peace.'

Repeat this as often as you like. Boost this charm with self-hypnosis and other forms of help as mentioned above.

Charm Two For this you will need a balloon and a marker pen. Choose a balloon of the colour you think most appropriate – yellow for fear, black for depression, etc. Blow up the balloon and tie it so it will not deflate.

Write or draw on it the thing you want to be rid of (be careful as you may not want to advertise your problem to the world). Take the balloon to a hilltop when there is a breeze and let it go into the atmosphere. Say:

> 'Fly balloon, fly
> Into the sky.
> My problems blown away
> This happy day.'

Repeat this charm as often as you like, although you may need to adapt it for frequent usage. The sad thing about this charm is that it is not environmentally friendly as balloons have their drawbacks. If you know a place where you can obtain biodegradable balloons, then use as many as you like. Otherwise you could make a little kite from lolly sticks and tissue paper (if your fear is of balloons you would need to do this anyway!). Alternatively, you could capture a windblown seed, name it for your problem and let it fly off into the wind, taking your troubles to seed good things instead. This charm will also need to be helped by self-hypnosis.

self-hypnosis for coping with problems

Self-Hypnosis for De-stressing

[Usual induction.]

Now you are so wonderfully relaxed. Your whole body is beautifully and pleasantly relaxed and your mind feels so tranquil and peaceful. You are floating gently down a blue stream, following the gentle ripples, rocking sweetly, softly, serenely. Down, down, down the stream and with every ripple you become more relaxed. Everything is smooth, everything is easy. You have a blissful feeling of total relaxation flooding your mind and your body. Green leaves cast soft shadows on you as you float down the stream, down and down and down.

You are so beautifully relaxed, and because you are so deeply relaxed, the feeling of relaxation is staying with you. In ordinary life you are keeping with you as much of this relaxation as you need. It feels so good; it feels wonderful; it feels right. With each day you feel calmer, more serene, and that means that everything and everyone is dealt with positively by you; everything and everyone leaves you calm. Your mind is clear and sharp and you focus on things in a quiet, sensible and efficient way. Of course, at times things and people may challenge you – that is to be expected. It is perfectly natural. But everything and everyone is easier to deal with. Your mind feels free and able to concentrate on what is important in your life. You keep things in perspective.

With each day that goes by, you are feeling and you are becoming more and more relaxed. And with each day that goes by you are feeling and becoming more and more mentally calm. And with each day that goes by you are feeling and becoming more and more confident. When you are mentally calm and physically relaxed, confidence is a natural outcome. You are able to be yourself. You are able to keep in mind your own priorities. You keep things in perspective. You know how to look after yourself. You are more confident in yourself, more confident in your ability to cope with people and situations, more able to enjoy life, much happier about the future.

With each day that passes, you are feeling and you are becoming more and more mentally calm, more and more relaxed in your body, so all tension disappears. All fear disappears. All negativity disappears. When you feel mentally calm and physically relaxed there is no room within you for tension or for negative feelings. There is simply a pleasant sensation of relaxation, optimism and feeling ready for anything. With each day that passes, you are feeling and you are becoming more and more mentally calm and more and more physically relaxed.

Think now about your body. Feel the relaxation flowing down, from the top of your head, over your face and neck, over your shoulders, down your arms and hands, down over your chest, your back, your abdomen, your pelvis, your thighs, calves and feet. Feel the warm, pleasant relaxation flowing down through your body. With each day that passes, this pleasant feeling stays in your body. Every day you keep with you this feeling of relaxation. Through each ordinary day you retain this wonderful feeling of physical relaxation. And you are dealing with everything, with every person, with every circumstance, so much more calmly, in a so much more relaxed a way, so serenely. And you are noticing, perhaps by only small signs at the beginning, but definitely noticing that you are truly coping so much more calmly and easily and effortlessly with everything, everybody and every situation. So you know that you are truly becoming a calmer, more relaxed, happier individual, a more positive, serene and optimistic individual.

The problem that you have been experiencing is fading, it is receding, it is dying. You are leaving it behind, in the past, and that is where it belongs. And you feel fine, you feel good, you feel great. The many, many benefits of this increased feeling of confidence and serenity are steadily growing. Everything and everyone has a more positive effect on you than in the past. It feels as if a weight is being lifted up off your shoulders, leaving you free to make choices, to move forwards, to enjoy yourself more and to achieve more – all in a state of pleasurable relaxation. And so you continue to enjoy this wonderful feeling of mental calmness and physical relaxation. Beautifully relaxed, wonderfully relaxed, pleasantly relaxed…

[Usual waking-up procedure.]

Self-Hypnosis for Disposing of Fear

This example addresses a fear of using a lift – basically claustrophobia – but it can be adapted to fit any fear. For instance, if you are dealing with fear of flying, start with thinking about the holiday, booking the flight, packing, driving to the airport in as much detail as you can. If you are dealing with agoraphobia, start with thinking about someone phoning up and asking you to go out, making plans, setting a time, getting up and getting ready, putting your coat on, etc. It is particularly valuable to be helped by a friend to compose and record a script to help you face your fear.

[Usual induction.]

You are wonderfully calm, feeling serene and contented. Enjoy this feeling of comfort, enjoy the sensation of tranquillity, enjoy this feeling of peace. Beautifully relaxed now, deeply relaxed. Relaxed in mind and relaxed in body. Feeling in harmony with the Universe, feeling a sense of optimism, feeling positive.

Now imagine your fear in front of you – see it as an animal or an object. See it any way you want – it cannot hurt you. Now make it shrink. See, it is becoming smaller and smaller. How weak and powerless it is! Now make it disappear altogether – you do not need it; it is not important; it is gone.

Now imagine you are walking towards the building where you know the lift will be – very calmly, very happily. You are remembering which floor you need to get to; you know that you want to get to this floor. It is important; it is pleasurable; it is something you want to do. You know the only way to get there is in the lift and you feel relaxed, you feel fine, you feel okay.

[Pause while you keep affirming okayness.]

Now you are going in to the building and you feel very serene. There is a smile on your face. You are making progress towards the place you want to be. You will be going in the lift like everyone else and that is fine. It is perfectly okay and you feel relaxed. In fact there are important and pleasurable things on your mind. You are looking forward to being where you want to be, doing what you have to do.

[Pause and continue with positive affirmations.]

Now you can see the lift in front of you. People are waiting to use it. They are relaxed, they look pleasant, they are smiling. You are smiling, you are serene, you are contented. You can see the light is flashing. The lift is coming. Soon the lift will be here and that is good because soon you will be able to go to the important appointment you have that you are looking forward to keeping.

[Pause and continue with positive affirmations.]

The lift has arrived, the bell rings and the door opens. You feel very calm, very tranquil and poised – that is good, everything is fine. You are smiling, feeling happy and content to be getting were you need to be. Along with everyone else you get into the lift. You get into the lift. You simply get into the lift.

[Pause and continue positive affirmations.]

Now the lift doors are closing and there is a swishing noise as the lift starts to move. All around you the people are looking pleasant. You feel truly calm, very relaxed and happy, thinking about the place you want to be, glad that things are going forward smoothly. You smile as the lift takes you to where you want to be.

[Pause and continue positive affirmations.]

The lift is stopping and the door slides open. You feel good, satisfied to be where you are going, very pleased. Serene and contented. It has been smooth and easy to get where you need to be. You are looking forward to your trip back down in the lift when you have completed your assignment.

Wonderfully relaxed, beautifully relaxed, feeling pleased with yourself that you have done what you set out to do, that you have gone about your business without hindrance, that you have kept things in perspective. Feel pleased with yourself for this victory. Feel pleased with yourself for being calm and relaxed. Feel pleased with yourself for doing what you set out to do in a serene and easy manner.

[Usual waking-up procedure.]

ten

Living a Charmed Life

'Happiness is not having what you want,
it is wanting what you have.'

'Happiness is a choice, not a result.'
Popular sayings

being happy

Much of this book has been about getting things you want, such as a relationship, or a job. It is very easy to believe that if we had certain things, then we would be happy. Naturally it is easier to be happier under fortunate circumstances, but nonetheless some of the most depressed people have everything going for them. Everything rests on the way we look at things.

I must say I am fascinated and humbled by the things I can learn from those people who come to me for help. One of the most memorable comments was made by a young man who came to me for treatment due to a fear of enclosed spaces. During the therapy we worked on his general relaxation and coping mechanisms. Although his phobia appeared to be easing, he did not have the opportunity to test this out thoroughly before the therapy had to end, due to his going abroad. But he said to me, 'I have learned to look at life in a different way. I am so much more serene and really it doesn't matter if I do still have my phobia!'

Nothing in life is bad or good, but thinking makes it so. So how do we achieve that positive state of mind that finds happiness natural? Many of the visualisations and hypnotherapy scripts in this book will help you on your way towards this – if not all the time, then more of the time. Here are a few practical things you can do.

* Take every opportunity to get out into Nature.
* Touch trees – they really do have a healing presence!
* Try to be positive and count your blessings. It is so easy to take things for granted. My eldest son once went missing for a night. All that had happened was that I had got my wires crossed over a message he had left, but I was up all night worrying. When he rang the next morning it was like being re-born! I try to imagine that feeling whenever I'm starting to get negative – how wonderful life really is!
* Try to live in the moment as much as you can – notice the scent of a rose, the beauty of the full moon.
* Prioritise friendships and human bonds – they are more important than routines and commitments.
* Be prepared to review your life priorities, even on an hourly basis.

Remember, no-one ever said on their deathbed that they wished they'd spent more time at the office, or cleaning the bathroom!

* If you have children, spend time with them. They won't be children for long.
* If you love doing something, do it as often as you can.
* If you find something beautiful, bring it into your life.
* Always have something to look forward to.
* Live each day as if it were your last.

> **Top Tip**
> *Being spiritual doesn't have to mean that you withdraw from the world – it can mean that you actually enjoy it more!*

a spiritual path

The wonderful thing about having a spiritual path is that it makes sense of the Universe and puts things into perspective. It gives you a feeling of belonging, and of being part of the scheme of things; it connects you to all that is around you and makes it glow. The pros and cons of different types of spirituality are outside the scope of this book. However, if you feel that spirituality is lacking in your life, the various forms are certainly worth exploring. Do not be put off by rules and dogmas – these are man-made and have nothing to do with spiritual awareness. If the conventional monotheistic religions do not appeal, look into Buddhism or Paganism. It is written, 'Seek, and ye shall find.' Not everyone has a road to Damascus experience and it is possible to find one's way by beginning with intellectual research. When you find your spirituality, make time in each day, however small, for your observance.

visualisation and meditation for living a charmed life

Finding your Spirituality

This is a visualisation you may like to do over and over again as you explore what your spirituality means.

Sit in your auditorium until the curtains open and you see before you a beautiful courtyard. Go up the steps and find yourself within the courtyard. The stone is white marble. Fountains play and many-coloured flowers cascade over the pearly walls. There is an atmosphere of peace and sanctity. Your courtyard may have other people within it or it may not.

Ahead of you there is a wide flight of shallow steps, leading to a smooth path. The path winds ahead, between rows of blossoming trees. You climb the steps and begin to walk along the path. Blossom is strewn over the path and as you walk upon it a sweet fragrance is released.

Walk the path slowly, noticing everything you see. Are you alone or are there people accompanying you? What does the landscape beyond the trees look like?

Ahead of you there is a small structure that is entered through an archway. The path is leading up to this archway. Around the structure many beautiful flowers grow, and within there shines a light. The structure is a shrine.

Walk slowly towards the shrine, with a feeling of reverence and expectation. As you come close, take off your shoes. Feel your feet on the cool, smooth floor as you enter into the shadows and the interior becomes clearer.

In front of you there is an altar and upon it burns a lamp. What else is on the altar? Is anyone else there? There may be a teacher or guru waiting for you, or this may be a solitary visit. Look at the altar and all around the shrine. What is the shrine there to worship, honour or commemorate? How do you feel? What do you wish to do?

As you look at the altar, the light upon it grows in brightness and splendour until it fills your vision. You close your eyes but the warmth rises within you until you feel that you are the light, shining and radiant. Feel the light coming from you; feel joyful and energised.

When you are ready, open your eyes and see that the light has dimmed to its former brightness. But now there are three gifts waiting for you. One is a book, one is a crystal and the other is a key. You also must leave an offering – what would you like this to be? Is there a pledge you feel prepared to make?

Pick up your three gifts. Taking your leave respectfully, turn around and make your way back to the courtyard. Go down the marble steps. The fountains still play and peace pervades. Find your entrance point. You are back on the stage. Go down into the auditorium as the curtains swing shut and the sound of the fountains disappears.

Take your three gifts into the auditorium and sit with them. Place the book on your lap. What is its title? Open it – what is in it? What does it say? Can you see any of the writing? Maybe the writing is invisible, but you hear some words in your head. Take your time. Take note of whatever you see, however meaningless it may seem.

Put the book to one side and take up the crystal. Feel its cool, smooth surface. Cradle it in your hands. Can you feel anything on its surface? Look deep within it. It is beautiful. Can you see anything inside its depths? Look carefully and take note, however unimportant it may seem.

Place your crystal safely to one side and pick up the key. Examine it – what sort of key is it? How does it feel? Are there inscriptions on it? What sort of gate or door do you think it opens? Are you prepared to use it?

Place your objects safely in your auditorium and come back to everyday awareness when you are ready.

a charm for a charmed life

Charm for Spirituality

Charm spirituality into your life simply by making space for it. All you need for this is a small shelf or cupboard top that you can use as an altar. Cover it with a cloth if you like. Set a night-light on this, in an attractive holder. Place flowers here, burn joss-sticks and ask yourself what else would seem appropriate. These things may include small statuettes, symbols, plants, precious or semi-precious stones, pictures, etc. These may be a key to your spirituality. Do not worry if they are unformed or do not seem to you to make sense. You may like to tend your altar regularly by renewing the flowers or joss-sticks, by putting a different colour cloth in place or in any way that appeals. Decide what days are most suitable to you to mark. Does it feel right to do this on Sundays? Or days of the full or new moon? Sunny days, rainy days, your birthday or that of a loved one, anniversaries – the choice is yours. Keep a diary of what you have done with your altar to see how you develop.

self-hypnosis for a charmed life

Any self-hypnosis that relaxes you is likely to help you in a spiritual search because it will relieve tension. Tension is the great barrier between us and our instinctive perceptions of the Eternal. Dissolve yours!

appendix one

charm correspondences

Here is a short list of correspondences for your charms. You can use it to make up your own charms if you wish!

Business Bloodstone, malachite, red for energy, green for commercial growth, yellow for creative ideas, almond, oak, pecan, honeysuckle, pine, the God Mercury.

Clarity/Cleansing Salt, white, lavender, benzoin, running water, flame.

Fertility Moonstone, green, figs, grapes, peaches, rice, the Goddesses Ceres and Demeter, the moon – especially waxing and full.

Friendship Turquoise, rose quartz, pinks, blues, lemon, sweet pea, the Goddesses Venus and Kuan Yin.

Health Amber, amethyst, red for energy, blue for soothing and calming, green for healing and new growth, orange/gold to cheer and hearten, lemon balm, eucalyptus, garlic, the Goddess Isis.

Love Rose quartz, lapis lazuli, pink, red, sometimes blues and greens, roses, thyme, ylang ylang, lavender, jasmine, doves, swans, rings, hearts, the Goddesses Venus, Aphrodite and Freya.

Money Emerald, jade, green, gold, almonds, patchouli, cedarwood, wheat, Mercury (the God of commerce), Venus (the Goddess of cash) and Jupiter (the God of prosperity).

Peace Amethyst, aquamarine, sapphire, blue and lilac, hyacinth, rose, lavender, gardenia, the Goddess Kuan Yin.

appendix two

a few more helpful scripts

Here are some more visualisation and self-hypnosis scripts that you may find useful generally or for dealing with specific issues, such as increasing your sense of self-esteem or stopping smoking.

Meditation for Coping with Abuse and Negative Experiences in a Relationship

Prepare yourself for your meditation by ensuring that you have space for yourself, physically and mentally, and that you cannot be disturbed – certainly not by the abuser. Take a bath with lavender oil, heat the same oil in your burner and light a white or blue candle, if you wish.

Settle yourself peacefully and let a dreamy feeling come over you. Close your eyes. Find yourself in the auditorium. The stage is before you and the curtains swing wide. Go up the steps, onto the stage and into quiet, shaded woodland.

The woodland is sweetly fragrant. Underfoot the soil is springy and the healing presence of the trees enfolds you. The air rings with birdsong and is pleasantly cool against your skin. Wander around the woodland, touching leaves, tree-trunks and flowers and noticing all you see. *[Pause.]*

Ahead of you, you spot a tangled path, going deeper into the wood. You decide to follow it. You move slowly, pushing away fronds and branches as you go. The song of the birds is even more beautiful here, and ahead you are sure you can catch the sound of running water.

You come to a crystal stream and stop for a moment to look into the water. Never have you see water so pure and clear. In it dart small fish, brightly coloured and shining silver. You stoop to put your hand in the water and it feels fresh and silky. You put a drop to your lips and it tastes sweet.

The stream now runs beside the path. You walk on and soon come to where a waterfall cascades over rocks into a silver pool. You decide that you will take off your shoes and paddle in the pool. The bottom of the pool is smooth rock and your toes spread out in the pure water. You walk towards the waterfall – you have never seen water with such a sparkle. A million rainbows dance in the cascade. *[Pause.]*

Do you wish to be bathed by this magical water? If so, take off your clothes and stand beneath the waterfall. Feel the enchanted water taking away all the hurt, the fatigue, the fear and oppression you feel in your relationship. Feel it washing off all the negative feelings you have about yourself, such as guilt, lack of self-esteem and weakness. Stand under the waterfall for as long as you like, naming everything you want the water to take away. Feel it all leaving you, so you are fresh and purified.

When you are ready, step through the waterfall and find yourself in a grotto. The walls are slightly luminous and precious stones glint in the nooks and crannies. You walk into the grotto and become aware of a wonderful presence. Ahead of you a female figure sits on a rock, radiant with love, robed in blue. She motions you to sit down on a rock in front of her and you do so, finding the rock smooth and surprisingly warm.

You know that you can tell this being all the troubles and hurts that you have. Tell them all slowly and listen for any answers that come. These may not be specific solutions, but they will be insights. Ask what your part in the relationship is, why are you being treated this way, why are you allowing it, what there is within you that attracts this. Give this time – you may not get all the answers at once.

When you are ready, respectfully take your leave. Pledge a small offering, such as planting some seeds or doing something good for yourself as an act of worship to the Powers of Life, such as having a massage or buying a hyacinth. The being herself may give you a gift. Take it with you. Pass through the cave and come out through another entrance, finding yourself back on the stage.

Come down the steps and into the auditorium, where you may leave your gift, if you were given one. Come back to everyday awareness and make a note of your experiences, the answers you got and the nature of your gift, which is probably symbolic.

Self-Hypnosis for Luck

[Usual induction.]

Because you are now so beautifully relaxed, there are no barriers between you and all the luck that is out there waiting for you. You are open to luck, you welcome luck into your life, you know that you can be lucky, that you will be lucky. You deserve only the best, and the best is coming towards you. You welcome it, because you know that is what you want. It is what you need, what you have been waiting for.

You smile when you realise how lucky you are. Your whole being opens to welcome these new and wonderful experiences. How wonderful life can be! How much you are able to enjoy life! How many wonderful experiences there are, out there, waiting to be had! You are going to sample them all, in due time, one by one.

You are open to new experiences now; you are willing to try anything that is sensible. Fresh ways of doing things attract you; you want to explore, you want to try things out. How interesting it is to see what works for you, what new things you can do, what you can feel and enjoy. You are smiling as you think of all the new things that are waiting for you.

With everything that happens, you are able to see a positive side. You are open with yourself about how you feel. You do not conceal your emotions, but you are able, always, to see a positive side to the events that occur. There is a good side to everything. Something beneficial comes, and will come, from all circumstances. There is always an advantage, even to the most challenging circumstances. You smile as you meet the world; you know that you can turn anything to your advantage, even if this is only a very little bit at first. But you know that you can make anything good.

You are beautifully open to all the blessings of life that are out there waiting for you. Think about how wonderful life is. Think about flowers, rainbows, sunshine. Think about music and dancing. Think about fragrance, taste, touch. Think about anything that you especially like, anything that gives you pleasure. What a wonderful world this truly is. How lucky you are to be able to enjoy it! How much luckier you are becoming, because you are now even more open to all the positive things that are waiting for you.

You smile when you meet life. You are smiling now. A smile comes readily to your lips at all times. You are ready to welcome life, to appreciate it, to see the positive in all you have contact with. Whatever happens, you feel optimistic about the outcome – you know it will be for the best. Because you are so open, so optimistic, so positive, you know that you can turn anything to your advantage. Even when things do not look so good for a while you find a way to turn them to the good, and you keep trying, in different ways, in sensible ways, until you succeed. You have a calm and relaxed attitude, a confident attitude, a pleasantly self-assured attitude.

As the days go by, you notice changes in your life, changes for the better. At first this may be in small ways, and these grow. You notice the difference; other people notice the difference. You are aware that things are getting better, and you smile, because you welcome this. You enjoy smiling; smiling gives you pleasure.

Now imagine one thing you are going to do in the near future. Imagine it in as much detail as you can. *[Pause.]* Imagine completing this task, completing it in just the way you would like to. Imagine you are doing it well. *[Pause.]* Imagine you are doing it excellently. *[Pause.]*

When you have completed this task to your satisfaction, when you are pleased, when you feel good about what you have achieved, then you can wake up. Come back to everyday awareness, feeling really good about what you have done, what you are going to do. Feel truly confident and optimistic about your lucky, lucky future.

[Usual wake-up procedure.]

Self-Hypnosis for Self-Esteem

Before doing this hypnotherapy session, think of three things you have done in life that make you feel good. If you feel so low that this is hard, think as far back into the past as you need to – there will always be something. Nothing is too small to pat yourself on the back for, from the time you gave 10p to charity to making a sandwich for a friend. Start with this sort of thing if you have to – as time goes by you will realise there is so much more to feel good about.

238 ✳ a charmed life

[Usual induction.]

You are now so wonderfully relaxed that there is room only for the positive within you. You feel in harmony with yourself and the world. There is peace within you and without you. You see the beauty in all things, especially yourself.

At all times you focus on the good things that you have done. You remember your achievements, however small they may be or however large. You feel good about these achievements. Well done. You did well! Think about these achievements and the positive effects they had. Feel good about them. Feel a glow start within you and grow. Think about the good things you have done and feel pleased.

[Short pause.]

Now you are so beautifully relaxed, you understand the importance of being positive. From now on you focus only on the positive. At all times you recall your abilities, your talents and your achievements, and you build upon them. Strength is growing within you. How strong you are! And you are growing stronger each day. When challenges come along you find a way to deal with them. You remember past successes, however small, and you know that you can build on these, so that you deal with everything, and with everybody, more calmly, more sensibly and more effectively, and that effectiveness is growing.

You are feeling more confident. There is a glow of confidence around you, whether you are at home, at work, socialising or doing ordinary things like shopping. You feel calm, confident, relaxed and determined to do your best and get the best out of life. At all times you recall your successes, your achievements, your good deeds, and you know you can build on them. You do build on them. You feel pleased with yourself for building on all the good things you achieve.

Imagine yourself standing on a hill in the sunshine. You feel free, positive, optimistic, peaceful and happy. Feel the sunlight on you. Feel it settle on you and surround you, like a corona. How you glow, from tip to toe. This is your glow of confidence. This is the glow that comes from your knowledge of all that you have achieved, are achieving and will achieve. Feel this glow within you and around you.

You are confident and relaxed. Of course, there are always challenges in life but you have a new way of meeting them. You imagine a positive outcome to situations. You fill your mind with positive images. You create positive mental images for situations you are going to face. You go into that situation calm and relaxed, with your glow around you. You simply relax and feel your glow. Whenever you need to be, you are relaxed and glowing. Confident, happy, relaxed and positive.

[Waking-up procedure.]

Self-Hypnosis for Stopping Smoking

[Usual induction.]

Beautifully relaxed now, wonderfully relaxed. Relaxed in mind and relaxed in body. Feeling so good, so comfortable, so peaceful. Because you are now so wonderfully relaxed, you know that anything you wish to do is within your grasp, because you are deeply in tune with your true needs and instincts. Think about all the things you have achieved. *[Elaborate here on as many good things as you can – academic and career achievements, relationships, children, sports, circle of friends.]* How well you have done! Allow yourself to feel really good about these achievements. Feel proud of yourself. Let a glow of pride surround you. You know you can do anything to which you really put your mind, and now you have put your mind to stopping smoking.

You are relaxed, you are confident and you reach all the goals that you set yourself, including that of being a non-smoker. You are pleased with yourself for making that decision. Allow a feeling of pleasure to flow over you at your decision. It is a good decision, one that is right for you. You now choose to be a non-smoker. Smoking is not a suitable habit for someone such as you – someone who appreciates clean, clear air, smoke-free lungs, a healthy body. Smoking is not right for a person who has achieved the things you have and who chooses a healthy lifestyle. You have made up your mind. You are leaving behind you all the things associated with smoking – you no longer choose them, you no longer want them to be a part of you. You are determined to go forward and leave the habit of smoking behind you.

Imagine that you are holding a packet of cigarettes in your hand.

Imagine all the undesirable effects of smoking are there, within that packet. The toxins, the choking, the bad smell, the lack of health, the craving, the expense, the bother of having to find somewhere to smoke when you are in a place where it is not allowed – all these things and everything linked to cigarettes are what you no longer want or need. *[Insert more drawbacks that are particularly important to you, if you wish.]* See this packet as full of these nasty things. You do not want it. You reject it utterly. Imagine yourself standing on a hilltop on a sunny day. Throw the packet towards the blue sky – see the packet taken by the breeze up to the sun, where it is burnt up and all its toxins disappear. Now you are free!

Take a deep breath and let yourself feel very pleased with your decision. It is the right one for you and you feel positive and determined. You choose healthy air – clean, fresh air. You choose to have your lungs working efficiently and comfortably. You choose to have your body working at its best. Instead of having a cigarette in the morning you will *[insert other options]*. Instead of smoking in the car you will *[insert other options]*. Instead of smoking after meals you will *[insert other options]*. Instead of smoking when you go out you will *[insert other options]*. *[Insert as many circumstances as you can think of, giving your chosen other option each time.]* Imagine yourself going through a day and meeting all the usual circumstances as a non-smoker. You are smiling, you feel happy, confident and pleased and are enjoying life. Really be there, feel that sensation of freedom and confidence. You feel fine, you feel pleased with yourself. You feel more and more pleased with yourself with each hour and each day that goes by. Your confidence is growing all the time. You can now face all your day-to-day situations with total confidence in the fact that you are a non-smoker, and you feel so pleased with yourself – so very, very satisfied and pleased. In any situation where, in the past, you might have chosen to have a cigarette, you now renew that choice to be a non-smoker, and it feels wonderful.

Now you are a non-smoker; you choose to be a non-smoker. Before you began smoking, you were a non-smoker and quite happy to be that way. Now again you are a non-smoker, and that feels great, it feels wonderful, it feels right. You are a non-smoker and you enjoy all the benefits of being a non-smoker – fresh breath, clear lungs, increased health, more money. You have made a conscious decision that you are indeed a non-smoker. Wherever, in the past, you might have chosen to smoke a cigarette, now you renew your choice to be a non-smoker. You feel great about yourself. Very pleased and content with your decision to be a non-smoker.

You feel so good now that you are a non-smoker. Imagine once more a typical day for you, going through it as a non-smoker and feeling confident and full of pleasure. See yourself smiling. The more time passes with you as a non-smoker, the better you feel. Soon you notice, maybe in quite small ways at first, but you definitely notice that all areas of your life are improving steadily, with every day and every night that passes. Your lungs expand beautifully, your sense of taste improves, your vitality and enthusiasm increase. It feels wonderful to be a non-smoker; it feels right for you. You are a non-smoker and it feels great. See yourself in a pleasurable situation, having fun, smiling, as a non-smoker – feel good about it, delight in it. You are a non-smoker, a non-smoker. With each day that passes there are more and more situations for you to enjoy as a non-smoker. You feel better and better about your decision to be a non-smoker with each day that passes.

[Waking-up procedure.]

(Parts of this script were inspired by the excellent book *Hypnosis for Change* by Hadley and Straudacher, which is highly recommended for further reading and also for many other hypnotherapy scripts such as those for pain control, creativity, childbirth and athletic performance.)

further reading

Books by Teresa Moorey

Silver Moon, Rider, 2003. A comprehensive guide to living with the moon and the effects of her cycles on nature and on the human being. Factual, practical, looking at astrology, magic, mythology and lunar living.

The Little Book of Moon Magic. A pocket-sized companion volume to the above.

Witchcraft, A Beginner's Guide, Hodder & Stoughton, 1999. Many background questions to the whole idea of charms are answered in this book.

Witchcraft, A Complete Guide, Hodder & Stoughton, 2000. More detailed and extensive information on the spiritual path of witchcraft.

Herbs for Magic and Ritual, Hodder & Stoughton, 1999. You will find this useful if you want to make your own incense, use a variety of oils, etc.

Spells & Rituals, A Beginner's Guide, Hodder & Stoughton, 1999. More charms and rituals for you to try out.

The Wheel of the Year, Myth and Magic Through the Seasons, Capall Bann, 2003. This is co-written with artist Jane Brideson. Lots of ways to celebrate the eight seasonal festivals which were touched on in Chapter 6 of this book.

Spellbound! The Teenage Witch's Essential Handbook, Rider, 2002. All about charms and magic for teens.

Magic House, Ryland, Peters & Small, 2003. Turn your home into a magical haven with this full-colour practical guide.

Zodiac Spells Ryland, Peters & Small, 2003. Spells for your sign of the zodiac, plus how to get some of the best of the other signs for yourself!

Love Spells, Ryland, Peters & Small, 2003. Spells for all the stages of romance.

Seduction Spells, Ryland, Peters & Small, 2004. Spells to put the 'ooh!' in 'oomph'!

The Goddess, Hodder Mobius, 2003. The many facets of the Divine Feminine explored, with practical hints.

Contacting the Author

You can e-mail me at undines@freeuk.com. I try to give a brief reply to all e-mails, but I do not have the time to answer specific queries in a lengthy fashion. I'm sorry about this.

I am available for private consultation by anyone who lives within travelling distance of Gloucester. If you wish you may find out more on-line at www.gloucesterhealth.co.uk.

Books by other Authors

Baird, Lori (ed), *Cut the Clutter and Stow the Stuff*, Rodale, 2002.

Boston, Graham, *Astrology, A Beginner's Guide*, Hodder & Stoughton, 1998.

Carr, Allen, *Allen Carr's Easy Way to Stop Smoking*, Penguin, 1999.

Casement, Patrick, *On Learning from the Patient*, Tavistock Routledge, 1986.

Cheiro, *Cheiro's Palmistry for All*, Herbert Jenkins, 1966.

Conran, Shirley, *Superwoman*, Sidgwick & Jackson, 1976.

Dobson, C.B., *Stress, The Hidden Adversary*, MTP Press, 1983.

Edwards, Gill, *Living Magically*, Piatkus, 1991.

Ford, Bill, *High Energy Habits*, Bill Ford Pocket Books, 2002.

Fordham, Frieda, *An Introduction to Jung's Psychology*, Penguin, 1985.

Gawain, Shakti, *Creative Visualisation*, Whatever Publishing, 1978.

Hadley, Josie, and Straudacher, Carol, *Hypnosis for Change*, New Harbinger, 1996.

Hay, Louise, *You Can Heal Your Life*, Eden Grove (UK Edition), 1988.

Jacobs, Michael, *Psychodynamic Counselling in Action*, Sage Publications, 1989.

Jeffers, Susan, *Feel the Fear and Do It Anyway*, Vermilion, 1997. Also available on tape.

Jung, C.G. *Analytical Psychology*, Ark, 1986.

Liedloff, Jean, *The Continuum Concept*, Arkana, 1989.

Markham, Ursula, *Hypnotherapy, A Guide to Improving Health and Wellbeing Through Hypnosis*, Vermilion, 1997.

Marne, Patricia, *Teach Yourself Graphology*, Hodder & Stoughton, 1986.

Mayne, Brian and Sangeeta, *Life Mapping*, Vermilion, 2002.

Mayo, Jeff, and Ramsdale, Christine, *Teach Yourself Astrology*, Hodder & Stoughton, 1996.

Montignac, Michel, *Eat Yourself Slim...and Stay Slim!*, Montignac Publishing, 1999.

McTaggart, Lynne, *What Doctors Don't Tell You*, Thorsons. 1996. (The newsletter *What Doctors Don't Tell You* and its accompanying publication on alternative medicine *Proof!* is available from 4, Wallace Rd, London, N1 2PG, England, and also on-line.)

Olivier, Suzannah, *500 of the Most Important Stress-Busting Tips You'll Ever Need*, Cico, 2002.

Ozaniec, Naomi, *Teach Yourself Meditation*, Hodder & Stoughton, 1998.

Peiffer, Vera, *Principles of Stress Management*, Thorsons, 1996.

Salzberger-Witenberg, Isca, *Psycho-Analytic Insight and Relationships*, Routledge & Kegan Paul, 1986.

Skynner, Robyn, and Cleese, John, *Families and How to Survive Them*, Methuen, 1987.

Skynner, Robyn, and Cleese, John, *Life and How to Survive It*, Mandarin, 1994.

Sleet, Roger, *Hypnotherapy, Is It for You?*, Element, 1988.

Stewart, William, *An A–Z of Counselling Theory & Practice*, Nelson Thornes, 2001.

Too, Lillian, *Discover Yourself*, Rider, 2002.

Winnicott, D.W. *Playing and Reality*, Routledge, 1982.

Wiseman, Dr Richard, *The Luck Factor*, Century, 2003.

useful addresses

THE ASSOCIATION OF NATURAL MEDICINE
19A, Collingwood Road, Witham, Essex CM8 2DY. Tel: 01376 502762.

AL-ANON (for families of those with alcohol problems)
61, Great Dover Street, London SE1 4YF. Tel: 020 7403 0888.

ALCOHOLICS ANONYMOUS
PO BOX 1, Stonebow House, Stonebow, York YO1 2NJ.
Tel: 01904 644026.

BRITISH ASSOCIATION FOR COUNSELLING
1, Regent Place, Rugby, Warwickshire CV21 2PJ. Tel: 01788 550899.

CENTRE FOR STRESS MANAGEMENT
156, Westcombe Hill, London SE3 7DH. Tel: 020 8293 4114.

INSTITUTE OF FAMILY THERAPY
24–32 Stephenson Way, London N1 2HX. Tel: 020 7391 9150.

NATIONAL COUNCIL FOR ONE-PARENT FAMILIES
255, Kentish Town Road, London NW5 2LX.

RELATE MARRIAGE GUIDANCE, NATIONAL HQ
Herbert Gray College, Little Church Street, Rugby, Warwickshire CV21 3AP.
Tel: 01788 573241.

resources

Most oils can be obtained from your local health-food store, along with good-quality herbs. Crystals may be found in any New Age shop.

Herbs and oils can be ordered worldwide from the following, but sometimes you may have to send a small sum for a catalogue.

Starchild, The Courtyard, 2–4 High Street, Glastonbury, Somerset BA6 9DU, UK. Tel: 01458 834663. Catalogue £1.50.

The Sorcerer's Apprentice, 6–8 Burley Lodge Road, Leeds LS6 1QP, UK. Tel: 0113 245 1309. Send two first class stamps or international reply coupons for a catalogue. The Sorcerer's Apprentice has a large web-site at http://www.sorcerers-apprentice.co.uk and you can order supplies on-line. However, much of the equipment they supply is likely to seem rather over-the-top for your simple charms.

Enchantments, 341 East Ninth St (Between 1st & 2nd Avenue), New York City, NY 10003, USA. Tel: 212 228 4394. Catalogue $3 USA, $5 elsewhere.

Mystery's, 386, Darling Street, Balmain, NSW 2041, Australia.

Eye of the Cat, 3314 E Broadway, Long Beach, CA 90803, USA. Catalogue $10 550c refundable on first order.

Lunar Calendars and Goddess Cards

Dark Moon Designs, Rainbow Cottage, Clonduff, Rosenallis, Co Laois, Eire e-mail morrigan@mac.com

index

Abuse 64, 65ff, 87ff, 102, 119, 136, 234
Accident 3, 26, 65, 160, 204, 219
Accounts 166, 195, 199ff, 204, 208, 209
Addiction 117ff, 202
Affair (love) 68ff, 88
Agate 7
Agoraphobia 224
Alcohol 97, 117ff, 150
Alcoholics Anonymous 245
Alone 12, 26, 56, 76ff, 90ff, 111, 118, 143, 171, 230
Altar 33, 230, 231, 232
Amber 7, 39, 233
Amethyst 37, 233
Anal retentive 203ff
Anorexia 116
Anxiety 103, 111, 114, 127, 200, 213, 216ff, 217, 221
Apache tear 7
Arthritis 218
Astral plane 33
Astrology 48, 136ff, 242, 243, 244

Balloon (phobia) 215, 222
Basil 83
Bay 87, 123
Beltane 85, 158
Besom 87
Body 3, 35, 42, 60, 62, 80, 91ff, 103ff, 106ff, 132, 141, 142, 143, 160, 162, 163, 175, 189, 193, 218ff, 219, 222, 223, 225, 239, 240
Buddhism 229
Bullying 66, 174ff
Bulimia 111, 115ff

Business 25, 26, 28, 154, 226, 233

Calendar
  Of lunar phases 7, 246
Calm 59, 80, 143, 163, 164, 182, 191, 202, 209, 223, 224ff, 233, 237, 239
Calories 106, 107, 108
Cancer 202, 218
Candle(s) vi, 6, 7, 32, 34, 36f, 41, 80ff, 122ff, 139, 156ff, 164, 186ff, 202, 204, 207ff, 234
Cannabis 118
Career 15, 55, 149, 152, 154, 180, 239
Carnelian 7
Censer 7, 34
Charm(s) 2, 4, 5ff, 12, 22, 30, 31, 36ff, 45, 73, 74, 76, 79ff, 110, 116, 122ff, 137, 139ff, 154, 156ff, 164, 175, 180, 186ff, 193, 207ff, 219, 221ff, 231ff, 233, 242, 246
Childhood 9, 26, 35, 47, 53, 55, 56, 71, 74, 75, 115, 150, 174, 180, 185, 214, 219
Children 19, 25, 28, 29, 31, 37, 49, 60, 62, 67, 69, 75, 88, 105, 111, 129, 140, 141, 145ff, 161, 164, 179, 204, 208, 215, 229, 239
Cinnamon 40
Claustrophobia 219, 224
Cleansing 81, 158, 233
Colour
  Meanings of 2, 180ff
Compulsion 198, 202, 216ff
Confidence 20, 39, 81, 93, 94, 95, 110, 115, 126, 143, 181, 184, 223, 224, 237, 238, 239, 240, 241

Control 47, 56, 67, 87, 104, 111, 115, 135, 136, 172, 203, 210, 216, 217, 218
Counsellor / Counselling 8, 24, 29, 53, 99, 115, 118, 152, 178, 183, 204, 219, 243, 244, 245
Creativity 41, 45, 49, 66, 150, 158, 168, 170, 181, 182, 201, 203, 218
Crystal(s) 7, 34, 37, 38, 77, 78ff, 84, 140, 160, 164, 187, 220, 221, 230, 231, 234, 246
Cypress 89

Debts 199, 203
Dependency 135, 136
Depression 25, 99, 100, 123, 217ff, 221, 228
Diary 30, 51, 176, 177, 232
Diet 100, 106ff
Dill 157
Divorce 48, 153
Dream 20, 21, 56, 89, 197
Drug 101ff, 117

Eating disorder 111, 115ff, 123
Eleusis 36
Energy / Energised 111, 115ff, 123
Envy 20, 21, 134ff, 153
Equinox 85, 158, 159
Eucalyptus 8, 89, 122, 123
Exercise 4, 6, 34, 51, 97, 104, 113, 114, 178, 180, 202

Family 9, 18, 37, 49, 53, 81, 111, 114, 117, 120, 129, 144ff, 168, 169, 170, 174, 179, 197, 244, 245
Fat 106ff
Fear 21, 22, 41, 55, 56, 62, 66, 67, 76, 82, 100, 116, 118, 147, 153, 156, 175, 185, 204, 213, 214, 215, 216, 218, 219ff, 221, 224, 225, 228, 235
Fertility 150, 157, 158, 160ff, 233
Fibre, dietary 109
Food / Feeding 71, 87, 97, 106ff, 118, 120, 123, 124ff, 140, 193
Flower(s) 2, 35, 42, 43, 78, 79, 83, 84, 85, 139, 140, 157, 158, 160, 187, 189, 205, 230, 231, 234, 236
Frankincense 8, 80
Friendship 51, 64, 71, 72, 89, 114, 128ff, 152, 208, 220, 224, 228, 233
Fulfilment 14, 20, 47, 69, 76, 94, 100, 170

Garlic 124, 233
Ginger 123, 157
Goal(s) 14, 16, 22, 23, 31, 147
Goddess 19, 49, 77ff, 83, 84, 158, 160, 193, 233, 243, 246
Graphology 98ff, 244
Greedy 17, 18, 49, 83
Guilt 17, 49, 54, 72, 87, 106, 107, 109, 135, 147, 150, 156, 196, 235

Hadley, Josie 241
Hallowe'en 85, 159
Happy / Happiness 13, 14ff, 18, 30, 56, 61, 90, 95, 103, 125, 132, 142, 145, 146, 148, 152, 156, 162, 163, 180, 208, 222, 227ff, 238, 239
Hay, Louise 103, 243
Hazel 40
Health / Healthy 16, 24, 41, 70, 76, 93, 96ff, 147, 150, 151, 193, 208, 233, 240, 241,
Heart
  Broken 70ff, 73, 89ff
Herb(s) 2, 7
Horseshoe 40, 187, 189
Hypnosis / Hypnotic state 4, 8ff, 11, 22, 100, 114, 116, 118, 119, 216, 217, 218, 219, 228, 243, 244
  Induction 10ff, 41, 43, 91, 94, 125, 141, 162, 189, 209, 222, 224, 236, 238, 239

Imagination 3, 31, 33, 54, 71, 164, 169, 170, 172, 183, 188

index ✷ 249

Imbolc 85, 158
Induction, hypnosis *see* hypnosis / hypnotic state
Infertility 150ff
Interview 176, 186, 189
Intuition 6, 30, 41, 133, 136, 182
Irritable bowel 103, 127, 214, 218ff

Jasmine 8, 37, 139, 233
Jealousy 37, 55, 63, 66, 74ff, 89, 90, 132ff, 135, 153, 174
Joss-stick 7, 187, 208, 209, 231
Jung, C.G. 85, 243

Lammas 85, 159
Lapis lazuli 77, 233
Lavender 7, 8, 32, 35, 41, 80, 81ff, 88, 89, 90, 98, 123, 200, 209, 234,
Laziness 10, 21, 65, 82, 187, 188, 202, 233
Life script 27ff, 38ff, 55, 76, 197
Lifts (phobia of) 218ff, 224, 225ff
Love 6, 8, 23, 46ff, 97, 137, 139, 146, 157, 159, 163, 164, 193, 202, 206, 233, 235, 242
Luck 24, 29ff, 40, 45, 108, 162, 187, 189, 191, 236ff, 244

Mandala 85ff
Mars 157
Massage 80ff, 235
Meditation 4, 5, 30, 32ff, 38, 77ff, 120ff, 137ff, 154ff, 184ff, 205, 219ff, 229, 234ff, 244
Mercury 157, 233
Midsummer 85
Migraine 103
Mint 157
Money 16, 20, 48, 54, 60, 62, 70, 97, 114, 164, 166, 169, 172, 178, 179, 192ff, 233, 241
Montignac, Michel 108, 244
Moon 7, 38, 40 81, 82, 84, 86, 89, 90, 91, 122, 124, 139, 157, 158, 160, 161, 164, 186, 20, 221, 228, 232, 233, 242, 246,
Mother 25, 49, 61, 71, 110ff, 114, 115, 127, 145, 148, 215, 216, 219
Myrrh 81ff

Nature 85, 128, 150, 156, 159, 160, 168, 182, 183, 193, 210, 228, 242
Network(ing) 22, 164, 167, 173, 176
Nutmeg 123

Oak 3, 123, 185, 233
Obesity 106, 109
Obsession 116, 216ff
Oil-burner 2, 3, 32, 37, 88, 89, 234
Oil(s), essential 2, 8, 39, 41, 80, 81, 84, 89, 90, 122, 160, 242, 246
Organise / Organisation 28, 131, 149, 176
Overweight 106ff

Palmistry 200ff, 243
Parent, single *see* Single
Patchouli 8, 38, 83, 88, 160, 161, 164, 186, 233
Perspective 2, 5, 28, 29, 41, 42, 43, 47, 75, 163, 190, 191, 223, 226, 229
Phobias 213ff, 215ff, 221, 228
Pollyanna 23ff
Positive thinking 9, 11, 19, 23ff, 42, 67, 94, 114, 132, 141, 142, 152, 159, 177, 178, 191, 224, 225, 226, 228, 236, 237, 238, 239
Pregnant / Pregnancy 8, 105, 150, 160
Problem(s) 33, 52, 79, 111, 115, 119, 130, 145, 150, 205, 212, 224

Quantum physics 3
Questionnaire(s) 4, 14ff, 17ff, 36, 50ff, 57, 67, 71, 76, 82, 97, 111, 118, 130ff, 137, 146, 166ff, 168ff, 194ff, 213ff

250 ✳ a charmed life

Reality 2, 3, 27, 29, 100, 219
Relationship(s) 19, 26, 47ff, 111, 129, 175, 178, 228, 234, 235, 239
Relaxation 10ff, 30, 32ff, 41ff, 91ff, 98, 114, 116, 124, 125, 141ff, 150, 162ff, 163, 164, 180, 189, 209, 214, 216, 217, 218, 220, 222ff, 228, 232, 236, 238, 239
Rescue 26ff, 135
Retail therapy 202ff, 208
Ritual 2, 84, 156, 216, 242
Rose 80, 83, 84, 89, 90, 139, 193, 228
Rose quartz 7, 84ff, 137, 138, 139, 164, 233

St John's wort 36, 123
Science 3, 98
Self-esteem 20, 28, 29, 45, 48, 49, 51, 55, 61, 64, 68, 74, 75, 79, 81, 95, 115, 116, 135, 177, 191, 234, 235, 237ff
Self-hypnosis 2, 32, 34, 41ff, 45, 79, 91ff, 120, 125ff, 141ff, 163ff, 177, 180, 189, 209ff, 21, 221, 222ff, 232, 234ff, 236, 237ff, 239
Selfish 17, 18, 49, 65, 69, 136, 194
Sex / Sexual 54, 59, 67, 91ff, 97, 99, 111, 115, 116, 181
Shrine 33, 230
Single 53, 81, 82
 Parent 25, 147, 162
Sleep 9, 10, 11, 70, 83, 97, 217
Sleeplessness 70, 213, 217
Slimming World 108ff
Smoking 97, 119ff, 123, 124, 150, 178, 234, 239, 243
Solstice 158
Spiritual / Spirituality 14, 17, 19, 47, 50, 52, 103, 117, 140, 156, 157, 182, 193, 229ff, 242
Statue 8, 77ff, 184, 231
Step-families 37, 153ff, 161
Stone, semi-precious 7, 88, 140, 231

Straudacher, Carol 241
Stress 16, 34, 42, 62, 114, 116, 118, 127, 145, 203, 213, 214, 216, 217, 221, 222, 243, 244, 245
Subconscious 2, 9, 11, 23, 27, 67, 76, 79, 83, 84, 85, 119, 124, 160, 189

'Talking stick' 161ff
Talisman 84ff
Tension 32ff, 41ff, 62, 98, 103, 161, 213, 232
Therapy 8, 27, 53, 55, 85, 103, 107, 114, 119, 127, 134, 202, 215, 216, 219, 228
Thyme 123, 157, 233
Top Tip(s) 3, 5, 14, 20, 24, 28, 52, 72, 98, 111, 129, 135, 145, 148, 176, 180, 194, 199, 218, 229

Unconscious 2, 32, 47, 148, 215, 217, 219, 221
Unemployment 177ff

Venus 8, 84, 157, 233
Victim 67, 68
Visualisation 2, 4, 5, 6, 11, 31, 32ff, 40, 45, 77ff, 120ff, 137ff, 154ff, 180, 184ff, 205, 219ff, 228, 229, 234ff, 243
Vocation 177ff, 184ff, 189

Waking up procedure 11, 43, 45, 94, 95, 126, , 143, 191, 211, 224, 226, 237, 239, 241
Wellbeing 96ff
Wiseman, Richard 30, 244
Work 165ff, 210, 213

Ylang ylang 8, 80, 89, 233
Yule 85, 157ff

Zodiac 86, 136, 242